Illinois Central College
Learning Resources Center

THE NEW GROVE

SCHUBERT

Maurice J. E. Brown

WORK-LIST
Eric Sams

W. W. NORTON & COMPANY
NEW YORK   LONDON

First published in
The New Grove Dictionary of Music and Musicians,
edited by Stanley Sadie, 1980

First American Edition 1983

ISBN 0-393-01683-8

Printed in Hong Kong

Contents

List of illustrations

GENERAL ABBREVIATIONS

A	alto, contralto [voice]	org	organ
acc.	accompaniment	ov.	overture
add, addl	additional		
add, addn	addition	perf.	performance
arr.	arrangement	pr.	printed
aut.	autumn	pubd	published
		pubn	publication
B	bass [voice]		
b	bass [instrument]	qnt	quintet
bc	basso continuo	qt	quartet
bn	bassoon		
		R	photographic reprint
cl	clarinet	r	recto
conc.	concerto	rec	recorder
cont	continuo	recit	recitative
db	double bass	red.	reduction
		repr.	reprinted
edn.	edition	rev.	revision
f. ff.	folio(s)		
facs.	facsimile	S	soprano [voice]
fl	flute	str	string(s)
Fr.	French	sum.	summer
frag.	fragment	sym.	symphony
		T	tenor [voice]
gui	guitar	timp	timpani
		tpt	trumpet
hn	horn	tr	treble [instrument]
		trbn	trombone
inc.	incomplete	transcr.	transcription
inst	instrument		
		U.	University
kbd	keyboard		
		v, vv	voice(s)
lib	libretto	v., vv.	verse(s)
		v	verso
tmovt	movement	va	viola
		vc	cello
ob	oboe	vn	violin
obbl	obbligato		
orch	orchestra		
orchd	orchestrated		

BIBLIOGRAPHICAL ABBREVIATIONS

AcM	*Acta musicologica*
AMw	*Archiv für Musikwissenschaft*
BMw	*Beiträge zur Musikwissenschaft*
GfMKB	*Gesellschaft für Musikforschung Kongressbericht*
JAMS	*Journal of the American Musicological Society*
JMT	*Journal of Music Theory*
Mf	*Die Musikforschung*
ML	*Music and Letters*
MMR	*The Monthly Musical Record*
MQ	*The Musical Quarterly*
MR	*The Music Review*
MT	*The Musical Times*
NZM	*Neue Zeitschrift für Musik*
ÖMz	*Österreichische Musikzeitschrift*
PMA	*Proceedings of the Musical Association*
PRMA	*Proceedings of the Royal Musical Association*
RBM	*Revue belge de musicologie*
ReM	*La revue musicale*
RIM	*Rivista italiana di musicologia*
SH	*Slovenská hudba*
SM	*Studia musicologica Academiae scientiarum hungaricae*
SMw	*Studien zur Musikwissenschaft*
VMw	*Vierteljahrsschrift für Musikwissenschaft*
ZIMG	*Zeitschrift der Internationalen Musik-Gesellschaft*
ZMw	*Zeitschrift für Musikwissenschaft*

Preface

This volume is one of a series of short biographies derived from *The New Grove Dictionary of Music and Musicians* (London, 1980). In its original form, the text was written in the mid-1970s, and finalized at the end of that decade. For this reprint, the text has been re-read and modified by the original author (or in some cases his representative) and corrections and changes have been made. In particular, an effort has been made to bring the bibliography up to date and to incorporate the findings of recent research.

The fact that the texts of the books in this series originated as dictionary articles inevitably gives them a character somewhat different from that of books conceived as such. They are designed, first of all, to accommodate a very great deal of information in a manner that makes reference quick and easy. Their first concern is with fact rather than opinion, and this leads to a larger than usual proportion of the texts being devoted to biography than to critical discussion. The nature of a reference work gives it a particular obligation to convey received knowledge and to treat of composers' lives and works in an encyclopedic fashion, with proper acknowledgment of sources and due care to reflect different standpoints, rather than to embody imaginative or speculative writing about a composer's character or his music. It is hoped that the comprehensive work-lists and extended bibliographies, indicative of the origins of the books in a reference work, will be valuable to the reader who is eager for full and accurate reference information and who may not have ready access to *The New Grove Dictionary* or who may prefer to have it in this more compact form.

✽

As Maurice J. E. Brown had, unhappily, died before the article appeared in print, the revisions undertaken by the late Mr Brown's friend and colleague, Eric Sams, for this publication in book form draw on Mr Brown's other writings on Schubert, in particular his critical biography (published by Macmillan).

S.S.

We are grateful to the following for permission to reproduce illustrative material: Bibliothèque Nationale, Paris (fig.1); Gesellschaft der Musikfreunde, Vienna (figs.2, 5); Historisches Museum der Stadt Wien (figs.4, 6, 7, cover); Richard Macnutt, Tunbridge Wells (fig.8); Curtis Institute of Music, Philadelphia (fig.9); Pierpont Morgan Library (Mary Flagler Cary Music Collection), New York (fig.10); Österreichische Nationalbibliothek, Vienna (fig.11).

Cover: Watercolour portrait by Wilhelm August Rieder
(Historisches Museum der Stadt Wien)

1. Background and childhood

Vienna, in Schubert's day, consisted of an inner city bounded to the north-east by the Danube Canal and enclosed by a rampart; these enclosing walls were to give place to the wide boulevards of the modern Ringstrasse. The real life of the capital was passed in this small and crowded area. Franz Peter Schubert was born in the district of the Himmelpfortgrund, lying to the north-west of the city, on 31 January 1797.

Schubert's father, Franz Theodor Florian, was a schoolmaster. He was a man of probity, a devout Catholic, industrious in his profession and undeniably successful. His ancestors were Moravian peasant farmers: he was born in Neudorf, near Märisch-Schönberg in the Altstadt district of Moravia. He migrated to Vienna to become an assistant to his brother Karl, who had a school in the Leopoldstadt suburb, and in 1785, when he was 25, married Maria Elisabet Katherina Vietz, the composer's mother. We know little of her except that she was born in Zuckmantel, in Austrian Silesia, and before her marriage was in domestic service. Soon after his marriage, Franz Theodor was appointed master of a school in the Himmelpfortgrund district of Vienna and in June 1786 he moved into a house there called 'Zum roten Krebsen'. In the years that followed, no fewer than 12 children were born, of whom only four survived infancy: Ignaz (b 1785), Ferdinand (b 1794), Karl (b 1795) and Franz Peter. A daughter, Maria Theresa (b 1801), was the last of the family. The house was later renumbered and the street renamed: it is now 54 Nussdorferstrasse, and since 1912 has been maintained by the city authorities as a Schubert museum. In 1969 it was reopened, after several years, fully restored to its original condition as the boy Schubert knew it.

Soon after the birth of Maria Theresa, the family moved into a new house in the nearby Säulenstrasse (now no.3), which Franz Theodor had bought a few months earlier. It was a smaller house, but more rooms were at his disposal for the growing number of his pupils. We learn from the memoirs of Schubert's father and of his brother, Ferdinand, of his boyhood in the Säulengasse schoolhouse. Franz Theodor's position offered no social standing and was ill-paid. It is not difficult to see that when he induced his sons, as they grew old enough, to become his assistants in the school, the primary aim was to save money. But the relations between father and sons were clearly affectionate, as their extant letters reveal; and Schubert as a boy experienced neither harsh discipline in his training nor exploitation of his obvious musical gifts. His father taught him the violin, his eldest brother Ignaz the piano, and he quickly outstripped them both. Ignaz wryly admitted that the boy told him as much, and that he intended to make his own way in the future. When he was nine or ten his father placed him under the tuition of Michael Holzer, organist at the parish church of Liechtental. Holzer is sketched amusingly by Anton Holzapfel (a schoolfellow of Schubert's) as somewhat bibulous but a sound contrapuntist. In addition to lessons on the piano and violin, young Franz was taught the organ, singing and harmony, and under Holzer's care both his singing and violin playing earned him a local reputation. Holzer said of his pupil: 'If I wished to instruct him in anything fresh, he already knew it. Consequently I gave him no actual tuition but merely conversed with him and watched him with silent astonishment'.

Schubert's extraordinary aptitude for music enabled him to absorb with ease this elementary instruction, and no further progress was possible on that road. But another lay before him, and was to lead him to an environment which awakened his genius and showed him the full possibilities of self-realization. Towards the end of 1808 he was accepted as a choirboy in the imperial court chapel, and this meant admission as a scholar to the Kaiserlich-königliches Stadtkonvikt (Imperial and Royal City College). His examiners were the court musical directors, Antonio Salieri and Joseph Eybler, and the choirmaster, Phillip Körner; Schubert also distinguished himself in general subjects. The college was the principal Viennese boarding-school for commoners. The tutors were men in holy orders (although the college was not a religious foundation) and the boarders, about 130 in number, were either scholars at the grammar school or students at the university. Music was a compulsory subject for the choristers, but the principal, Dr Innocenz Lang, was an enthusiastic musical amateur and he encouraged all scholars to practise the art. A young university student, Josef von Spaun, had formed a students' orchestra, which was conducted by a visiting music master, Václav (Wenzel) Růžička, and by the time the young Schubert came to the college, its standard was excellent. Schubert's violin playing greatly impressed Spaun and in a short time he was promoted to be leader of the first violins. The friendship between Schubert and this student, some eight years his senior, was to be one of the happiest things in his life, and it lasted until his death. Schubert was composing in those years, and some of the music has survived (he confessed to Spaun that he was too poor to buy all the music manuscript paper he needed, and Spaun's first act of kindness was to provide it).

When Růžička was absent, Schubert conducted the orchestra – a rare opportunity for a boy such as he to master orchestral techniques. The orchestra played overtures and symphonies by Mozart and Haydn and the first two symphonies of Beethoven. Růžička, like Holzer before him, was nonplussed at the rapidity with which Schubert absorbed his instruction. To him the explanation was simple: 'He has learnt everything from God, that lad'. Eventually Salieri took over the supervision of Schubert's work, a supervision which extended beyond the college years. The association is interesting: it was, indeed, fitting that Salieri, friend of Haydn and rival of Mozart, in a small way a pupil of Gluck and in a smaller way tutor to Beethoven, should have supervised the work of Schubert, the last of these Viennese masters.

The supposition that Schubert neglected other studies to devote himself to music is contradicted by the extant records from Dr Lang of his progress in these years. All subjects are rated 'good' or 'very good' and the comment 'a special musical talent' occurs year after year. Schubert impressed everyone at the college by his musical gifts and an equally deep impression was made by his moral qualities; he was privileged to leave the building for his lessons with Salieri because of his general reliability. The compositions which date with certainty from these years are the Fantasie in G for piano duet (D1; 8 April–1 May 1810), the Six Minuets for wind instruments (D2*d*; 1811, recovered in 1969) and the song *Hagars Klage* (D5; 30 March 1811). It was this song, in Schubert's scena form, which is said to have aroused Salieri's interest. On 8 July 1811, Spaun took Schubert to his first opera, Weigl's *Die Schweizerfamilie*, at the Kärntnertor-Theater (which was to figure in Schubert's own operatic ventures). His first settings of Schiller date from this time, *Des Mädchens Klage* (D6) and *Leichenfantasie* (D7).

In the following year, on 28 May 1812, Schubert's mother died. That he and his father had quarrelled and were reconciled at her graveside is purely fictitious; so is the assertion that he composed the wind nonet *Eine kleine Trauermusik* (D79) to her memory. The eight undated and incomplete numbers of his first operatic composition, *Der Spiegelritter* (D11), to a text by August von Kotzebue, were completed in 1812. In the summer that year his voice was breaking; after the performance of a mass by Peter von Winter, he scribbled on his part, 'Schubert, Franz, crowed for the last time, 26 July 1812', though he remained a pupil at the college for another year or so. There were two terms in the college year, the main holiday occurring in early autumn. It was during Schubert's holidays that a family string quartet was formed, with the composer playing the viola, his brothers Ignaz and Ferdinand the violins, and his father the cello. For this family quartet the early string quartets of 1811–14 were composed.

The compositions of 1813 are numerous and their variety indicates the wealth of his musical experience. Salieri's tutelage is apparent in the many vocal canons, which are primarily contrapuntal exercises, and in the varied settings of verses by Metastasio. Songs of the year include settings of Schiller, Hölty and Matthisson, and a translation by Herder of Pope's *Vital Spark of Heavenly Flame* (*Verklärung* D59). There are German Dances (*Deutsche*) for strings (D90) and six string quartets. The finest of these, in E♭ (D87), with a finale of true

Schubertian quality, was published in 1840 as op.125 no.1.

On 25 April 1813, Schubert's father remarried. His wife, Anna Kleyenböck, was a kindly woman who in later years helped Schubert with loans from her house-keeping money. For his father's name day, 4 October, Schubert wrote the words and music of a trio (D80). The finest of these early works was finished on 28 October, the First Symphony, in D (D82). It is the consummation of those years of absorption in music at the college and of his vital contact with its orchestra; it was his justification for the future. Two days after its completion he began work on a three-act opera *Des Teufels Lustschloss* (D84), to a libretto by Kotzebue. He is said to have stayed away from his lessons until the opera was finished in the following year, and then to have presented the fully scored work to his astonished master. Salieri's criticisms were heeded, for a revised, second version of the opera is dated five months after the completion of the first.

2. Beginning of career

At the end of 1813, probably late in October, Schubert left the Kaiserlich-königliches Stadtkonvikt; unable to withstand family persuasion, he entered a training-school for elementary teachers in the Annagasse, near St Stephen's Cathedral. By autumn 1814 he was teaching in his father's school. It is not true that he adopted the profession of schoolmaster to evade military conscription: assistants, in any case, were not exempt. He was rejected by the military authorities because he was shorter than the minimum height of five feet. His sight was defective, too; by then he was wearing the spectacles familiar from his portraits.

Although he continued to take lessons with Salieri until the end of 1816, his musical tuition was finished. In those years at the college he was able to draw in abundance on the rich resources of orchestral practice and church choral singing, of piano playing and song and chamber music with his fellows, of string quartet playing in his own home, and of frequent visits to some of the finest opera in Europe. These powerful stimuli were about to produce a staggering result. He was on the threshold of an outburst of composition without parallel in the history of music: the means of self-expression had been acquired and his genius sought utterance.

The early months of 1814, however, produced little work of significance: some string quartet sketches, a few songs, and the arrangement, including a new trio (D96) for the minuet, he made in February of a *Notturno*

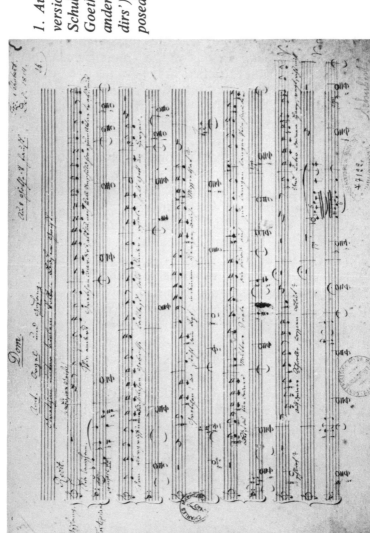

1. Autograph MS of version a of Schubert's 'Szene aus Goethes Faust' ('Wie anders, Gretchen, war dirs') D126, composed December 1814

op.21 by Wenzel Matiegka, for flute, guitar, viola and cello – it is called the 'Guitar' Quartet, and its attribution as a whole to Schubert is unfortunate. Between 17 May and 22 July he composed his first Mass, in F (D105). Another string quartet, in B♭ (D112), followed in September. The first movement was written in four and a half hours, as Schubert indicated on the autograph.

This was the period of the Congress of Vienna, and it coincided with the centenary celebrations of the Liechtental Church. Schubert's Mass in F was performed in the church as part of these celebrations on 14 October 1814; Holzer's choir sang, Ferdinand played the organ and Schubert himself conducted. The soprano solos were sung by Therese Grob, a young girl with a delightful lyric soprano voice. Ten days later the mass was repeated, in the court church of St Augustine, and both performances brought the young composer a welcome public acclaim. But something took place after those ten days more significant than the adulation surrounding the performances of his mass: he had been reading Goethe's *Faust*, and on 19 October 1814 he set the verses now universally known as *Gretchen am Spinnrade* (D118). It was his first masterpiece. The figure in the piano accompaniment represents the spinning-wheel, but as the song proceeds it gathers into itself all Gretchen's changing emotions as she recalls her lover, and the greatest moment is when, under the transported spirit of the suffering girl, the wheel comes to a standstill, falteringly beginning its motion again as she recovers. It is a song which, unlike several others, has never suffered eclipse during the passing years but rather has grown in stature. Another popular song to a Goethe text followed later in the year, *Schäfers Klagelied* (D121). In December, the song *Am See*

(D124) was composed to verses by Johann Mayrhofer. Spaun had given the poem to Schubert, and soon afterwards he took him to Mayrhofer's lodgings in the Wipplingerstrasse and introduced him to the poet. There began a friendship that was to affect Schubert deeply. Mayrhofer's poetry reveals the conflict between the idealism of the spirit and the actualities of life; it was, in later years, to evoke noble and profound music from the composer.

Schubert was, in 1815, a schoolmaster, feeling the irksome duties of the classroom as an intolerable barrier between him and the freedom to compose. But he evidently found time to put down on paper the music which, throughout that year, welled ceaselessly in his mind. There can have been scarcely a day when his pen was idle, and no other year in his life approached this one for its sheer volume of work. His Second Symphony, in B♭ (D125), begun the previous December, was finished in March. The Third, in D (D200), was written between 24 May and 19 July. There were numerous dances for piano solo, two sonatas, a set of ten variations on an original theme in F, and a sturdy little string quartet in G minor. Besides much varied choral music of secondary value, there were two masses. The first, in G (D167), was performed in spring 1815, soon after its completion. Depths are sounded in the Agnus Dei unknown to the earlier Mass in F. It is a *lento* movement in E minor, and solo passages for soprano and bass alternate with the chorus quietly intoning 'miserere nobis' to gracious, falling phrases. The violas are used expressively to link these solos and choruses. The second mass of the year, no.3 in B♭ (D324), looks to the later Schubert in page after page. The use of short, lyrical episodes, picturesquely orchestrated, between the vocal phrases foreshadows *Lazarus* of five years later; the use of descant-like melodies in violin or oboe hints at the slow movement of the 'Unfinished' Symphony. Above all, there are bravura passages, for example in the Gloria and Benedictus, which suggest the 'Wanderer' Fantasy and the finale of the 'Great' C major Symphony. This is the most consistently interesting of his four early settings of the Mass. The story put forward by Josef Doppler that the style of this work caused a break between Schubert and Salieri is a fabrication.

In the course of the year, Schubert set four dramatic texts to music. No doubt the successful production of an opera in Vienna appeared to him as the gate to freedom. Since Vienna possessed four theatres at which operas and plays with music were produced, he must have felt confident of eventual success. The four stage works are: *Der vierjährige Posten* (D190), to a one-act play by Theodor Körner, the music composed between 8 and 19 May; *Fernando* (D220), to a one-act play by Albert Stadler, composed 27 June to 9 July; *Claudine von Villa Bella* (D239), to a three-act play by Goethe, which was begun on 26 July, and survives in only an incomplete form, since the manuscript came into the possession of Josef Hüttenbrenner, whose servants, in 1848, unwittingly used the pages of Acts 2 and 3 to light fires; *Die Freunde von Salamanka* (D326), to a two-act play by Mayrhofer, which occupied the composer from 18 November to 31 December. The last of these four is the finest and, although Mayrhofer's text is lost, it is perfectly easy to follow the story from the extant musical numbers and so provide the necessary dialogue.

In addition to these larger musical forms, he composed in 1815 145 songs. The range is tremendous and the accomplishment outstanding. There are tiny songs

like *Die Mainacht* (D194) and *Der Traum* (D213) on the
one hand, and very long ballads such as *Adelwold und
Emma* (D211) on the other. The poets include Schiller,
Klopstock, Ossian and Kosegarten. He set 30 poems by
Goethe, and some of these are among his finest and most
famous songs: *Heidenröslein* (D257), *Erster Verlust*
(D226), *Wandrers Nachtlied* (D224) and *Rastlose
Liebe* (D138). The last of the Goethe settings, the song
by which the year will always be remembered, is
Erlkönig (D328), composed in late autumn 1815. The
story of its composition as told by Spaun and others is
full of incredible details; it is, in fact, impossible to
separate what is factually correct from subsequent ac-
cretions. Spaun called on his friend one afternoon (he
wrote) and found him excitedly reading Goethe's ballad.
Schubert then wrote the song out in the shortest possible
time, and the two of them (possibly with Mayrhofer)
hurried to the college and gathered a few congenial
spirits to hear the composition. The enthusiasm of the
students was tremendous and Růžička justified his
pupil's use of the discordant minor 9ths at the cry 'Mein
Vater!'. When the song was eventually published, some
six years later, it spread Schubert's fame far beyond his
native city. In his own lifetime and for generations afterwards it was considered his greatest song. Today, perhaps, some of the more subtle songs of his final years
spring to mind before *Erlkönig*, but the wealth of harmonic resource, its masterly structure and the mount-
ing tonal climaxes of the threefold lure will always
keep it high among his masterpieces of song.

During the autumn Schubert became acquainted with
Franz von Schober, who had come to Vienna to study
law. He had heard some of Schubert's songs and now
came to seek out their composer. According to his own

account, he found Schubert in the classroom correcting pupils' exercises. Of the same age as Schubert, he was a cultured, worldly young man and it was typical of his easy-going nature and wealthy upbringing that he urged Schubert to abandon the drudgery of teaching and devote himself to composition. It was not for another year that the composer could bring himself to make the break, but after his encounter with Schober, the step was inevitable. He attempted to do so in April 1816 by applying, unsuccessfully, for the post of music master in a training school for elementary teachers at Laibach (now Ljubljana), some 65 km north-east of Trieste. In the same month he completed his Fourth Symphony, in C minor (D417); the title 'Tragic' is his own. While he was engaged on this work, Spaun sent to Goethe, at Weimar, a group of Schubert's settings of the poet's verses. It included all the finest of the Goethe songs of the previous two years. The attempt to interest the poet in Schubert's work failed. In musical matters, Goethe was greatly influenced by Zelter. Both men shared the feeling of the north German musical world that in 'true German song' the accompaniment should be subordinate to the vocal part; all extravagances of harmony and modulation were categorized as 'bizarrerie' and eschewed. Schubert's songs were returned, and his appeal for recognition ignored. After Schubert's death, Goethe again heard *Erlkönig*, which was sung to him by Wilhelmine Schröder-Devrient on 24 April 1830; he told her: 'I have heard this composition once before, when it did not appeal to me at all; but sung in this way the whole shapes itself into a visible picture'.

In May 1816 Spaun took lodgings with his friend Josef Witteczek, who later became a devoted Schubertian and amassed a superb collection of

2. *Page from Schubert's diary of 10 June 1816 containing references to Mozart*

Schubert first editions, manuscripts and press cuttings. The house, in the Erdberggasse, was the scene of many of those domestic evening concerts devoted to the music of Schubert which came to be known as *Schubertiade*.

They were symptomatic of a new and vigorous social phenomenon, the cultivation of music by the educated middle class; though altogether humbler than the aristo-cratic employment of quartets and orchestras in the 18th century, its energetic growth is apparent from the ubiquitous piano and the vast mass of suitable music which poured from the publishing houses. A cantata, *Prometheus* (D451), was composed on 17 June for private performance; it was Schubert's first commis-sioned work and earned him a fee of 40 gulden. The music was given in the garden of the Erdberggasse house on 24 July 1816 and impressed its hearers profoundly. Whether or not this impression was deserved we have no means of knowing, as the score was lost without trace just before Schubert's death. Leopold von Sonnleithner sang in the chorus and thereby made Schubert's acquaintance; the composer was to be fortun-ate in this contact with so influential and musical a family as the Sonnleithners.

Several pages of a diary which Schubert kept that year have survived. The entries for June have some interest, since they contain references to Mozart and Beethoven. If anything were needed to demonstrate that music was his only medium of self-expression, we have only to turn from the diary pages of September to the work on which he was engaged at this time – the Fifth Symphony, in B♭ (D485), the best and most popular of his six early symphonies. It was finished on 3 October and performed soon afterwards by a private orchestra which had developed from the family string quartet and which met in the house of its conductor, Otto Hatwig.

3. Growing reputation

In October 1816, after a four-month visit to his birthplace in Sweden, Schober returned to Vienna, and he persuaded the composer to make a move towards independence. There was no clean break with teaching, but by December Schubert was installed in rooms in the house of Schober's affluent mother – a temporary respite. 1816 had been almost as prolific as the previous year. In addition to the compositions already mentioned there was a further Mass, in C (D452), composed during June and July and published nine years later with a dedication to Michael Holzer. The three sonatas for violin and piano (D384, 385, 408), published by Diabelli in 1836 as 'Sonatinas', and the String Quartet in E (D353) were composed that year. The songs, over 100, include *Der Wanderer* (D489), after *Erlkönig* the most popular of his songs for many years, and masterpieces to poems by Goethe such as the three Harper's Songs from *Wilhelm Meister* (D478–80) and *An Schwager Kronos* (D369). It is one of the enigmas of his music that these songs so richly reveal his personal style, whereas in his contemporary instrumental works it appears only fitfully. A few months after Schubert was installed in his new house, Schober prevailed upon the operatic baritone, Johann Michael Vogl, to visit him and make the acquaintance of the composer and his songs. Vogl was well-to-do, a man of culture with a distinguished, even stately bearing. Schubert was overawed and painfully embarrassed, but the singer, very much at his ease, took the proffered songs: the newly composed

Ganymed (D544) was one of them. His parting remark was to the effect that, although there was much fine stuff in the songs, it was ill-presented; Schubert, he said, was too little of the charlatan. But he was more impressed than he admitted. Shortly afterwards he revisited the composer and the two men soon became the delight of the Viennese drawing-rooms. Vogl, his days in the theatre nearly over, was not averse to the plaudits of the salons and initially he looked upon the songs as vehicles for his voice. Occasionally he altered them, adding flourishes and introducing wide skips in voice parts. He once embellished a new song of Schubert's, also transposing it to suit his voice, and on presenting the copy a fortnight later was greeted by the composer with 'A good song. Whose is it, then?'. Generations have chuckled over this anecdote, seeing only the 'clairvoyant' genius (Vogl's word) who forgets his own production when the trance is over; they have missed Schubert's implied protest.

An effort was made during the spring of 1817 to publish *Erlkönig*. The song was sent to the Leipzig firm of Breitkopf & Härtel. Knowing only one Franz Schubert, a musician in Dresden, they sent him the manuscript for confirmation. He replied:

With the greatest astonishment I beg to state that this cantata was never composed by me. I shall retain the same in my possession to learn, if possible, who has so impertinently sent you that sort of rubbish and also to discover the fellow who has thus misused my name.

The manuscript was returned to Schubert without comment.

The spring and summer of 1817 were devoted to the composition of piano sonatas. The wide range of piano styles and the use of unusual keys show that Schubert was experimenting in both form and medium during his months of freedom. Three of the sonatas were published posthumously: the one in A minor (D537) as op.164 (c1852); the one in E♭ (D568) as op.122 (1829); the one in B (D575) as op.147 (1846). A work in E minor (D566 and 506) has an extraordinary history of publication: each movement appeared separately over the years between 1848 and 1929, and the whole work, edited by Kathleen Dale, was published only in 1948. The Sonata in E♭ (D568) was first planned in the key of D♭; Schubert himself decided on the transposition and he completed the work probably by June 1817. By November he had returned to the parental home and resumed his teaching duties; he had been obliged to vacate his rooms in Schober's house the previous August. The autumn of 1817 saw the composition of the Sonata in A for violin and piano (D574) and the String Trio in B♭ (D581). Both works show clear evidence of the establishment of his style in the growing harmonic complexity, the exuberant melody and (more subtly) in the spontaneity of the modulations and the obvious delight he took in expanding a new rhythmic or melodic idea.

Vienna at that time was in the grip of one of its furores, this time for Rossini, whose operas had been received in the city with frantic enthusiasm. Schubert himself was not unmoved, and signs of the genial Italian's style appear markedly in the work he was then writing, his Sixth Symphony, in C (D589), which was begun in October. It is a transitional work and shows him attempting to express his mature vision, while still using, and being inhibited by, the language of his earlier symphonies. Two overtures 'im italienischen Stile' (D590–91), finished in November, set out to imitate, almost parody, Rossini. They are attractive and tuneful works; Schubert later re-used material from the introduction and the coda of the first in the work now known as the overture to *Rosamunde*. In December, he arranged both overtures for piano duet (D592 and 597). Besides settings of Goethe and Schiller, whose *Gruppe aus dem Tartarus* (D583) evoked one of Schubert's grandest conceptions, there are songs that year to words by his own friends, among them the immortal *An die Musik* (D547) to Schober's text. Two famous songs of 1817 are *Der Tod und das Mädchen* (D531) and *Die Forelle* (D550), which from the first won all hearts. Both melodies later served Schubert as themes for equally beloved instrumental variations. Of the Mayrhofer settings, the finest is *Memnon* (D541); a slighter song is *Erlafsee* (D586), printed in January 1818 as a supplement to a periodical – Schubert's first published work.

In December 1817, Schubert's father was appointed master of a school in the adjoining district of Rossau. The family, augmented by two sons and two daughters of the second marriage, had moved to the new house by early 1818. Schubert remained there as a teacher until the following July. It must have been doubly irksome to him, this resumption of a task he hated after a year of freedom from routine, and a return to the family circle in which he must have felt deep affection but no true kinship after his recent contact with congenial spirits. No wonder he was to say of himself during this period, 'I should have become nothing but a thwarted [*verdorbener*] musician'. His work of that spring reflects his depression. A sonata in C (D613) and a symphony in D (D615) were both left unfinished. Only a little Rondo in D for piano duet from that period (D608) has any sparkle; it was a tribute to his new friend Josef von Gahy, an excellent pianist with whom Schubert loved to play duets. (The title on the first edition, 'Notre amitié est invariable', does not, however, derive from Schubert.) The second 'Italian' overture, in C, was performed in the hall of the Zum römischen Kaiser restaurant on 1 March and again in May – his début in the concert room. These performances secured press notices in Vienna, Dresden and Leipzig.

In July he was able to leave the Rossau school. He was offered and accepted the post of music master to the children of Count Johann Esterházy: his pupils were the young princesses Marie and Caroline. The count's summer residence was at Zseliz, then in Hungary, about 480 km east of Vienna. Schubert resigned from his father's school and never returned to teaching.

The first weeks at Zseliz were very happy. On 3 August he wrote to his friends in Vienna:

I am quite well. I live and compose like a god, as though that were as it should be. Mayrhofer's *Einsamkeit* is ready, and I believe it to be the best I have done, for I was without a care . . . Thank God, I live at last, and it was high time . . .

Einsamkeit (D620) is a long, discursive ballad of mixed value, and few people would endorse the composer's opinion of it. Other compositions reveal the fact that he was in charge of two young pianists, for they are almost all for piano duet: a Sonata in B♭ (D617), a set of variations (D624) and a fine but little-known set of polonaises (D599). The variations, on a song called *Reposez-vous, bon chevalier*, were published in 1822 as his op.10 and dedicated to Beethoven 'by his admirer and worshipper, Franz Schubert'. As time passed, Schubert grew discontented with life at Zseliz. He felt that none of the people he met there really cared for music, and his existence began to seem unendurably empty compared with the society he had enjoyed in the capital and the stimulus of his Viennese friendships. He wrote to Schober on 8 September:

At Zseliz I am obliged to rely wholly on myself. I have to be composer, author, audience and goodness knows what else. Not a soul here has any feeling for true art, or at the most the countess now and again (unless I am wrong). So I am alone with my beloved and have to hide her in my room, in my pianoforte and in my bosom. Although this often makes me sad, on the other hand it elevates me the more. Have no fear, then, that I shall stay away longer than is absolutely necessary.

While at Zseliz Schubert composed the *Deutsches Requiem* (D621) for his brother Ferdinand who, possibly to enhance his reputation as a music teacher, passed off the work as his own. In a letter of October he referred to this 'sin of appropriation'. Schubert's reply is one of the most affectionate and sweet-natured letters he wrote: he made nothing of Ferdinand's act, saying only that it was his greatest reward for composing the *Requiem*. It was only with the discovery of this letter by Grove on 26 October 1880, announced in his article 'Schubert' in the first edition of this dictionary, that the true author of the *Deutsches Requiem* was revealed. His Sonata in F minor (D625, ?505) was composed at Zseliz in September 1818; it is not quite complete, and of very different quality from the unfinished and inferior sonata of the previous April. In November the Esterházy family returned to Vienna for the winter, Schubert with them. The association was not broken, however, and he continued to give the children lessons during the winter months. There was no return to school-teaching, although for some years he was officially designated 'school assistant at the Rossau'.

4. Vienna friends and patrons, 1819-20

On his return to Vienna, Schubert went to lodge with Mayrhofer in the Wipplingerstrasse. Relations between the two artists were cordial, and even happier was their association in the songs of that year, for Mayrhofer's verses drew from Schubert a music whose grandeur is surpassed only by his settings of Goethe and Schiller. It is moreover an interesting facet of Schubert's work in lieder to find how the greater Mayrhofer settings often led to even greater Goethe settings – as though Mayrhofer had tapped the springs in Schubert from which Goethe could draw a finer music.

Schubert next began work on Georg von Hofmann's one-act play *Die Zwillingsbrüder* (D647); the overture is dated 19 January 1819. Vogl, for whom the leading roles (the twin brothers) were designed, secured its performance at the Kärntnertor-Theater the following year. On 8 January, a performance of the *Prometheus* cantata was given in the house of Ignaz von Sonnleithner, the father of Schubert's friend Leopold. The elder Sonnleithner was a rich patron of music and in his rooms in the Gundelhof regular and lavish concerts were given. In private circles Schubert's name was becoming widely known, and in public circles, too; an overture of his (probably that in E minor, D648, composed in February 1819), was played at Müllers Hall on 14 March, and a tenor of the Theater an der Wien, Franz Jäger, sang the *Schäfers Klagelied* several times during the spring; the performances received favourable notices in the press, one even in Berlin.

Anselm Hüttenbrenner, who had made Schubert's acquaintance when they were both pupils of Salicri's, had left Vienna for his home in Graz during autumn 1818. Schubert's relationship with him was cordial and his letters very friendly; on 19 May 1819 he wrote: 'In spite of Vogl it is difficult to outwit such *canaille* as Weigl, Treitschke etc. That is why instead of my operetta, they give other rot, enough to make your hair stand on end'. The younger brother, Josef Hüttenbrenner, remained in Vienna and gave Schubert the slavish devotion which frequently provokes snubs; Schubert's earned him the nickname 'The Tyrant'.

The summer of 1819 was one of the happiest periods of Schubert's life. He accompanied Vogl to Steyr at the beginning of July and spent nearly three months in a district which he described as 'inconceivably lovely'. Steyr, some 145 km west of Vienna, was Vogl's birthplace and whenever possible he spent the summer there. The popular 'Trout' Quintet (D667), for piano and strings, was begun there, commissioned by the town's most eminent music patron, Sylvester Paumgartner, a cellist. By the following autumn in Vienna it was finished and despatched to Paumgartner; the variation movement which gives the quintet its nickname owed its inception to Paumgartner's love of the song. It has been well suggested that the Steyr countryside was a secret collaborator in the quintet; it is even fortunate in its nickname, with its suggestion of cool, sun-flecked water.

The friends departed for Vienna in the middle of September. The record of the next six months is a chronicle of composition. Schubert rejoined Mayrhofer and in October set three of his friend's poems, including *Nachtstück* (D672). Two Goethe songs followed: one of them, *Prometheus* (D674), is the finest of his lyrico-dramatic songs. A charming song to verses by Schiller is *Strophe aus Die Götter Griechenlands* (D677, 'Schöne Welt, wo bist du?'), written in November. The fifth mass, in A♭ (D678), was begun in November, but set aside and not completed until September 1822. Another work, unfortunately, was also left unfinished, and Schubert never returned to this fragmentary score. It is the setting, dated February 1820, of August Niemeyer's sacred poetic drama *Lazarus, oder Die Feier der Auferstehung* (D689). Although a little too full of Schubert's softer, more easy-going lyricism, it is written in a style which is endlessly fascinating; it contains hints of leitmotif, and the orchestral web which forms the accompaniment, colourful and inventive, hints at Wagnerian practice.

Die Zwillingsbrüder was staged on 14 June at the Kärntnertor-Theater with Vogl doubling the roles of the twin brothers. It had only a moderate success and was withdrawn after five further performances. But these performances did bring Schubert's name into greater prominence, and in July he was commissioned by the management of the Theater an der Wien to compose music for a three-act play, *Die Zauberharfe* (D644). It is an extravaganza, full of mechanical stage effects and burdened with a complicated plot. The text was also by Hofmann. Schubert is said to have been as little interested in *Die Zauberharfe* as he had been in *Die Zwillingsbrüder*. The music was composed in a fortnight and the work presented on 19 August 1820. The overture, now known as the *Rosamunde* overture, is Schubert's finest work in this genre and deservedly popular (the reason for its misnaming will be discussed later). The music of *Die Zauberharfe*, entirely unknown to the public, is often very beautiful and had a profound effect on Schubert's development. He was compelled by the nature of the work to write *Melodramen* (i.e. music to accompany spoken words), and for the first time in his operatic pieces was obliged, as it were, to think instrumentally rather than vocally, to develop his themes and thematic figures according to symphonic rather than to lyrical demands. We owe the 'Unfinished' Symphony to *Die Zauberharfe*. That the music was beyond the understanding of the conservative musicians of the day is clear from the words of the critic of the Leipzig *Allgemeine musikalische Zeitung*: 'most of it is much too long, ineffective and fatiguing, the harmonic progressions are too harsh, the orchestration redundant, the choruses dull and feeble'. There were eight performances, the last on 12 October 1820. A poem written by Schubert during September 1820 entitled *Der Geist der Welt* is an enigmatic piece of writing, attacking 'those . . . who with wrangling fill these days'. Many attempts have been made to explain the contemptuous dislike Schubert expressed in these words. Rudolf Klein has convincingly suggested that it was the composer's response to the philistine reception of the music he had written for *Die Zauberharfe*.

Through his association with the Esterházy family, Schubert met Baron von Schönstein in 1820. The possessor of a fine baritone voice, Schönstein was, after Vogl, the most notable interpreter of Schubert's songs during the composer's lifetime, and he later introduced them to Liszt. The poet Matthäus von Collin, a cousin of Spaun, introduced Schubert to Ignaz von Mosel and Count Moritz Dietrichstein, two important officials at the imperial court, and also to Ladislaus Pyrker, Patriarch of Venice. In December 1820, at one of Sonnleithner's concerts, August von Gymnich, accompanied by Anna Fröhlich, sang *Erlkönig*. It was received with overwhelming enthusiasm. The performance was to have far-reaching results. The immediate outcome was that Schubert made the acquaintance of the four Fröhlich sisters, Barbara, Kathi, Josefine and Anna, a cultivated and musical family; through them he met Franz Grillparzer, Austria's most eminent dramatist.

Mayrhofer is the poet of several fine songs written during the autumn of 1820; one is the little-known *Freiwilliges Versinken* (D700), which reveals Schubert's growing power of subtle yet picturesque comment in the accompaniment. The year ends with an outpouring of music of the finest quality. The sketch in C♯ minor of Goethe's *Gesang der Geister über den Wassern* (D705), of superb promise, remained unfinished. Its stormy piano accompaniment, which recalls *Gruppe aus dem Tartarus*, might have been Schubert's finest exposition of this passionate style; the choral work is contrapuntal yet transparently clear. The same exalted mood is recaptured in the extended song *Im Walde* (D708), to words by Friedrich von Schlegel (it is sometimes called *Waldesnacht* to distinguish it from the similarly entitled song of 1825 to words by Ernst Schulze). *Im Walde* is almost impracticable in the concert room, but the Schubertian turns again and again to its outpoured splendour. The setting of Psalm xxiii for female voices (D706) was composed in December 1820 for the singing pupils of Anna Fröhlich, who taught at the Vienna Conservatory. Finally that month there was the first movement of an unfinished String Quartet in C minor, known as the 'Quartettsatz' (D703), in which Schubert

3. Franz Schubert (right) with Anselm Hüttenbrenner and Jenger: drawing by Josef Teltscher

achieved the lyrical radiance of the 'Trout' Quintet with the dramatic intensity of his finest songs. It is the first of the instrumental masterpieces of the 1820s. 41 bars of the slow movement, an Andante in A♭, are extant.

5. Events of 1821-2

In the early part of 1821, Schubert decided to leave Mayrhofer and he moved into a house nearby in the Wipplingerstrasse. He became very friendly with a young painter named Moritz von Schwind, some seven years his junior, who was in after years to paint the most famous of the Schubert pictures: it was called *Schubert-Abend bei Joseph von Spaun* and enshrines for ever the Biedermeier atmosphere of the Schubertiads. The settings of Goethe which he composed that spring have become famous: the songs range from the delicacy and charm of *Geheimes* (D719) to the grandeur of *Grenzen der Menschheit* (D716). A new treatment of *Gesang der Geister* for double male chorus with accompaniment for low strings (D714) was finished in February 1821. The poem held a great attraction for Schubert and this finished setting is a sublime work, though the earlier sketch holds even greater promise. At a public concert in the Kärntnertor-Theater on 7 March 1821, Vogl sang *Erlkönig*; it was a masterly performance which created a profound impression.

The continual performances of Schubert's songs and vocal quartets that year and their enthusiastic reception make it difficult to understand why publishers were so reluctant to issue his work. Songs, string quartets and piano pieces by such people as Anselm Hüttenbrenner, Benedikt Randhartinger, Franz Volkert, Ignaz von Moscheles and hosts of other minor composers were readily accepted and published, and one has to accept the fact that, at this period in Vienna, fame as a performer was the key to publication, not merit as a composer for one as obscure as Schubert. Leopold von Sonnleithner and other friends took matters into their own hands and determined to issue *Erlkönig* by private subscription. The response was overwhelming; not only was the cost of the song covered, but also that of engraving *Gretchen am Spinnrade*. The firm of Cappi & Diabelli was commissioned to engrave the works. In this manner 20 songs were published, as opp.1–8, by the end of 1821. *Erlkönig* appeared on 31 March, dedicated to Count Dietrichstein, *Gretchen* on 30 April, dedicated to Moritz von Fries. The other songs include *Der Wanderer*, *Heidenröslein*, *Rastlose Liebe* and *Der Tod und das Mädchen*; dedications were offered to Pyrker, Vogl and Salieri. Schubert did very well from some of these carefully directed dedications; he wrote to Spaun at Linz: 'but I must now tell you that my dedications have done their work; that is to say, the Patriarch has forked out 12 ducats, and, through Vogl's intervention, Fries 20, which is a very good thing for me'.

He composed two supplementary numbers, an aria and a duet (D723), for a performance at the Kärntnertor-Theater on 20 June 1821 of Hérold's *Das Zauberglöckchen* (originally *La clochette*). Their almost symphonic stature is ill-fitting in such a light work, and they made little impression. Soon after this luckless operatic venture, Schubert went to Atzenbrugg with Schober. The property was managed by an uncle of Schober's, and each summer a party of young people met there and spent a holiday together with excursions, concerts, dances and charades. The 1821 visit is the most notable of the three which Schubert made, since it is recorded pictorially by three drawings made by a new friend, the painter Leopold Kupelwieser. Two of these arc charming watercolours depicting activities of the holiday party (see fig.4), and the third is a pencil drawing of the composer, signed and dated by him 'July 1821'. The half-dozen waltzes known as the 'Atzenbrugger' Dances (D145 nos.1–3, D365 nos.29–31) were written during this holiday. Back in Vienna he began, in August, the seventh of his symphonies, in E (D729), completing a part of the first movement in score and sketching, sometimes in detail, the remainder of the four movements. No hint of the standard reached in the

4. Charade at Atzenbrugg: watercolour (1821) by Leopold Kupelwieser; Schubert is seated at the piano with Philipp Karl Hartmann to his left, Schober, Kupelwieser and Jenger (left and right) in the doorway, and Josef von Spaun seated second from the right

Quartettsatz can be found in this slender production. The symphony has been 'realized' by J. F. Barnett (1883) and Felix Weingartner (1934) but neither attempt is convincing.

During September 1821 Schubert accompanied Schober to St Pölten; they stayed nearby at the castle of Ochsenburg (owned by the Bishop of St Pölten, a relative of Schober's), seeking in this rural retreat the peace and seclusion necessary to embark on the work they were undertaking together, the composition of a full-scale opera, *Alfonso und Estrella* (D732). In later years, Schober wrote that they undertook this opera 'in a state of happy enthusiasm but with great innocence of heart and mind'. The first act was written between 20 September and 16 October. They returned to Vienna towards the end of October, and Schubert finished the second act in November; the opera was completed by 27 February 1822. Schober's libretto has been too readily accepted in the past as the reason for the total neglect of this work. The music is first-rate, full of Schubert's most endearing lyricism and dramatic genius.

The well-known set of waltzes op.9 (D365) was published in November 1821, and shortly after that Schubert began the first of his settings of the poet Rückert, *Sei mir gegrüsst* (D741). From the beginning of 1822 Schubert lodged with Schober in his house in the Spiegelgasse. There Schwind introduced him to Eduard Bauernfeld, later famous as a playwright and translator of Shakespeare and Dickens. Bauernfeld greatly admired Schubert's music and had ardently wished to meet him. These three young men, Schubert, Schwind and Bauernfeld, unlike in character yet united in their artistic ideals and love of music, became inseparable.

During February, Schubert met Weber, who was in Vienna to conduct the first full performance in the city of *Der Freischütz* at the Kärntnertor-Theater. The theatre had just come under the management of the famous Italian impresario Domenico Barbaia, who later leased the Theater an der Wien. These moves did not promise particularly well for Schubert's new opera, on which he was placing high hopes. His published songs, however, were making their mark. They were favourably reviewed in January by the Vienna *Allgemeine musikalische Zeitung*, and in March a long, sympathetic and comprehensive criticism by Friedrich von Hentl appeared in the *Zeitschrift für Kunst*. The variations op.10 (D624) were published in April. Schubert himself is supposed to have taken a copy to Beethoven, but the accounts of this event are so contradictory that it is doubtful whether they have any factual foundation. On 3 July Schubert wrote the strange document describing the dream of a quarrel and reconciliation with a father. It is embroidered with sentimental descriptions of a mother's death and burial, and the entombment of a 'gentle maiden'. The title *Mein Traum* was added years later by Ferdinand. Attempts to look upon the tale as autobiographical have given rise to the fiction of a rupture with his father and a reconciliation at his mother's graveside.

A letter from Spaun's brother Anton, written to his wife on 20 July, gives an unpleasant account of Schubert's relations with Schober and Vogl during summer 1822. Schubert seemed to be behaving in a manner at odds with his true nature; he aped the man of the world, became offhand to his friends (discourteously so to Vogl) and extravagant and loose in his way of life. Vogl considered the libretto of *Alfonso und Estrella* to be thoroughly bad; the absence of his backing, together with the fact that Barbaia was engrossed with Rossini, led to its rejection. Apparently Schubert and Vogl were reconciled by the autumn. 12 of his songs were published in Vienna during the year, the three Harper's Songs (op.12, D478–80) and *Geheimes* (op.14, D719) appearing on 13 December. The songs of 1822 include settings of Mayrhofer, composed in the spring, one of which is the charming *Nachtviolen* (D752); towards the end of the year there were settings of Goethe, not of the stature of *Prometheus*, but containing such sublime specimens of his lyric art as *Der Musensohn* (D764) and *Am Flusse* (D766). The Mass in A♭ (D678) was finished in September, and November saw the first example of his maturity in piano composition, the 'Wanderer' Fantasy (D760).

The outstanding work of that autumn is the eighth of Schubert's symphonies, the 'Unfinished' in B minor (D759). Only one other work among his instrumental compositions up to that time, the Quartettsatz, is not dwarfed by the two movements of the symphony. They were composed during October and the scherzo set aside for the composition of the 'Wanderer' Fantasy.

Many theories have been evolved to account for the fact that Schubert never finished the symphony. That he intended it to be a two-movement work is disposed of by the existence of a substantial part of the third movement. It has been suggested that the symphony was in fact finished: T. C. L. Pritchard put forward the idea in 1942 that Anselm Hüttenbrenner had lost the manuscript of the last two movements, but more recent documentation and discoveries leave no ground for this theory; more recently Gerald Abraham has suggested that the finale of the symphony is the movement used by Schubert as

5. Autograph sketches for the projected scherzo of Schubert's Symphony no.8 in B minor D759 ('Unfinished'), composed October 1822

the B minor entr'acte of the *Rosamunde* music, but his arguments are slender and are contrary to the weight of palaeographic evidence. The truth about Schubert's failure to complete the symphony may lie in psychological factors, and particularly in the tragic event which occurred at the end of 1822. He then contracted syphilis, and by the late spring of 1823 he was desperately ill. To a sensitive man like Schubert the association of the composition of his symphony with the events which led to his illness might have made a return to it repugnant. The fate of the manuscript has also been bedevilled by theorizing on scanty facts. The recent disclosure of documents from the Hüttenbrenner family archives shows that Schubert gave the manuscript of the 'Unfinished' Symphony, in its incomplete state, to Josef Hüttenbrenner some time in 1823, to pass it on to his brother Anselm as a private gift (not, as long believed, as an acknowledgment of his election to the Styrian Music Society). This was probably in payment for a debt or an obligation; Anselm had a perfect right to retain the score. It was eventually, in 1865, handed over to the conductor of the orchestra of the Vienna Musikverein and performed in December that year.

6. Illness

The onset of his unpleasant illness forced Schubert to leave Schober's home. By the end of 1822 he was living in his father's house in the Rossau. In the early weeks of 1823 he was too ill to leave the house, as we learn from a letter which he wrote to Ignaz von Mosel asking him to send *Alfonso und Estrella*, with a letter of recommendation, to Weber at Dresden. On this same day, 24 February, the 'Wanderer' Fantasy was published as op.15.

The pressing need for money forced Schubert into a bad business move that winter. He sold to Cappi & Diabelli, for a lump sum, all his rights in the publication of opp.1–7, and in February offered them the remaining opp.12–14. He suspected the publishers of dishonest dealing with him, and not only in the strict account of sales. He broke with the firm in a letter of 10 April 1823, a letter with an edge which is new in Schubert. His first publication from another house was op.20, issued by Sauer & Leidesdorf; it included *Frühlingsglaube* (D686) and *Sei mir gegrüsst* (D741). His next piano sonata, in A minor (D784), was written in February 1823; it is the first of his mature sonatas, restrained and economical compared with the 'Wanderer' Fantasy, and breaking completely with the graceful, ornamental style of his earlier sonatas. A one-act operetta, *Die Verschworenen* (D787), to a libretto by Ignaz Castelli, was completed in April (in deference to a touchy political censorship the title was changed to *Der häusliche Krieg*). It was not performed in Schubert's lifetime, but has proved to be thoroughly stageworthy, as well as melodious, witty and delightfully scored.

By now, Schubert's condition had grown so serious that he was admitted to the Vienna general hospital. A poem of his, written on 8 May, makes painful reading; it ends:

> Take my life, my flesh and blood,
> Plunge it all in Lethe's flood,
> To a purer, stronger state,
> Deign me, Great One, to translate.

Yet during this depressing period the first songs of the *Schöne Müllerin* cycle were composed; they grace this unhappy year, in truth, like 'a sunny archipelago of songs'. The author is Wilhelm Müller, and the story told in the sequence of poems originated in a family charade.

On 25 May 1823 Schubert turned once more to the composition of a full-length opera, *Fierabras* (D796). The original play had a complicated plot, set in the time of Charlemagne although its ideas and atmosphere are medieval. The libretto was by Josef Kupelwieser, brother of Leopold. Schubert's inability to visualize how ineffective this play would be as a theatrical proposition suggests that there was no genuine theatrical urge behind his repeated operatic ventures. It can never have occurred to him that to earn a living in this way would be as arduous a task as routine class-teaching. He spent the weeks from the end of July to mid-September revisiting Linz and Steyr, where he met Spaun, Mayrhofer and Vogl. His life was regular and quiet; that and the summer air of this idyllic countryside restored him somewhat, though even there he suffered a bout of severe illness. He was elected an honorary member of the Linz Musical Society and met the president,

Friedrich von Hartmann, whose two sons, Fritz and
Franz, later came to Vienna and kept copious diaries
which contain many references to Schubert and his
friends. *Fierabras* was finished on 26 September, and
the overture completed on 2 October. The rejection
by Barbaia was inevitable: no discerning manager could
have accepted the play, in spite of the excellence of its
music – music which haunts the mind more than that of
Alfonso und Estrella, which Schubert is supposed to
have preferred to all his other operas.

Weber was in Vienna that autumn for the first performance of *Euryanthe* on 25 October. In Schubert's
opinion its bad reception was justified, and when he met
Weber at the Zur ungarischen Krone inn he told him
so, adding that he preferred *Der Freischütz*. Relations
between the two men cooled, but there is no trustworthy
evidence that this frankness on Schubert's part led to a
quarrel between him and Weber. In November Schubert
was again seriously ill; but he rallied, and wrote on 30
November to Schober (who was at Breslau attempting
to make a name as an actor) that his health seemed to be
firmly restored at last. In those days, of course, a cure
was out of the question; the disease never again racked
him outwardly, but it steadily undermined his central
nervous system. His temperament, too, was altering.
With his resilient good humour there would always be
periods in which he knew no care; but he had also to
contend with pain and giddiness which understandably
induced fits of irritability and depression. He told
Schober that he had composed more *Schöne Müllerin*
songs; the cycle was completed soon afterwards. The
remaining Rückert songs, including the celebrated *Du
bist die Ruh* (D776) and *Dass sie hier gewesen* (D775),
were also probably composed that autumn.

In spite of the object-lesson of *Euryanthe*, he accepted in October a commission to write incidental music to a romantic drama by the same author, Helmina von Chézy. The drama, *Rosamunde, Fürstin von Zypern*, is lost, but a synopsis of the plot, surviving in contemporary records, shows its worthlessness. Fortunately most of Schubert's music is instrumental (D797). Produced on 20 December, *Rosamunde* was a failure, and it achieved only two performances. The orchestral parts for the vocal numbers lay in oblivion until 1867, when they were rescued by Grove and Sullivan. Today the entr'actes and ballet music, although written in an incredibly short time, are among Schubert's most popular orchestral works. The fact that he wrote no overture to *Rosamunde* has led to two of his other overtures' being wrongly attributed to the play. For the actual performance he used the overture to *Alfonso und Estrella*, possibly in revised form; it is this work, in D (D732), which was wrongly printed in the Breitkopf & Härtel complete edition at the start of the *Rosamunde* incidental music and so was looked upon as the authentic *Rosamunde* overture. The second misnamed work, now universally performed as the *Rosamunde* overture, is actually the overture composed for the performance of *Die Zauberharfe* in 1820.

Although Schubert never abandoned his ambition to write a successful opera, *Rosamunde* is his last completed dramatic work. He then turned again to purely instrumental forms, and in them achieved masterly success. At the beginning of 1824 he composed his first chamber works for over three years. On 13 February Schwind wrote to Schober: 'Schubert now keeps a fortnight's fast and confinement. He looks much better and is very bright, very comically hungry and writes quartets and German dances and variations without number'. The quartets were the favourite one in A minor (D804), finished in March 1824 (published the following September as op.29 no.1), and the one in D minor (D810) with variations on the song *Der Tod und das Mädchen* as its slow movement, also finished in March 1824; because of a mistake by Franz Lachner the date 1826 is still often assigned to it. Among the variations mentioned by Schwind is the set for flute and piano (D802) on *Trockne Blumen* from the *Schöne Müllerin* cycle, which Schubert composed for Ferdinand Bogner, professor at the Vienna Conservatory. During February he was also at work on the Octet in F for wind and strings (D803) which had been commissioned by Ferdinand, Count Troyer, a clarinettist and a member of the Archduke Rudolph's musical establishment. The Octet, deservedly popular, was modelled (at Troyer's request) on Beethoven's Septet, and although the work is highly characteristic of Schubert there are links, both obvious and subtle, between the two. The theme of the variation movement is from the duet 'Gelagert unter'm hellen Dach der Bäume' in *Die Freunde von Salamanka*. On 14 March a quartet led by Ignaz Schuppanzigh gave a public performance of the A minor String Quartet; three days later the first part of *Die schöne Müllerin* was published as op.25. Schubert dedicated neither of these works to a rich patron, who might have made some financial return, but instead paid tribute to two fine artists: the first was dedicated to Schuppanzigh, the second to Baron von Schönstein.

7. Schubert's circle of friends

Letters exchanged between his friends often touch on Schubert or his activities; Schwind wrote to Schober on 6 March: 'If you go to see him during the day, he says, "Hullo, how are you? – Good" and goes on writing'. Reading parties, instituted by Schober in autumn 1822, had become so swollen with new and uncongenial acquaintances that not even custom could prolong their existence. Doblhoff wrote to Schober on 2 April: 'Yesterday our reading circle was formally suspended. It had grown so much that in the end it devoured itself . . . Schubertiads are hardly mentioned any more. Schubert himself cannot sing, and Vogl will sing only in agreeable and respectable society'. Schubert's circle had disintegrated and another one was in the process of forming. While we cannot altogether regret the departure of Schober, it is quite another matter to consider Spaun's absence in Linz, Kupelwieser's departure for Italy and the estrangement of Mayrhofer (which occurred that spring). With Schwind he was on terms of affectionate intimacy, and soon Bauernfeld came into prominence; but in the composer's mind the breaking of his friendships and the wreck of his health became associated, and with almost unbearable misery he wrote to Kupelwieser on 31 March 1824:

In a word, I feel myself to be the most unhappy and wretched creature in the world. Imagine a man whose health will never be right again, and who, in sheer despair over this, ever makes things worse and worse, instead of better; imagine a man, I say, whose most brilliant hopes have perished, to whom the felicity of love and friendship have nothing to offer but pain . . . Thus joyless and friendless I should pass my days, did not Schwind visit me now and again and turn on me a ray of those sweet days of the past.

Schubert went that summer to Zseliz for a second time as music master to the Esterházy family, leaving Vienna on 25 May. It was a grudging move on his part, for he wrote to Schober on 21 September: 'Now I sit here alone in the depths of the Hungarian country whither I unfortunately let myself be enticed a second time without having a single person with whom I could speak a sensible word'. In this letter we again have that aching cry for the past: 'I want to exclaim with Goethe: "Who will bring me back an hour of that sweet time?"' (an allusion to *Erster Verlust*, which he had set in 1815). Family letters survive from 1824 as from 1818. Ferdinand and Franz were always devoted brothers, and the composer's illness had drawn them even closer. On 3 July Ferdinand wrote to his brother that a musical clock in the Zur ungarischen Krone inn had played several of his (Franz's) waltzes, and that hearing them he was moved to . . . but he could not finish the sentence. Schubert replied, 'Did all the tears come to your mind which you have seen me weep?'. To Schwind, during August, Schubert wrote:

I am still well, thank goodness, and should be quite comfortable here, if only I had you, Schober and Kupelwieser with me, but as it is, I often long damnably for Vienna, in spite of the certain attractive star. By the end of September, I hope to see you all again. I have composed a grand sonata and variations for four hands, which latter are having a great success here.

Both works mentioned are for piano duet. The 'grand sonata' was composed in June and published posthumously under the title 'Grand Duo' as op.140 (D812). The variations are those in A♭ (D813), published the following spring as op.35. Another piano duet

6. *Franz Schubert: watercolour portrait (1825) by Wilhelm August Rieder*

of the period is the famous *Divertissement à l'hongroise* (D818) whose best moments are among the most superb passages in Schubert's music for piano duet. The 'attractive star' of his letter is certainly Caroline Esterházy, then nearly 20 years old, with whom he was believed to be in love. The vocal quartet *Gebet* (D815) was written for her during one September day, Schubert receiving Fouqué's words after breakfast and presenting the finished composition for rehearsal that evening.

He arrived back in Vienna, with Baron von Schönstein, on 17 September, and once more went to live in the Rossau. He was considerably better for having spent those quiet summer months in Zseliz, and Schwind wrote to Schober on 8 November: 'Schubert is here, well and divinely frivolous, rejuvenated by delight and pain and a pleasant life'. The Sonata in A minor (D821) for piano and arpeggione (a six-string cello-like instrument with frets) was composed in November and played shortly after by the man for whom it was written, Vincenz Schuster; it is a secondary work compared with the giants of the year, but not to be despised. Anna Milder-Hauptmann, whom Schubert in his youth had revered for her operatic singing, wrote to him on 12 December from Berlin. She had come to know and admire his songs, and asked whether she might use her good offices to secure the performance of one of his operas in Berlin. Schubert sent her the score of *Alfonso und Estrella*, but without success.

His growing intimacy with Schwind led him in February 1825 to move into the suburb of Wieden, where he occupied rooms in a house close to Schwind's home. Schubert was fond of the volatile young painter and called him his 'beloved'; Schwind, for his part, idolized the composer and daily sought his company. In his own sphere as painter and illustrator, Schwind was to achieve notable work, but through Schubert we encounter him in his turbulent youth, and he shows a tiresome strain of adolescent gracelessness, particularly in his childish quarrels. According to Bauernfeld he behaved with studied rudeness to Vogl. Bauernfeld's close friendship with Schubert began during February. It is easy to see how attractive to Schubert was the company of this lighthearted youth, who chaffed him over his love affairs, fraternized with him in taverns and promised him a new operatic libretto.

8. 1825-6

Schubert's reputation grew steadily. Songs and vocal quartets were given in Vienna by the Gesellschaft der Musikfreunde (the Musikverein) and at the Vienna Conservatory. Schubertiads, with Vogl once more supreme, were more popular than ever, taking place in the houses of Witteczek or Weintridt and, on one occasion, in the house of Katherina von Lászny, a former soprano at the Kärntnertor-Theater, courtesan and patron of the arts. To her Schubert dedicated op.36, containing *Der zürnenden Diana* (D707). Another famous singer whom Schubert met that spring was the popular and much loved Sofie Müller. Extracts from her diary tell of frequent visits by Schubert and Vogl to her home in Hietzing, a district which includes the Schönbrunn estate. She herself sang many of his songs, including *Die junge Nonne* (D828) on 3 March 1825, soon after it was composed.

Anna Milder-Hauptmann wrote from Berlin on 8 March and quickly dispelled any hopes Schubert may have had that his opera would be done there. It is evident, reading between the lines, that she had hoped for an opera with a big leading role for herself and had looked upon Schubert as a possible provider of congenial show-pieces. At her concert in Berlin on 9 June she included *Erlkönig* and the second Suleika song (D717). The *Berlinische Zeitung* commented appreciatively on the music, and Anna sent the cutting to Schubert, then on holiday in Gmunden. In both Berlin and Dresden, Viennese correspondents reported favourably on his songs.The publications in Vienna during 1825 make an impressive list, both in quantity and in quality. They include, besides such songs as *An Schwager Kronos*, *Ganymed* (both op.19, D369, 544) and *Die junge Nonne* (op.43, D828), the C major Mass (op.48, D452) and the A♭ variations for piano duet (op.35, D813). Quite as interesting is the variety of publishers. Schubert still had no dealings with Diabelli; the works issued by that firm had been acquired before the break in 1823. But Cappi & Co., Sauer & Leidesdorf and Pennauer published his work and before the end of the year Artaria was negotiating with him.

In spring 1825, the fine Piano Sonata in A minor (D845) was composed; but a potentially even finer one in C, known as the 'Reliquie' (D840) was left unfinished. We may regret this the more deeply since the magnificent first movement is accordingly little known. Some of the songs from Scott's *The Lady of the Lake* were composed that month, in a translation by P. Adam Storck; Schubert hoped that the addition of Scott's original text, when the songs were published, would help to make his name known in England.

Towards the end of May he left Vienna for a holiday with Vogl in Upper Austria; the summers of 1824 and 1825 thus parallel the summers of 1818 and 1819. He spent over four months in this district, a supremely happy period in his life; everywhere he found new friends and old admirers of his songs and piano pieces. To facilitate reference, it may be well to list his movements during the period:

Steyr (20 May–4 June; there was a short visit to Linz during this period); Gmunden (4 June–15 July; including a visit to Ebenzweier); Linz (15–25 July; a visit to Steyregg); Steyr (25 July–13 August); Gastein (14 August–4 September; via Werfen and Lake Traun); Gmunden (10–17 September); Steyr (17 September–1 October); Linz to Vienna (1–3 October).

According to a letter of 19 July to Spaun from Anton Ottenwalt, Schubert's host at Linz, the composer 'worked at a symphony at Gmunden'. This is the first mention of the supposedly lost work of 1825, called the 'Gastein' or 'Gmunden–Gastein' Symphony (D849). Interpretations of the documents vary, but certainly a symphony was sketched (Reed, 1972, believed that the work was practically completed), and the sketches probably became the Symphony in C (D944). There is no evidence, however, to connect the 'Gastein' Symphony with the Grand Duo of 1824.

The songs of *The Lady of the Lake*, particularly *Ellens Gesang III* (popularly known as *Ave Maria* D839), frequently featured in the song recitals which Schubert and Vogl gave for their friends that summer. The performance of these two men, playing and singing as if they were one, was something new and unheard of, and they had tremendous success (so Schubert wrote to his brother Ferdinand in September). His letters to his family are long and interesting, coloured as they were by his journeyings through this lovely region, and by the warmth of his reception at the hands of people who were strangers, but who looked upon him, because of his music, as a valued friend. He wrote to his parents on 25 July:

In Upper Austria I find my compositions everywhere, especially at the monasteries of Florian and Kremsmünster, where with the aid of a gallant pianist I produced my four-hand variations and marches with notable success. What pleased especially were the variations in my new sonata for two hands, which I performed alone and not without merit, since several people assured me that the keys became singing voices under my hands.

At Gastein he finished another piano sonata in D (D850), a work full of the overflowing romanticism so typical of that summer; we find it again in two magnificent songs to words by Pyrker, composed in August: *Das Heimweh* (D851) and *Die Allmacht* (D852), Schubert's rapturous creation in music of the summer beauty of the landscape about him, which had so fortified him in spirit and body during these months.

On 3 October Schubert arrived in Vienna, accompanied by Gahy. He found awaiting him not only Bauernfeld and Schwind, but also Schober, returned from Breslau, and Kupelwieser from Italy. Schober quickly assumed his old place in the centre of the stage, and Bauernfeld recorded in his diary that the reunion led to celebrations in inns and coffee houses, often until 2 or 3 a.m. An acknowledgment of Schubert's growing reputation that year is the fact that his portrait was on sale in December at the house of Cappi & Co. An 'extremely good likeness', the firm called it; it is an engraving by J. H. Passini of the best-known portrait, the watercolour by Wilhelm Rieder made from sketches in May 1825 (fig.6).

In January of the following year, Schubert produced the last of his settings of Goethe, the Songs from *Wilhelm Meister* (D877). All are to lyrics of Mignon which he had set before, but which he now supplemented with more mature if not necessarily more endearing settings. The following month the String Quartet in D minor (D810) was performed at the residence of Josef Barth; it was published posthumously in 1831. The publication, early in 1826, of the A minor Piano Sonata (D845) as op.42 by Pennauer widely established Schubert's status as a composer for the piano; there were favourable notices in Leipzig (1 March) and Frankfurt (26 August). The Zurich publisher Hans Nägeli mentioned Schubert in a series of lectures, purely as a piano composer; he also wrote to

Carl Czerny on 18 June saying that the A minor Sonata
was a 'capital piece' and asking him to invite Schubert to
contribute to a projected series of piano works by
contemporary composers. On 4 July Schubert accepted
the invitation, but did nothing further in the matter –
unless it is to Nägeli's offer that we owe the composition
of the Sonata in G major (D894) in the following
October.

The publications of the year are more numerous and
impressive than those of 1825, and among his publishers Artaria and Thaddeus Weigl make their appearance. The former published the *Lady of the Lake* songs
(op.52), the D major Sonata (op.53, D850) dedicated to
the pianist Karl von Bocklet, and the *Divertissement à
l'hongroise* (op.54, D818). Weigl, in addition to songs,
published as op.63 no.1 a Divertissement for piano duet
on supposedly French motifs (D823); Schubert intended
this to be the first part of a three-section work, the other
two parts being an *Andantino varié* and a *Rondeau
brillant*. These two, through a mistake, were published
as op.84, and the work has remained in this
dismembered state ever since. Op.51, from Diabelli in
August, contains the favourite *Marche militaire* (D733).
On 12 August Schubert wrote to Breitkopf & Härtel and
to H. A. Probst, offering to the two Leipzig firms songs
and instrumental pieces. Both replied courteously, but
there the matter ended. On 7 April 1826, Schubert
petitioned the emperor to be appointed as vice-director
of the imperial court chapel; it was a move clearly
directed by financial need, but equally clearly he
genuinely wanted the post and was disappointed when
he heard of his failure to secure it.

Bauernfeld spent the summer in Carinthia, and at
Villach he wrote *Der Graf von Gleichen* as a libretto for

Schubert. Once again we are faced with the extraordinary inability of the composer to assess the merit of
opera texts: *Der Graf von Gleichen* (D918) is a lifeless
hotch-potch of stock stage situations with, moreover, a
bigamous marriage as the central theme. It was
prohibited by the censor, but Schubert continued to
make sketches, often in considerable detail, for the
music. Spaun had returned to Vienna during April and
resumed his friendly relations with Schubert; we see the
two friends at a new haunt, the inn Zum grünen Anker,
near St Stephen's Cathedral. To the composer's closer
acquaintance with the poet Johann Seidl we owe a group
of songs including *Das Zügenglöcklein* (D871) and the
Vier Refrainlieder (D866) and two vocal quartets,
Nachthelle and *Grab und Mond* (D892–3). There was
also a fine series of songs in 1826 to poems by Ernst
Schulze, among them *Über Wildemann* (D884) and the
ever fresh *Im Frühling* (D882). During July, while stay-
ing at the Schober house in Währing, he composed the
three Shakespeare songs (the German versions were cast
in the original metre, and neither Shakespeare nor
Schubert needs to be modified when the songs are sung
in English). The well-known story of Schubert's composing *Hark, hark the lark* on the back of a menu card,
where a resourceful friend had pencilled staves to
accommodate his sudden inspiration, derives from
Doppler and is fictional, as are most of his reminiscences of Schubert. If other familiar Schubert anec-
dotes are missing from these pages, it is because of
similar dubious provenance.

His last String Quartet, in G (D887), was finished on
30 June. He had written to Bauernfeld the previous
month: 'I am not working at all'; when the period of
inactivity passed it was followed by a burst of creation,

7. *Schubert Abend bei Joseph von Spaun: sepia drawing by Moritz von Schwind;*
Schubert is at the piano, with Vogl on his right, and Spaun on his left

and the quartet was begun and finished in ten days. In spite of the publications of this year, he had no money for a holiday; a journey with Vogl was out of the question: the aging singer had married on 26 June. Kupelwieser, too, married that year, on 17 September. Schubert improvised dance music during the wedding celebrations; we read that he would not let anyone else go near the piano. A curious sequel to the wedding ceremony has come to light. One of the waltzes he improvised (AI/14) was remembered by the bride, Johanna Lutz. It was handed down in the family, and successive descendants of Johanna learnt the waltz-tune by ear. Eventually, in 1943, it was heard by Richard Strauss, who wrote it down and arranged it for piano.

For a short time in autumn 1826 Schubert lodged with Schober, but at the end of the year was again in rooms of his own. There is an almost day-to-day account of his doings during December in Franz von Hartmann's diary. He was surrounded by his friends, able to meet them at the Zum grünen Anker or Bogner's café, where more often than not they heard the chimes at midnight. There were Schubertiads at Schober's home or at Spaun's, culminating in the imposing event of 15 December. Here, in Spaun's house, a large and distinguished company gathered and heard Vogl, during the course of the evening, sing about 30 songs (Schwind's famous sepia drawing of 1868 was inspired by this concert; see fig.7). On 2 December the overture to *Alfonso und Estrella* was performed at the Kärntnertor-Theater; the performance was reported in the London *Harmonicon* the following June (1827).

9. Period of 'Winterreise'

Schubert and his friends met in 1827 at the inn Zum
Schloss Eisenstadt, but he felt himself bound by no
social obligations. Schwind, Sonnleithner, Ottenwalt
and even Schober suffered from his neglect, and the
Hartmann brothers recorded that in March Schubert
invited them to his rooms at Schober's but never put in
an appearance. A hostess, writing to a friend in June,
said: '[Schubert] was most amiable and talkative, but
escaped suddenly before anyone had an inkling'.
Engrossment in the work of composition was frequently
the cause of this non-compliance, though not always.
According to Bauernfeld, he would fail to keep
engagements if an evening walk or the chance of a
sociable gathering with his friends tempted him to do so.
He heard in January of his failure to secure the court
chapel appointment. The successful applicant was Josef
Weigl; Schubert's comment was generous: 'Much as I
would have liked to receive the appointment, I shall have
to make the best of the matter, since it was given to so
worthy a man as Weigl'. The first part of the song cycle
Winterreise (D911) was composed in February. The
poems are by the author of *Die schöne Müllerin* and
there is no need for the evidence in letters and memoirs
by his friends to make us realize how eagerly Schubert
seized this renewed opportunity to treat Müller's picturesque and limpid verses. Soon after the composition of
these songs he rejoined Schober, who had moved into a
new house, 'Unter den Tuchlauben'. In March of that
year, Beethoven, ill and near to death, may have been

given some of Schubert's songs to read while on his
deathbed. The story is told by Anton Schindler, who
related that among the songs were such masterpieces as
Die junge Nonne, Die Allmacht and *Grenzen der
Menschheit*, besides the lyrics of *Die schöne Müllerin.*
He was impressed by the songs and, if we are to believe
the untrustworthy Schindler, said: 'Truly in Schubert
there is a divine spark'. Schubert, in the company of the
Hüttenbrenner brothers and other friends, visited the
dying Beethoven on 19 March, and for the first and last
time the two men, who had lived for years as strangers
in the same city, met for a brief moment. A week later
Beethoven died and was buried in the Währing
cemetery. Schubert was one of 36 torch-bearers in the
funeral procession.

He resumed negotiations with Diabelli in spring 1827
and the firm published the Mignon songs of 1826
(D877) as op.62 on 2 March. Together with the re-
appearance of this old name in the list of his publishers
is a new one, that of Tobias Haslinger, who published
several sets of songs, the *Valses nobles* (op.77, D969; 22
January) and the G major Sonata (op.78, D894; 11
April), dedicated to Spaun. Haslinger gave op.78 the
spurious title 'Fantasie, Andante, Menuetto und
Allegretto'; the name 'Fantasy' has ever since haunted the
work, one of Schubert's noblest essays for the piano.

The Viennese press continued to report on performances of his songs and to review his publications, but
there was in 1827 a remarkable and widespread increase
in similar reports and reviews in the provincial press of
Germany in Frankfurt, Leipzig, Berlin, Mainz and
Munich. Not all were favourable, but those that were
spoke of the composer with high praise. The Leipzig
Musikalische Zeitung (26 December) devoted nearly

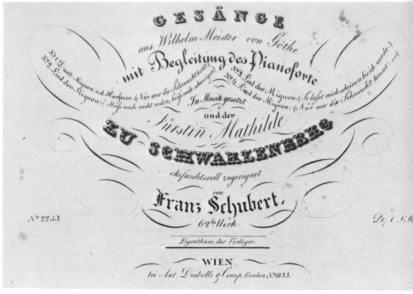

8. Title-page of the 'Gesänge aus Wilhelm Meister von Göthe' D877, published by Diabelli on 2 March 1827

2000 words to a discussion of op.78; the criticism is still readable and convincing. The numerous press notices belie the 19th-century view of Schubert as a composer with a tragically limited reputation; but their isolation from the context of contemporary documentation produces an equally false view of his fame in Austria and Germany. Its shallowness is proved by the decades of neglect and oblivion which followed his death.

Schubert spent a few weeks in the early summer, possibly with Schober, in the village of Dornbach; he stayed at the inn Zur Kaiserin von Österreich. Vienna was within easy reach, and there were occasional convivial evenings at Zum Schloss Eisenstadt. The only composition known to belong to the period is the lovely *Das Lied im Grünen* (D917), written in June, but probably some of the short piano pieces, later published as 'Impromptus', were also composed then. His election as a representative to the Vienna Gesellschaft der Musikfreunde was made that month, his own city honouring him as Linz and Graz had already done. An opportunity to visit the latter town in the coming autumn arose through his friendship with Johann Baptist Jenger, which dated from 1825. Jenger was a prominent member of the Styrian Music Society; he and Schubert were invited to spend a few weeks in the home of Dr and Frau Pachler at Graz. Schubert wrote to this lady on 12 June: 'I cannot forbear to accept an invitation whereby I shall not only set eyes at last on much vaunted Graz, but have the privilege, moreover, of making your honour's acquaintance'. The first performance of *Ständchen* (D920), to Grillparzer's words, was given by Anna Fröhlich's pupils on 11 August at Döbling. The occasion was the birthday of one of the pupils, Louise Gosmar, who later married Leopold von Sonnleithner. Anna received the poem from Grillparzer and asked Schubert to set it to music. He did so, for contralto solo and male-voice chorus; the mistake was pointed out to him and he quickly rewrote the chorus parts for female voices. The performance, in the garden of the Gosmar residence on that summer evening, would no doubt have delighted the composer, had he troubled to attend it. The new haunt that summer was the inn called Zum Wolf, der den Gänsen predigt; Schwind's and Bauernfeld's names are missing from the records of the meetings. Both were out of touch with Schubert that year; in fact, Schwind left in August for a visit to Munich, and Bauernfeld wrote in his diary:

'What is to become of us all? Shall we stick together?'.

Schubert and Jenger arrived in Graz on 3 September. Their hostess, Marie Pachler, was an accomplished woman, an excellent pianist, who had known Beethoven. She sought to entertain at her home in Graz any notable artist who was visiting the town. The days were spent in excursions to various places in the lovely neighbour-hood of Graz, including the castle of Wildbach. Anselm Hüttenbrenner was an old friend, of course, and he, Jenger and Schubert were responsible for the Schubertiads held in the evenings. Schubert's famous nickname of the period, 'Schwammerl', Viennese dialect for 'little mushroom', is an allusion to his diminutive stature, not to his stoutness (which was denied by Spaun); it may still explain, perhaps, why he preferred to improvise dance music for his friends rather than to dance himself. The dances he composed that holiday were published as the *Grazer Galopp* (D925) and the *Grazer Walzer* (op.91, D924). The two songs of the month, *Heimliches Lieben* (D922) and Herder's trans-lation of the Scottish ballad *Edward* (D923), were both composed at the instigation of Frau Pachler, to whom Schubert dedicated op.106, which contains *An Sylvia* (D891) and settings of the poet Leitner (a personal friend of the Pachlers). Later in the year, their small son, Faust, received from Schubert a *Kindermarsch* for piano duet (D928).

The return to Vienna came on 20 September; in his letter of thanks to Frau Pachler, Schubert wrote of his happiness at Graz, and of his difficulty in settling down to life in Vienna. He was, in fact, in poor health, suffer-ing from severe headaches and frequent suffusions of blood to the head. Both Spaun and Mayrhofer wrote of his depression and drawn looks during October, but

they were misguided in associating them with the composition of the concluding songs of *Winterreise*. The
sombre depths of these songs are the response of his
genius to the moods of Müller's verses, not a reflection
of his own sufferings. When Schubert sang the
Winterreise songs to his friends they were nonplussed,
and Schober confessed to liking only *Der Lindenbaum*.
His preference is illuminating: he cared only for the
straightforward, melodious side of Schubert's art, and
almost quarrelled with Spaun, earlier in the year, after
expressing his dislike of the sonatas opp.42 and 53
(D845 and 850). When Vogl, however, familiarized the
friends with *Winterreise*, it was as Schubert had
confidently foretold. Their indifference changed to keen
admiration. The exact date of composition of the Piano
Trio no.1 in B♭ (D898) is not known; it was probably
early in 1828. The second, in E♭ (D929), was begun in
November 1827. The latter was first performed on 26
December 1827, by Bocklet, Schuppanzigh and Linke.
Many years after his death several of Schubert's friends
alleged that he had used a Swedish tune in the work;
although accounts differ, the tale may have some
foundation.

Most of the short piano pieces published under the
titles *Impromptus* and *Momens musicals* (sic), as opp.90
and 142, and op.94 respectively, were composed in the
autumn of that year. They were in the tradition of
Tomášek's similar short lyrics, the 'Eclogues' and
'Dithyrambs', but Schubert owed little to Tomášek; nor
has the influence of his own piano pieces of this kind
been as great as simplifying historians have claimed.
Two pieces from the *Moments musicaux*, D780 nos.3
and 6, belong to earlier years, the first to 1823 and the
second to 1824. The last work of 1827 was the Fantasy

in C for piano and violin (D934), published in 1850 as op.159. Like the Rondo in B minor of 1826 (D895), for the same combination, it was designed for and played by the Bohemian violinist Josef Slavík. During the course of the Fantasy the song *Sei mir gegrüsst* is used as the basis for virtuoso variations which are not among Schubert's most successful essays in this genre.

10. The last year

The remarkable accomplishments of the year 1828 give to Schubert's death an overwhelmingly tragic aspect. His health was broken, and the feverish rate of production of these unparalleled 11 months before his death undoubtedly exhausted him. The work of 1828 is the *ne plus ultra* of his achievement. At the beginning of the year, and for the last time, his friends were all with him; even Mayrhofer was reconciled and made a brief appearance. The Schubertian circle has occasioned surprised comment on its predominantly non-musical character, but the musicians of that circle were so much less remarkable and articulate than the others that Schubert's quiet friendships with Gahy, Jenger, Lachner and the Hüttenbrenners tend to be overlooked. Under Schober's influence, the reading circles came into existence again, and there in January Schubert made the acquaintance of Heine's *Reisebilder*. Spaun was engaged on 6 January to Franziska Röner; at an evening concert on 28 January to celebrate the occasion – the last Schubertiad to be held at Spaun's house – the B♭ Trio was played by Bocklet, Schuppanzigh and Linke. The marriage took place on 14 April. Schubert's last letter to Anselm Hüttenbrenner, written on 18 January, asks for Anselm's good offices to procure for his brother Karl an appointment as drawing master in the training-school at Graz. He also inquired about two of his songs (*Im Walde* D834 and *Auf der Bruck* D853) which were being lithographed for publication at Graz by Josef Kreiner. They appeared the following May as op.90

(*recte* op.93). In January there were two public performances of his works: Slavík and Bocklet played the C major Fantasy on 20 January, and four days later, under the auspices of the Gesellschaft der Musikfreunde, the Grillparzer *Ständchen* was given; Schubert was present this time and remarked afterwards to Anna Fröhlich: 'Really, I never thought it was so beautiful'. The plan to give a full-scale public concert consisting solely of his own works, which had been maturing so long in his mind (the first mention of it had been in 1823) was put into effect at the end of March. The use of a room in the house Zum roten Igel, belonging to the Gesellschaft, was petitioned and granted, and on the evening of 26 March the concert was given to a packed and fervently partisan audience. The compositions and their performers were as follows:

1. First movement of a string quartet [? in G]: Böhm, Holz, Weiss and Linke;
2. Songs, *Der Kreuzzug* (D932), *Die Sterne* (D939), *Fischerweise* (D881), *Fragment aus dem Aeschylus* (D450): Vogl, accompanied by Schubert;
3. *Ständchen* (D920*b*): Josefine Fröhlich and her sister's pupils from the conservatory;
4. Trio in E♭ (D929): Bocklet, Böhm and Linke;
5. *Auf dem Strom* (D943): Ludwig Tietze, with horn obbligato by Josef Lewy;
6. *Die Allmacht* (D852): Vogl and Schubert;
7. *Schlachtlied* (D912): double chorus for male voices.

The event was called 'Franz Schubert's Invitation Concert', and it may be seen from the Deutsch numbers that nearly all the compositions were late ones. The programme gave no key for the string quartet but called it 'new'; the song with horn obbligato was written for the occasion. The concert received hardly a line in the press; it was eclipsed by the advent of Paganini. The great virtuoso threw Vienna into a frenzy greater than that which attended the advent of Rossini a dozen years earlier. Schubert, for a while prosperous (the concert had brought him 320 florins), went to hear Paganini in April and again in May, when he took Bauernfeld.

The 'Great' C major Symphony – probably, as we have seen, the work sketched at Gmunden in 1825 – was finished by March. It is likely that it was finalized for performance by the Gesellschaft der Musikfreunde; Schubert rarely composed without a performance of some sort in mind. The society, it is said, found the work too difficult, whereupon Schubert offered the earlier C major Symphony, no.6 of 1817–18. The manuscript of his last symphony, which came eventually into the possession of the Gesellschaft, shows more signs of revision than is usual in Schubert's fair copies, and all the alterations tend to give greater melodic significance to the work.

A more modest but likable work of the same month is his setting of Grillparzer's *Mirjams Siegesgesang* (D942), for soprano solo and chorus with piano accompaniment; it must originally have been intended for his concert (hence the piano rather than orchestral accompaniment). The repeated requests of his publishers for short and not too difficult piano works, coupled with his desire to find a market in Germany, may be the reason why he produced so many such pieces that year. In April the magnificent F minor Fantasy for piano duet (D940) was finished; it is the only work which he dedicated to the young Countess Caroline Esterházy (tradition has it that he once declared to her that such dedications were unnecessary, since all his work was dedicated to her). Two other piano duets are the sonata movement in A minor (D947), a superb essay, published as op.144 in 1840 and given the absurd, catchpenny title of *Lebensstürme*, and the very attractive Rondo in A (D951), finished in June and published as op.107 in December 1828. The *Drei Klavierstücke* (D946) were composed in the same year, but not published until 1868.

The few publications of 1828 were chiefly songs. Haslinger published the first part of *Winterreise* (D911) as op.89 on 14 January; the second part, beginning with *Die Post*, appeared in December after Schubert's death. Diabelli published on 14 March, as opp.85 and 86, settings of Andrew MacDonald's *Lied der Anne Lyle* (?1825, D830) and of Walter Scott's *Gesang der Norna* from *The Pirate* (1825, D831) and *Romanze des Richard Löwenherz* from *Ivanhoe* (?1826, D907). On 13 August Weigl announced the publication of *Vier Refrainlieder* (op.95, D866) as a new departure for Schubert: the composer in comic vein (though it is difficult to see how no.2, *Bei dir allein*, fits into this scheme). The *Moments musicaux* were published by Leidesdorf (11 July; op.94, D780).

Both in Berlin (25 June) and Munich (28 July) the *Winterreise* songs received lukewarm comment. Berlin was a stronghold of reaction where songs were concerned: it is a little difficult to see exactly what type of song they considered the 'true German song', but Schubert's did not come into that category and the Berlin journal was derisive in tone. Earlier that year a similar attitude had been adopted towards op.83 (D902), Schubert's three Italian songs dedicated to Luigi Lablache. But as usual the Leipzig *Musikalische Zeitung* was generous in its praise. Johann Rochlitz, the journal's founder, was very favourably disposed towards

Schubert, and had written to him on 7 November 1827 proposing his poem *Der erste Ton* as deserving of the composer's attention (it had already been set by Weber); his suggested treatment aroused no response in Schubert. Other letters from distinguished acquaintances, all expressing sincere pleasure in his work, reached the composer in 1828 and must have given him great satisfaction. Johann Schickh, who as editor of the *Wiener Zeitschrift* had initiated a series of song supplements with *Die Forelle* in 1821, wrote on 3 April, in the name of a number of admirers, urging Schubert to repeat his concert. Johann Mosewius, an opera singer and, in 1828, a lecturer in music at Breslau University, sent a glowing appreciation of the songs on 4 June. Later in the month, Karl Brüggemann, a publisher at Halberstadt, asked very deferentially for piano pieces. A letter which would have been of more interest to us than any of these was unfortunately never sent to him: it was written by Robert Schumann, then a boy of 18.

A bulky correspondence survives from 1828 between Schubert and two publishers, H. A. Probst of Leipzig and B. Schott of Mainz. Schubert was clearly doing his utmost to obtain recognition outside Vienna; the steady decline during these last two years in the amount and variety of work issued by the Viennese publishers showed that the market for his music needed some outside stimulus. By a strange coincidence, both publishers wrote to him on the same day, 9 February. Schott asked for piano compositions or songs, pointing out that the firm had an establishment in Paris and publications would be made known there too. Probst, who had already met Schubert in spring 1827, wrote a more personal letter, suggesting that it would be easy 'to disseminate your name throughout the rest of Germany and in the north, in which I will gladly lend a hand, considering talent like yours'. He replied to Schott on 21 February offering chamber music, impromptus and partsongs; eight days later the publisher expressed interest in several of these works. On 10 April Schubert, elated by the success of his concert, wrote again to both firms. To Schott he offered the E♭ Trio for 100 gulden, the second set of impromptus and a five-part chorus, *Mondenschein* (D875), for 60 gulden each; the same offer was made to Probst, except that the trio was unpriced and the other two works were not specified by name, although the same price was asked for each. It is exasperating to see the subsequent sharp practice of the two publishers, so offhandedly generous in their introductory letters. Schott, for example, accepted the smaller works for 60 gulden (the two); Probst accepted the trio for 60 gulden. The negotiations with Schott came to nothing; the Paris establishment rejected the impromptus as too difficult, and Schubert refused to sell *Mondenschein* for 30 gulden. Under protest, he accepted Probst's offer for the trio, and his two subsequent letters to the publisher (of 10 May and 1 August) are worth quoting:

The cuts indicated in the last movement are to be most scrupulously observed. Be sure to have it performed for the first time by capable people, and most particularly see to a continual uniformity of tempo at the changes of time signature in the last movement. The minuet at a moderate pace and *piano* throughout, the trio, on the other hand, vigorous, except where *p* and *pp* are marked.

The second letter was in reply to Probst's requests for the opus number and a dedication:

The opus number of the trio is 100 . . . This work is to be dedicated to nobody, save those who find pleasure in it. That is the most profitable dedication.

There was no holiday that year; ailing and wretched as he was, a few weeks outside Vienna would have been a godsend. But he had no money. Ferdinand Traweger, his former host at Gmunden, wrote on 19 May offering him a room and board at a nominal price; there was an invitation from Frau Pachler to spend the summer at Graz. Both had to be refused. Jenger, declining the second invitation in his friend's name, mentioned to Frau Pachler that Schubert was 'working diligently at a new mass'. This was the setting in E♭, begun in June (D950). Other church works were composed during the year, all rather superficial in expression and of no great moment. 13 songs of the group known as *Schwanengesang* (D957) were composed in August. The first seven are to poems by Rellstab; there follow six settings of poems by Heine, which Schubert had encountered at the reading circle. Another song, *Die Taubenpost* (D965*a*), with words by Seidl and composed in October, was added by the publisher. *Schwanengesang* is a rich and masterly epilogue to the long series of his songs: whether purely lyrical as in Rellstab's *Ständchen*, or creating unheard-of atmospheric effects as in *Die Stadt* or *Der Doppelgänger*, Schubert's hand was never more sure nor more powerful.

At the beginning of September he went to live with Ferdinand in the Neue Wieden suburb (the street is known today as the Kettenbrückengasse). His doctor, Ernst Rinna, hoped that his health would benefit from the semi-rural surroundings. He was suffering from acute headaches and giddiness. Unfortunately, the house was damp and unsanitary; far from having the desired beneficial effect, the move hastened the end. The last three sonatas, in C minor, A and B♭ (D958–60), were completed by 26 September; Schubert played from them the next day at the house of Dr Ignaz Menz. He had intended to dedicate them to Hummel, but when Diabelli published them, in 1838, Hummel was dead and they were dedicated to Schumann. His last instrumental work was the Quintet in C for strings (D956), using an extra cello rather than the more common extra viola and thus allowing of a more sonorous effect. The work may be ascribed to autumn 1828, since in a letter to Probst of 2 October Schubert mentioned the sonatas and the Heine songs, and went on to say that he had 'finally turned out' a quintet. As with the songs of *Schwanengesang*, the last instrumental works have a splendour in which there is no sign of decline; no sinking glow as of autumn or sunset lights these vigorous masterpieces. The song with clarinet obbligato *Der Hirt auf dem Felsen* (D965) was composed in October for Anna Milder-Hauptmann and sent to her the following year by Ferdinand. Either this or *Die Taubenpost* is the last song he wrote. Early in October he went on a three-day walking tour with Ferdinand and two acquaintances into Lower Austria, and on as far as Eisenstadt where Haydn was buried. It is doubtful whether, in Schubert's exhausted condition, the excursion was of any value. A cordial letter from Schindler, who was living in Pest, reached him on his return, inviting him to attend the first performance of Lachner's opera *Die Burgschaft* and suggesting that while at Pest he could give a concert of his songs. But by then any such visit was out of the question.

As the month of November drew to a close, Schubert's condition weakened. It used to be thought that his terminal illness was typhoid, known on the Continent as 'typhus abdominalis'; but it now seems beyond doubt (see Sams, 1980) that syphilis, from which

Schubert had suffered since 1822, was the cause of death. Signs of serious deterioration appeared on 31 October, when at the tavern Zum roten Kreuz he tried to eat fish and was nauseated by it. From then until he finally took to his bed he ate nothing. On 4 November he arranged to take lessons in counterpoint from Simon Sechter; whether he had lessons or not is uncertain, but a batch of his exercises was discovered in Vienna in 1969; they had been written for Sechter. A week later he was too ill to leave his room; on 12 November he wrote to Schober: 'I am ill. I have eaten nothing for 11 days and drunk nothing, and I totter feebly and shakily from my chair to my bed and back again. Rinna is treating me. If ever I take anything I bring it up again at once'.

His last occupation was the correction of the proofs of part 2 of *Winterreise*. On 16 November there was a consultation at his sick-bed between two doctors. Josef von Vering and Johann Wisgrill, Rinna himself being ill. There were now professional nurses in attendance, but Ferdinand gave him ceaseless care and Schubert's small stepsister, Josefa, was devotedly attentive to his needs. Randhartinger and Spaun visited him during those days, but Schober, for whatever reason, kept away. His last visitors were Bauernfeld, and Lachner who had returned from Pest. He was delirious, but during a lucid interval talked of Bauernfeld's *Graf von Gleichen*. On Tuesday, 18 November, the delirium persisted; Ferdinand recorded his brother's broken sayings, but no significance can be attached to them. He died the following day, 19 November, at 3 p.m., turning from Ferdinand with the words: 'Here, here is my end'.

The funeral took place two days later. Schubert's body was borne from the Neue Wieden by a group of

9. Schubert's death mask

young students and laid in St Joseph's Church in the
Margareten suburb. A chorus based on the 1817 song
Pax vobiscum (D551), to new words by Schober, was
sung. The interment was in the Währing cemetery,
Ferdinand having interpreted Schubert's deathbed
utterances as his desire to lie near the body of

Beethoven; the graves of the two composers are separated by three others.

In the valuation of his property an item labelled 'some old music' was priced at 10 gulden. This does not refer to his manuscripts, most of which were still with Schober, but to various items of printed music. His effects, as a whole, were assessed at 63 gulden. The expenses of his illness and funeral, and his debts, were together far more than the estimates usually given, amounting in fact to nearly 1000 gulden. All were discharged by the following June through posthumous publication fees.

His death was a blow, not only to his family, but also to his friends and acquaintances; they expressed their grief in diaries and letters. Memorial poems were written by Bauernfeld, Mayrhofer, Baron Schlechta and by many obscure admirers. On 23 December a memorial service was held at St Augustine's Church, at which a requiem by Anselm Hüttenbrenner was sung. A number of his friends, under the guidance of Grillparzer, Jenger and Schober, collected money to erect a monument for him; part of the fund came from a concert given by Anna Fröhlich, on 30 January 1829, at the Musikverein. It included Schubert's *Mirjams Siegesgesang* and the E♭ Trio, and also the first finale from Mozart's *Don Giovanni*. The monument, with Josef Dialer's bust of Schubert in bronze, was erected in the autumn of 1830 and inscribed with Grillparzer's epitaph: 'Die Tonkunst begrub hier einen reichen Besitz, aber noch viel schönere Hoffnungen' ('The art of music here entombed a rich possession, but even fairer hopes').

11. Posthumous publication

The wealth of unpublished work left at Schubert's death eventually came into the possession of Ferdinand, who made unremitting efforts to secure its publication. On 29 November he offered to Diabelli & Co. (later Spina & Co.) a large quantity of manuscripts comprising 'all the songs for solo voice with piano accompaniment', piano music (solo and duet) and chamber works. The offer was accepted. The songs appeared between 1830 and 1851 in 50 instalments under the general title 'Nachgelassene musikalische Dichtungen' (often abbreviated to 'Nachlass'). The masterpieces of chamber music lay unheeded on Diabelli's shelves until the 1850s: the String Quartet in G (D887) appeared as op.161 in 1851; the first three movements of the Octet (D803) as op.166 in 1853; the String Quintet in C (D956) as op.163 in 1853. Diabelli's bulk purchase still left Ferdinand with nearly all his brother's operas, symphonies and masses; the works not in his possession were *Alfonso und Estrella* (the original at Graz, the copy with Anna Milder-Hauptmann in Berlin) and the B minor Symphony in Anselm Hüttenbrenner's possession at Graz. In 1835, he appealed to Schumann, as editor of the *Neue Zeitschrift für Musik*, and on 26 April a paragraph appeared in that journal giving a list of the works available to publishers. There was no immediate result, but a few years later, when Schumann went to Vienna, he visited Ferdinand (on New Year's Day, 1837) and saw the piles of manuscripts for himself. The outcome of this famous visit was a performance, in a heavily cut version, of the 'Great' C major Symphony at the Leipzig Gewandhaus, under Mendelssohn, on 21 March 1839. The Leipzig firm of Breitkopf & Härtel published the work (parts, 1840; score, 1849), paying Ferdinand 180 gulden for it. Projected performances of the symphony in Paris under Habeneck (1842) and in London under Mendelssohn (1844) were brought to nothing by the blank refusal of orchestral players to master its difficulties at rehearsals. There are no records extant of a supposed first performance at Windsor by the private orchestra of Prince Albert. The publication of a complete edition of his works was inspired by the great Schubertian Nicolaus Dumba and carried out by Breitkopf & Härtel between 1884 and 1897. Their Kritisch durchgesehene Gesamtausgabe contained 39 volumes in 21 series, the last a supplementary volume. The operas, the early symphonies, over 200 songs and the smaller, unpublished piano and choral works appeared in print for the first time in three volumes. The editorial commentaries contain all Schubert's sketches then available for instrumental and vocal music; of outstanding interest are those for the 'Unfinished' Symphony of October 1822. In June 1967 the Internationale Schubert-Gesellschaft was founded in Tübingen, with the chief object of preparing the Neue Schubert-Ausgabe, a complete and authentic edition of the composer's work, to be published by Bärenreiter. Like the original Gesamtausgabe of 1884–97, it consists of series of classified works, eight in all, the last (entitled 'Supplement') including fundamental bibliographical works such as O. E. Deutsch's documentary biography and the thematic catalogue. The first volumes appeared in the late 1960s. The Neue

Schubert-Ausgabe has been in the care of a group of senior editors, including Walther Dürr, Arnold Feil and Christa Landon, and many Schubert scholars are also responsible for the production.

12. Posthumous performance

Schubert's fame as a songwriter was high in Austria and Germany, and it soon spread to France and England; for many years it seemed as if it were to be the only reputation allowed him. One recalls Spaun's words to Bauernfeld in 1839: 'For all the admiration I have given the dear departed for years, I still feel that we shall never make a Mozart or a Haydn of him in instrumental and church compositions, whereas in song he is unsurpassed'. This was an opinion which, happily, Spaun abandoned as the years passed and he grew more and more familiar with the instrumental masterpieces as they were published. There were occasional performances of the choral and chamber works in Vienna, chamber music in Berlin (the E♭ Piano Trio D929 and the 'Trout' Quintet D667) and in Paris (the B♭ Piano Trio D898). Schumann was indefatigable in his praise and propaganda for works for which he had a preference, such as the 'Great' C major Symphony or the Piano Trio in E♭; but even he was strangely unresponsive to the three fine sonatas of 1828, dedicated to him on publication, indeed almost flippant about them. The operas were ignored; the performances of *Alfonso und Estrella* under Liszt at Weimar (24 January 1854) and of *Die Verschworenen* at Frankfurt am Main on 29 August 1861 were travesties, although the latter opera was well received and reviewed. Not until the impact of the Johann Hellmesberger chamber concerts in Vienna in the 1860s, when the Octet and several string quartets were given, and of the performance of the 'Unfinished' Symphony, through Johann Herbeck's enthusiasm, in Vienna in 1865, was the musical world of mid-19th-century Europe forced to the conclusion that in Schubert there was an instrumental master of the front rank. The impression was of slow and by no means unopposed growth; even as late as the 1920s it was possible for a critic to write of the 'dreary passage-work' of the 'Great' C major Symphony. The new respect for Schubert in the 20th century is in part due to the realization that Beethoven's way with sonata form is not the only, Heaven-ordained way, and with that realization Schubert need no longer be considered as a mere offshoot from his great contemporary. It was not until broadcasting extended the orchestral repertory that Schubert's first six symphonies ever reached performance after their initial hearing: they began to be played during the 1930s and no.5, in B♭, quickly became popular. The sonatas were slower in making their way into public esteem. Artur Schnabel's attitude towards, and his performance of, these works proved to be a revelation. Nowadays the last of the sonatas, in B♭ (D960), is frequently played and has taken its place with the foremost examples of the Classical sonata. His operas still await discovery, and thus need to be discussed in more detail.

13. Music for the theatre

The failure of Schubert's operas to hold the stage, or even to win a hearing, is usually attributed to his librettos. Except for *Die Verschworenen*, these are somewhat pedestrian affairs, and their plots are complicated, often requiring elaborate stage machinery. Schubert matched these plays with music which is mainly of secondary value, though frequently, particularly in the later work, thoroughly characteristic. There is endless resource, and an astounding assurance in his balance of stage mood and movement against the development of his orchestral themes. As we proceed from *Des Teufels Lustschloss* (D84) to the final operas, there is the clear evolution of his own operatic style: the music grows in colour, fluidity and scope. It is unlike the evolution in his songs or instrumental work; it belongs entirely to this unknown sphere of his music. There is an extended use, for example, of richly accompanied recitative, which is quite his own; figuration grows more complex and weaves between voice and orchestra, as in the duets for Florinda and Maragond (*Fierabras*, no.9), or for Alfonso and Estrella (no.12), in a manner quite unlike anything in the songs. The exordia and ritornellos, negligible in early work, achieve the same individuality and importance as in the late songs, until in *Fierabras* there is a movingly sensitive moment where an A major passage, heralding the scene between King Karl and his daughter Emma, is beautifully modified in the orchestra when Fierabras enters and gazes in enraptured silence on the princess.

His handling of the orchestra, competent in *Lustschloss*, grows in skill and boldness until it has the true Schubertian quality, known chiefly from the *Rosamunde* music and the last two symphonies, a quality which was no 'clairvoyant' visitation but the outcome of his endless experimentation and exploration of possibility in the operas. Unlike the orchestra of his early symphonies, which was ordained by college or domestic resources, the orchestra of his operas acknowledged no limitations; he scored for full woodwind and from the first used three trombones. There is much 'nature' music in the operas: winds, storms, floods, birdsong, night and morning scenes, and in all of them the orchestral painting is vivid. *Alfonso* opens in the morning, before daybreak: soft shakes on flute and strings, with phrases on the oboe, depict the scene deliciously. One of the loveliest passages in the whole of his operas closes Act 1 of *Fierabras*: it is night, and Emma appears on a lighted balcony, while Eginhard serenades her from below. The whole of the music is fragrant with the atmosphere of this night in a garden of Spain, with the clarinet breathing its love-song above the plucked strings.

The device, so well known from his songs, whereby a striking word is translated into apt musical figuration for his accompaniments is found in the operas too. For example, the word 'schleiche' ('creep') in Olivia's aria (no.4) from *Die Freunde von Salamanka* (D326) is depicted by a slow chromatic rise and fall in the strings, ostinato, a vivid musical suggestion of slow footsteps. To come upon this aria in going through the early operas is like coming upon *Gretchen* among the early songs; it is the first appearance of the authentic voice amid efficient mediocrity. Mayrhofer drew Schubert to finer issues and this two-act Singspiel is full of interesting work; there is even a *Winterreise*-like pathos in the D minor duet for Olivia and Alonso (no.14).

Adrast, also by Mayrhofer, was not finished; of all the dramatic works before 1821 this is the finest. Noteworthy points of orchestration are the use of two cellos to accompany Croesus's air (no.2) and the use of four trombones in the following chorus. Accompanied recitative, characteristically rich in harmonic nuance, pervades the work. *Die Zwillingsbrüder* (D647) and *Die Zauberharfe* (D644) can be seen as transitional works, between the fruitful experimental work of the earlier operas and the individual fulfilment of the later ones. The benefit to Schubert, in the development and perfecting of his own orchestral style, brought about by the particular nature of the libretto of *Die Zauberharfe*, has already been touched upon. The Romance in the Act 2 finale (no.9, 'Was belebt die schöne Welt?') is a marvellously beautiful aria, which should not be allowed to remain in obscurity; it would grace any orchestral concert and repay an enterprising singer. Both works have worthy overtures: the second is famous as the '*Rosamunde* overture', and the other, which uses a theme appearing in the String Quartet in G minor (D173), also deserves revival.

Alfonso und Estrella was said to be Schubert's favourite opera; its period, 1821–2, is sufficient guarantee of its consistently good level, and many of its numbers rise above even that. The music associated with Adolfo, the conventional villain, is the best, his impassioned aria in E♭ minor (Act 2, D732 no.8*b*) being one of the finest things in the work. One intriguing fact connected with this opera is that six years later Schubert, perhaps unconsciously, took over the melody of Troila's song at the opening of Act 2, 'Das Lied vom Wolkenmädchen' (no.11), as no.19 of *Winterreise* (*Täuschung*). The words of Troila's song clearly show the link:

> Er folgte ihrer Stimme Rufen
> und stieg den rauhen Pfad hinan.
> Sie tanzte über Felsen-stufen
> durch dunkle Schlünde leicht ihm vor.

The words of *Täuschung* which provoked this reminiscence are:

> Ein Licht tanzt freundlich vor mir her
> Ich folg' ihm nach die Kreuz und Quer.

The one-act Singspiel *Die Verschworenen* (D787) is dramatically effective, with music that subtly reflects the atmosphere of this cynical text (based on Aristophanes' *Lysistrata*). A group of ladies, tired of their husbands' insatiable appetite for war-mongering, vow to withhold from them all matrimonial rights until they promise to abandon their exploits. The intrigue, the breaking of vows and the final resolution of the problem are all excellently wrought by the author, Castelli, and Schubert's music is tuneful, witty and colourful as occasion demands. The sad little Romance of Helene (no.2), the ensemble where Udolin tells the knights of their wives' vow (a delicious finger-to-lip quality in this passage), the puzzlement of the ladies (symbolized by a sinuous melody on the violins), and the vivacious play on 'für dich' and 'für mich' in the parallel arias for the Count and Countess – all these warrant an occasional performance of this sparkling operetta.

In *Fierabras*, there is little negligible work: page after page reveals the greater Schubert. One or two of the fine things in the opera have been mentioned. Others are the unaccompanied chorus 'O teures Vaterland' (no.14), also used in the overture, and the outstanding arias for Fierabras (no.6*b*) and Florinda (no.13), both of which could find a place in the concert repertory.

His last finished work for the stage, the celebrated *Rosamunde*, is mainly instrumental; had it been otherwise, the feeble libretto would have entombed it, excellent though the music is. The melodies of these ballets and entr'actes, and their poetic orchestration, so completely individual, are additional revelations of the Schubert of the B minor Symphony. Together these works herald the first period of his maturity which culminated in *Winterreise*. One point requires comment. Examination of the score of the B♭ entr'acte (D797 no.5) shows that the interlude in B♭ minor was drawn from an early song, *Der Leidende* (D432*a*), written as early as May 1816. By some strange chance, the first entr'acte, in B minor, one of the composer's masterpieces, seems to have disappeared from the concert room (Abraham suggested in 1971 that this was the original finale of the 'Unfinished' Symphony, as we have seen).

14. Church and other choral music

All Schubert's choral works, both sacred and secular, were written within a closely defined tradition of practical music-making. There was thus little place for innovation, and the established norms were not conducive to masterpieces. But the works were popular in every sense. The partsongs were frequently performed by friends; several were published in Schubert's lifetime. When in 1826 he applied for a post at the court chapel he testified that he had written five masses, all of which had been performed in various Vienna churches; one (D452) had already been published. In these genres Schubert was often content to satisfy demand, and his writing is accordingly sometimes routine, even perfunctory. But when his interest is aroused and his emotions are engaged, great music can result.

His partsongs begin in 1813 with male-voice trios (TTB). In 1815–16 these gradually give way to quartets (TTBB), and for the next ten years he composed only quartets or quintets, with an increasing use of women's voices. Most are *a cappella* or with unobtrusive piano accompaniment, though other instruments may be added for expressive effect or local colour, e.g. horns in *Nachtgesang im Walde* (D913). The first tenor usually predominates; the idiom is mainly harmonic with little or no counterpoint. Impetus is maintained by bold key-change and emphatic rhythms. The settings, as in the typical example mentioned, are mainly of poems depicting feelings of solitude or invigoration aroused by Nature, which is imagined as embodying the moods of the poet.

The supreme example is the setting of Goethe's *Gesang der Geister über den Wassern* (D714*b*) for double male voice chorus and lower strings; here the poetic fusion of pictorial and philosophical aspects, concrete and abstract together, is masterfully matched in music. Elsewhere it is more often the element of experimentation that elevates the style into such peaks of achievement as *Nur wer die Sehnsucht kennt* (D656), *Ruhe, schönstes Gluck der Erde* (D657), *Nachthelle* (D892) and *Grab und Mond* (D893). The Grillparzer setting *Ständchen* (D920), though perhaps overlong for its iterative thematic material, deserves special mention for its melodic charm and motivic scene- and mood-painting. Here the partsong form comes closest to the more characteristically Schubertian style of the solo lied, while such quasi-dramatic effects as the assembly and dispersal of a serenading chorus recall his most evocative operatic writing.

The sacred music more rarely arouses any such immediate feelings of presence or participation. Schubert's brother Ignaz was a notorious freethinker. The composer himself was highly heterodox; a letter to him from Ferdinand Walcher in January 1827 begins with a musical quotation above the words 'Credo in unum Deum' and continues 'You don't, as I very well know'. Further, Schubert went so far as to omit, from all of his masses, the words 'et in unam sanctam catholicam ecclesiam'. It is hardly surprising then that the church music can be plainly unconvincing, as in the harmonic clichés and conventional melodies of the *Hymnus an den heiligen Geist* (D948). Other works equally uninspired have enjoyed an abiding popularity, such as the vernacular *Deutsche Messe* (D872), eight separate religious songs for the intervals between the stages of the Office. Even in the Masses, some of which attain great heights of grandeur

and passion, there is much reliance on traditional for-
mulae, especially in the four early settings (D105, 167, 324
and 452). The Credo texts tend to be disposed of in brisk,
business-like sequences that sound like stock responses.
The Kyrie is typically in ternary form; the Gloria is
vigorously rhythmic, usually with a fugal treatment at
'Cum sancto spiritu'; the Benedictus employs solo voices;
and so on. As in the partsongs, which developed in
parallel with the liturgical settings, the texture is mainly
homophonic and the music is kept going by bold harmonic shifts rather than by contrapuntal procedures. But
the liturgical music too is often much redeemed by grace
of melody, as in the Mass in G (D167). And whenever the
words of the Mass take on a special meaning for the more
mature Schubert, the music attains a new spiritual stature,
as in the A♭ and E♭ Masses. Predictably, his response
remains essentially humanist. 'Crucifixus' and Agnus Dei
inhabit the everyday world of the suffering flesh; even the
'Et incarnatus' offers the human tenderness of the
Bethlehem story rather than any special sense of transcen-
dental mystery. But in the A♭ Mass (D678) in particular
the harmonies add a new grandeur to the 'Et incarnatus'
and a new poignancy to the 'Crucifixus' which suggest
that the sacred and the secular strains in Schubert could
have achieved a masterly synthesis. The late E♭ Mass
(D950), though arguably lacking in the universal qualities
that make the great Bach and Beethoven masses acts of
worship as well as works of art, is nevertheless rich in the
new sensibilities, both intellectual and emotive, that had
been stimulated and released by the composition of
Winterreise.

An earlier fusion of sacred and secular had informed
such fine works as the *Stabat mater* (D383) and the setting
for women's voices of Psalm xxiii (D706); and these

same qualities appear in the masterly Easter cantata *Lazarus* (D689). Most of Schubert's other essays in this form were occasional pieces composed for the purpose of honouring various individuals, and performed on an anniversary. These works, though rarely without their moments of attraction, are for the most part negligible. *Lazarus*, composed in 1820 but left unfinished, is in a quite different category. In 1863 the manuscript came into the hands of Brahms, who was deeply impressed; but despite his advocacy and that of other Schubertians the work still remains all but unknown, no doubt because of its unusual form. It consists mainly of richly accompanied lyrical recitatives for the six solo voices, a framework within which the formal aria is not a break or a contrast but a heightening of the musico-dramatic progress. Much of the music is characterized by devices found in the songs and ballads of this period, e.g. a deliberate restriction of the harmony to diatonic chords, and long-flighted melodies within which a short lyrical pattern is repeated. The orchestra has brief modulating figures flexibly used to emphasize the meaning of the words, to interconnect contrasting sentiments and to underscore powerful climaxes, in ways clearly evocative of the Wagnerian music-drama. The embellished recitative accompaniments of this unique work expand Schubert's song-writing techniques into those used in the non-lyrical sections of the operas, that is, those parts of the text where, by dialogue or ensemble, the action of the plot is urged forward. In *Lazarus* the long recitatives that precede and follow each of the four arias embody the best of Schubert's achievement in this style; only the greatest passages in *Alfonso und Estrella* and *Fierabras* surpass them in power and beauty.

15. Songs

One of the reasons for the abiding popularity of Schubert's songs is simple: whatever other elements may or may not be present, the primary essential, the melodic element, or (to put it plainly) an attractive and singable tune, is rarely absent. A second and deeper reason for their appeal is that they are firmly grounded, in idiom and procedure, in the 'Viennese symphonic' period of music, say from 1770 to 1830. One has only to think of such songs as *Halt!* from *Die schöne Müllerin* (D795 no.3), *Auf dem Flusse* from *Winterreise* (D911 no.7), or *Der Zwerg* (D771), with their exposition and development of thematic fragments, to realize that as long as this period remains the most congenial to a large number of listeners, so will his songs with it.

From the first the Schubert song was practically without ancestry; even before *Gretchen am Spinnrade* he was writing passages which have no precedent. Songs there certainly were before his, and in his youth he modelled his own efforts on those of men such as Zumsteeg and Zelter. Many of Beethoven's and Mozart's songs, considered as music, are equal to his own earlier efforts. The miracle he achieved was to match with a reality of music poetry whose depths of human emotion would have appeared to the older composers as rendering it unsuitable for song. Two factors are said to have helped Schubert: the late 18th-century outburst of lyric poetry, whose outstanding exponent is Goethe; and the establishment of the piano accompaniment with its inexhaustible possibilities of picturesque

comment. These factors are trifling compared with the
power of his genius: otherwise one might ask why
Beethoven and Weber, to whom these two possibilities
were equally available, composed no masterpieces of
song comparable to Schubert's.

The songs, more than 600, fall into four main groups:
the simple strophic song in which each verse is sung to
the same music; the modified-strophic song in which his
endless variety defies classification (examples are
Lachen und Weinen, D777 and *Das Zügenglöcklein*
D871); the *durchkomponiert* (through-composed) song
in which various melodies and interpolated recitatives
are welded together by the same, basically unchanging
accompaniment, like *Die junge Nonne* (D828) and
Auflösung (D807); and finally the 'scena' type of song,
such as *Der Wanderer* (D489) or *Kriegers Ahnung*
(D957 no.2), containing separate episodes of different
tempo and mood, of which his own scena, Käthe's aria
from *Der vierjährige Posten* (D190 no.5), may be cited as
a prototype. The poets range from Goethe, Schiller and
Heine at one end of the scale to versifying friends like
Mayrhofer and Schober at the other. This catholic
choice is sometimes taken to indicate that Schubert had
no literary taste; when he chose to set a poem to music,
however, he did so not to show his literary judgment but
because of its musical possibilities. The ready and sympathetic audience of the Schubertiads must not be overlooked in this connection. Schubert obviously favoured
the poem with a 'bite' in the last stanza, even in the last
line; as for instance in *Erlkönig*, *Der Wanderer* and *Der
Doppelgänger*. The way in which he absorbed the
quality of a poem and produced an analogous quality in
music can best be appreciated when one turns the pages
of his poets – of Goethe or Heine, for example. The

swift lyricism and movement of the one, the pith and
imagery of the other, are perfectly paralleled in the
music.

The refinement of later composers in their attention
to the poet's text, and in their balance of interest between voice and piano, is instinctive, but not uncon-
scious, with Schubert. His lyric and harmonic vitality
and his spontaneous reaction to the stimulus of the
poet's emotional or visual appeal give an almost abandoned quality to the music he poured out. Sometimes, as
in *An Schwager Kronos* (D369), the result is overpower-
ingly convincing; elsewhere, as in *Die Gebüsche* (D646)
or in *Fülle der Liebe* (D854), the result is less happy.
But always there is the firm grasp of the essential.
Schubert's periphery may sweep beyond, or not quite
reach out to, that of the poet, but it always encircles the
same central point. One perceives it in that quality of his
famous songs which can only be called 'atmosphere'.
The very first bars of *Im Abendrot* (D799), *An die Musik*
(D547) or *Nacht und Träume* (D827) take us to the
heart of the poem. Nor need the atmosphere be one of
abstraction or rapture: the lighthearted *An die Laute*
(D905), or the comfortable *Der Einsame* (D800), illustrate the point equally well.

Schubert's melodies, particularly in his songs, are the
most individual and revealing of all the factors in his
work. Of infinite variety and grace, they have a quality
of pathos, of direct appeal to the listener, which is a
reflection of the sweetness and sensitivity of his own
nature. They are often based on a juxtaposition of tonic
and dominant chords as in *Wohin?* (D795 no.2) and *Der
greise Kopf* (D911 no.14). The phrase built on a falling
dominant 7th is associated in his mind with weariness or
grief, so it is used in *Wandrers Nachtlied* (D224) and in

the first of the Harper's Songs (D478). The little figure sung at the start of *Frühlingsglaube* (D686) appears repeatedly in his songs whenever blissful contemplation of nature engrosses both poet and composer. The use of sequence is discreet and flexible, as is shown in *Ungeduld* (D795 no.7) and *An Sylvia* (D891); in the latter song the sequential treatment of the opening phrase is exquisite.

The most familiar characteristic of Schubert's harmony is his passing from minor mode to major and, less frequently, from major to minor; the change may be smooth or abrupt, but it always represents an emotional change. Another characteristic, equally important but insufficiently noticed, is his use of the Neapolitan 6th and relationships based upon it. A third is his fondness for passing, with little or no preparation, into the key a major 3rd below his tonic, as for instance in *Nacht und Träume* (D827; B major to G major). An awareness of these three fundamental processes gives an insight into the masterly way in which he handles his harmonic material, for example in the song *Stimme der Liebe* (D412). This flexible use of harmonic changes had its direct influence on his melody and modulation, but the processes were reversible: melody and modulation affected his harmonic spectrum. In addition to these personal harmonic characteristics, Schubert took over from the normal harmony of his day the augmented 6th (in both the 'German' and 'French' forms) and the diminished 7th, using both chords frequently and often with the most poetic effects: consider the use of the diminished 7th in its form C–E♭–F♯–A throughout the song *Die Stadt* (D957 no.11). Arpeggios based on the chord softly sweep the keyboard to depict Heine's 'feuchter Windzug' and are tenuously resolved at the end of the song by a single held *C* in the bass.

Schubert's accompaniments are celebrated for their graphic reinforcement of the inner meaning of the poem or of the external details of the poet's scene. He seems inexhaustible in contriving graceful pianistic figures to illustrate moving or glinting water or the shimmer of stars. Again and again he devised in his accompaniments a music which derives from both aspects of the poem and achieves thereby a powerful synthesis of which the poetry alone is incapable – the ranging arpeggios of *Auflösung* (D807) or the heartbreak in the gusty diminished 7ths of *Die Stadt* (D957) demonstrate such powers. The preludes of his songs can be remarkably apt: the most beautifully poised entry in them all is in *Ganymed* (D544); how the opening bars depict the glory and contentment of morning! The introductory chords of Goethe's *An den Mond* (D296) cloud the A♭ tonality and prepare the listener for the 'Nebelglanz' of the poet's address to the moon. But the last word has not been said about the Schubert song when its melody, accompaniment, atmosphere – all the beautiful externals of his music – have been surveyed. There yet remains the ineffable quality of textual illumination to which purpose all these factors are bent. Consider Heine's *Der Doppelgänger* (D957 no.13). 'The night is still', says the poet, 'the streets are deserted', but there needs no ghost to remind him of his anguish on 'so many nights long ago'. Schubert set the opening words to a falling B minor phrase, low in the compass of the voice; the final agony is implicit in this phrase, and it rings out at the end in a florid version an octave higher. Similar examples abound in the mature songs. There is the way in which the pure diatonic harmony at the start of *Du bist die Ruh* (D776) is tinged with colour as the poet turns from

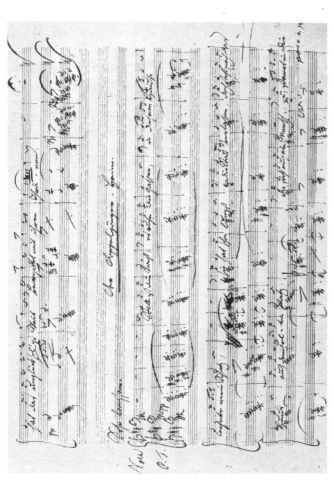

10. *Autograph MS of the end of 'Am Meer' and the beginning of 'Der Doppelgänger' from book 2 of Schubert's 'Schwanengesang', composed August 1828*

'du bist' to 'ich weihe'. The high opening phrase of *An die Entfernte* (D765) poses a question, 'Have I lost thee?', introduced by an enigmatic diminished 7th; it has an entirely different quality when it recurs later, after a decisive C major chord, to the words 'All my songs cry unto thee'. The refinement by which the main key of *Dass sie hier gewesen* (D775) is held back to coincide with the main statement of each stanza is well known, but this device is just as notably used in *Gruppe aus dem Tartarus* (D583), in which the whole discordant opening prepares for C major and the awesome word 'Eternity', and in *Grenzen der Menschheit* (D716), where the main key of the song is reserved for the declaration of Man's humility. On songs such as these his fame rests; but his stature is as surely revealed in innumerable tiny songs, page-long creations, few without touches of sublimity where with the most modest means he can encompass greatness in a score of bars.

16. Song cycles

Schubert created and perfected not only the lied form but its further development, the song cycle; here too his masterpieces *Die schöne Müllerin* (D795) and *Winterreise* (D911) were practically without ancestry and have never been surpassed. Again this music grew from the German poetic renaissance, this time the original work of Wilhelm Müller in the form of the narrative lyrical sequence. Though there is no direct evidence, it seems likely that Schubert was familiar with Beethoven's *An die ferne Geliebte* (Vienna, 1816), a set of love-lyrics composed in continuous cyclic form, essentially an extended song beginning and ending with the same music. Schubert wrote a masterpiece of this new genre also, in his *Viola* (D786, 1823). But his musical treatment of Müller's versified story eschews all such overt structural devices. The poetry's naive but effective realism, with its depiction of simple and powerful human emotions mirrored in external nature, also includes elements of dramatic conflict, even character study, which seized Schubert's imagination more strongly and held it more consistently than any of his opera librettos. The cycle of poems had been written under the influence of Goethe, and contains much of his scenic and dramatic quality that had already so inspired Schubert in the solo song. Indeed, the verses had begun as a form of domestic literary charade or playlet, and the five-part publication of Schubert's musical setting was not an arbitrary subdivision but a deliberate attempt to present the work in five small 'acts': I, the arrival at the mill (songs 1–4); II, the falling in love (5–9); III, brief happiness (10–12); IV, jealousy and despair (13–17); and V, resignation and death (17–20). As a complement to this objective approach, the composer's own state of mind was perhaps especially receptive to the idea of youthful passion blighted by tragedy. Schubert found Müller's sequence of 24 poems (four of which were left unset) in the summer of 1823, at the very period when he must have realized that his own recently contracted syphilis was certainly grave and possibly mortal. There is an undocumented but perhaps not unfounded tradition that some of the Mill songs were written in the Vienna general hospital during the time of Schubert's emergency treatment there. Whatever the reason, Müller's poems are given, here and in *Winterreise*, a musical universality and power that they could never have attained unaided. The verses need not be decried on that account. Their many felicities of metre and onomatopoeia, their direct and vivid imagery, their limpid diction and versification, their deep roots in traditional folksong, all help to inspire music of mythopoeic quality (see Reed, 1978) with a strong structure articulated far more by verbal narrative and description than by any manifest musical device. No Schubert songs have ever been so consistently beloved and popular; but their apparent simplicity distracts attention from their exquisitely wrought variety of structure, from strophic verse repetition (as in *Mit dem grünen Lauten-bande*) via added refrain (*Trockne Blumen*) or recitative (*Am Feierabend*) or other modification (*Pause*) to the 'scena' song (*Der Neugierige*) or the wholly through-composed *Eifersucht und Stolz*. In *Die schöne Müllerin* the pastoral sound-language of walking, flowing and flowering so well defined by Richard Capell (1928) reaches a new pitch of expressiveness. This cycle dominates the lieder of Schubert's middle years, even though, considered as separate songs, none may be thought to equal the settings of Goethe in 1821 or those of Rückert in 1822–3. Their strength derives from their inseparable unity, which adds a new dimension of sustained drama and narrative to the song form.

In *Winterreise* (D911) of 1827, the whole is even more compellingly greater than its parts. It affords fewer occasions for overt musical characterization or dramatic conflict; the tragic themes of coldness and rejection are less varied than *Die schöne Müllerin*, and so are the modified-strophic song structures. But the identification of nature with human suffering is even more intense, and the central character is even more strongly mythopoeic in its union of three Romantic ideals – the wandering youth, the isolated artist and the unrequited lover. The opening words of Müller's verse-tragedy, 'fremd bin ich eingezogen,/fremd zieh ich wieder aus' ('I arrived here a stranger, a stranger I depart'), are designed from the outset to convey a sense of cosmic significance, to say with King Lear that men must endure their going hence even as their coming hither, and that ripeness is all. Schubert's music again reaches the poet's thought and expresses it far more trenchantly and poignantly than Müller himself; but the expressiveness undoubtedly owes some of its power to the poetry both in general outline and in particular detail. Thus the simple phrase 'Vom Abendrot zu Morgenlicht' (from sunset to dawn) in its context suggests the wider horizons of life and feeling, and inspires a great arching theme that traverses 12 slow beats and nearly two octaves. On a smaller scale, impressive effects are attained by a remarkable simplicity of means, as when the wanderer's climactic cry of 'Oh, were the whole world dark' in *Einsamkeit* is driven home with a steely point in a phrase of just two falling semitones. In such ways the verses, once lifted to the height of the composer's genius, are given new and continuing universality. It seems that Schubert himself was aware of a corresponding development in his creative powers. In the well-documented year of 1827, when the Hartmann brothers for example kept full diaries, Schubert's appearances in the journals and letters of his friends have a ghost-like and unreal quality. He seems so quiet and controlled, almost insignificant, whereas we know that all the time he is striving towards, and urging his powers to reach up to, his vision of the *Winterreise*.

Some of this triumph must be ascribed to pure chance. The song cycle was composed and published in two parts, each of 12 songs. The first part, dated February 1827 (though no doubt begun some weeks earlier), corresponds exactly to the order and text of Müller's poems as published in the Leipzig yearbook *Urania* of 1823. Presumably an old copy had come into Schubert's hands in early 1827. As Capell says, 'one can imagine his joy at the beauty of the chance that had brought him his collaborator back, at the countless fresh images provoked by this poetry of fire and snow, of torrent and ice, of scalding and frozen tears'. The eagerness with which he started composing these songs, and the exhausted state in which their composition left him, show how congenial Müller's verses were to his tastes and gifts. He was indeed evidently overjoyed to find another series of lyrics by the poet of *Die schöne Müllerin*, and he did not spare himself as poem after poem stimulated the creative power within him and extorted musical scene after musical scene from his imagination. Then, in the late summer of the same year, Schubert encountered Müller's complete and final version of the cycle, this time in book form as published in 1824, containing 24 poems; an extra 12 had been in-

terpolated at various points throughout the text. Schubert
set these also, with unabated enthusiasm and inspiration.
By that time however his first set was already in the
publisher's hands; and instead of intercalating the extra
songs as Müller had done, Schubert simply added them *en
bloc* as a second instalment. As John Reed says, had
Schubert discovered Müller's poems in the first place in
their final 1824 form, he would no doubt have kept to that
order – for reversion to which in performance a cogent
case can accordingly be made.

This second song cycle, like the first, dominates the
lieder of the period. Further, it heralds a new phase in
Schubert's work as a whole, one which he did not live long
enough wholly to fulfil. But the music of *Winterreise*, once
realized, revealed to the composer newer potentialities in
his genius. For the first time in his music we find tragedy,
not the wistfulness or luxuriating sadness of previous
work but the darkness of the genuine emotion; we find it,
numbed, in *Gute Nacht* and *Der Wegweiser*, whose
threnodic progressions are related to the slow movements
of the 'Great' C major Symphony and the E♭ Trio (D929),
despairing and passionate in *Erstarrung* and *Der stürmische Morgen*, whose anguish is found again in the slow
movement of the String Quartet (D956). Side by side with
this tragic utterance is a profound serenity first voiced in
Der Lindenbaum, which is so characteristic of his later
work, but neither *Im Abendrot* (D799) nor *Du bist die Ruh*
(D776) has quite the dream-like quality of the works just
cited. Technically his music gained from *Winterreise* a
greater harmonic piquancy, a discovery of wider yet
subtler uses of Neapolitan relationships, and a newer, one
might say a more intellectual, manner with thematic
development.

17. Mature instrumental music

The 'Trout' Quintet (D667) is the climax of Schubert's approach to maturity in instrumental music, and the Quartettsatz (D703) begins the last phase in his work here. With the exception of the sketched symphony in E of 1821 (D729), the next eight years produced a series of masterpieces marked by an intense lyricism, a chromatic modulation which, for all its spontaneity, moves within an inherent tonal system, an absorbed attention to textural detail and an imagination which moulds its own formal structures. Academic devices such as fugato, elaborately worked canon or invertible counterpoint, all of which can be found dutifully appearing in his early work, are quickly abandoned; but his treatment of subject matter grows more powerful and attains a poetry and an emotion unknown in the years before 1820. As a typical movement, the Quartettsatz stands fittingly at the start of these years. The key scheme of the exposition shows, for the first time, that tonal structure which Schubert was to find so congenial: the C minor and G major tonalities which bracket the section are fairly orthodox, but they enclose a second-subject stretch in A♭ major. His use of the string quartet medium in which cello and first violin have predominant interest is first seen in this movement, and in the demands which are made on the players Schubert is clearly no longer bound by the limitations of the family quartet (particularly in the case of the cello, which was the task of the modestly equipped Schubert *père*).

The next work of importance is the Symphony in B minor (D759), another unfinished essay. The affinities of the symphony's first movement with that of the quartet are remarkable: in the singing quality, the passionate contrasts and the pathos they are obvious, but two technical points have interest. The first is the withholding of the main theme at the start of the recapitulation, in order to use it with greater force for the coda of the movement; the second is in the choice of key for the second subject. In the case of the 'Unfinished' Symphony this has occasioned much comment, but it has precisely the same relationship with the main key as in the quartet: B minor–G major, C minor–A♭ major; and both are instances of Schubert's favourite shift of a major 3rd downwards.

Between the quartet and the symphony appeared the first important composition for piano, a work of an entirely different character. The 'Wanderer' Fantasy takes its name from the *adagio* section, which is based on a theme from the song *Der Wanderer* (D489), of 1816. It is the first of a series of works in C major which have the epic quality thenceforth associated in his mind with that key, and its massive structure, new to his keyboard writing, is rarely absent from his later compositions for the piano. There is an interesting and deliberate use of cyclic form, one aspect of which derives from the dactylic rhythm of the song theme. This rhythm pervades his mature work and is an indication of the profound impression made upon him by the Allegretto from Beethoven's Seventh Symphony. The three chamber works of 1824, the Octet for wind and strings in F (D803) and the string quartets in A minor (D804) and D minor (D810), have much in common. They were written in the short space of only two months, in February and March 1824. They are full of typical melody; all three contain movements based on themes which Schubert had composed for other media from past days, and this fact seems to reflect his mood. In a letter written at this time to Kupelwieser he spoke of a ray of sunlight from past sweet days; the emotion shades from cheerful good humour to pathos, and occasionally, in the D minor String Quartet, to a shuddering terror. Even the cheerful pages, those in the minuet of the Octet, or the finale of the A minor String Quartet, have that characteristic Schubert patina of near-pathos; he was, unlike Haydn or Beethoven, incapable of pure comedy, of Rosalind's 'holiday mood'.

The six piano sonatas (five for solo and one for duet) which belong to the mid-1820s constitute a unified group. To begin with, the main theme of the first movement is invariably the basis of the development section, with supreme effect in the two A minor sonatas (D784 and D845), in the 'Reliquie' Sonata (D840) and in the G major Sonata (D894). The slow movements, with one exception, are in rondo form, the opening songlike theme alternating with dynamic interludes; an attractive example is the Andante of the duet sonata in C (D812). The exception is the slow movement of the Sonata in A minor (D845), a set of variations on an original theme, one of the most successful of his essays in this genre. It contains a delicate use of those chains of suspensions which he had used to good effect in the song *Versunken* (D715) and which are found again in the slow movement of the 'Great' C major Symphony (D944) and in the C minor Impromptu (D899 no.1). The period closes with two magnificent pieces of chamber music. Of the first movement of the String Quartet in G (D887) it is difficult to write without extravagance: the quintessence

11. *Autograph MS of the first page of Schubert's String Quartet in G (D887), composed 20–30 June 1826*

of every Schubertian virtue is found in its pages. The slow movement (in E minor, though his manuscript shows that it was originally planned in B minor) contains his most daring harmonic adventure, where violin and viola persistently utter a figure in one key, while the music moves more and more remotely from it (bars 52–6, repeated in bars 131–5). The finale is sometimes alleged to show the influence of Rossini; there is as little justification for this as for the so-called 'Hungarian' influence in the finale of the A minor String Quartet.

The Piano Trio in B♭ (D898) nowhere reaches the heights of the G major Quartet, but its humanity (and hence its popular appeal) is greater. The remark that

Schubert's lyrical subjects are unsuitable for development is refuted by the first movement of this trio, as indeed it is by the first movement of the G major Sonata; nothing could be more songlike than these themes, yet each forms the basis of a superbly constructed movement. The instrumentation of the trio is admirable, particularly in the controlled use of the piano, which is neither overwhelming nor over-modest in its partnership with the strings. Its soaring flights in the finale are among the most picturesque of Schubert's touches in his chamber music.

Before the next important work, the Piano Trio in E♭ (D929), came the completion of *Winterreise* (D911); and the significance (already discussed) of that song cycle for Schubert's development can be seen by comparing the temper of the E♭ Trio with that of its predecessor. This closing period is also distinguished by signs that Schubert was concerning himself with two sections of his large-scale works which he had hitherto treated somewhat lightheartedly, the trio of the third movement and the finale. Another feature of these final works comes from his changed attitude to the development section of his first movements; no longer invariably based on the opening theme, as was the case in every one of the works between the 'Unfinished' Symphony and the B♭ Trio, they may derive from the introduction (C major Symphony), from subsidiary matter in the exposition (the Quintet) or even from a codetta phrase (E♭ Trio, A major Sonata). In the E♭ Trio the much maligned finale deserves a kindlier, more informed, judgment; as with other finales, the easy-going start leads on to better and greater things, and the introduction of the theme from the slow movement is a superb moment, and for Schubert a unique one.

We come to what is widely admitted to be his greatest masterpiece, the 'Great' C major Symphony. From any viewpoint the work bears the stamp of greatness, but the chief impression left by a study of it is of tremendous rhythmic vitality. No sketches are extant (this is usually the case with Schubert's finished work) and the manuscript suggests that some of the symphony was composed in full score as fast as the pen could travel. The development section of the first movement displays a remarkable synthesis of elements in the exposition section with the opening bars of the horn theme from the introduction. The Andante con moto can fairly claim to be his loveliest slow movement: in the duet for cellos and oboe, after the big climax; in the soft, repeated notes of the horn (a passage made famous by Schumann's eulogy) which lead to the recapitulation; in the varied string accompaniments to the melody of the A major section: all these have poetry and imagination which he never surpassed and never more ardently expressed. The Scherzo and Finale, the former in full sonata form, have a lively rhythmic energy which sweeps all before it: the first has great lyric beauty, the second a splendour of thematic development. In all four movements the use of the trombones, delicate or authoritative, is perhaps the most notable feature in an orchestration that abounds in felicities.

The last group of works for solo piano consists of eight impromptus, the Three Piano Pieces (D946) and three sonatas. Four of the impromptus (D899) were published as op.90 (nos.1 and 2 in December 1827; no.3, transposed from G♭ to G by the publisher, and no.4 in 1857), and four others (D935) as op.142 by Diabelli in 1839. The Three Piano Pieces appeared in 1868, anonymously edited by Brahms. The 11 pieces are realizations of various moods, dramatic, thoughtful or passionate, and all are supremely lyrical. As the first departure by a major composer from the dominance of the sonata over piano forms, and as the modest fore-runners of the Romantic composers' work in this field, they are historically important apart from their own intrinsic worth. But to rank them more highly and to play them more frequently than the sonatas is a folly of which this age is less guilty than the preceding one. And it is ill-informed to consider them as dismembered sonata movements: not only do they, for all their charm, lack the 'grand style' of his sonatas, but a study of their crude transitional passages is convincing of their lesser stature. Schubert's transitions in his sonatas have the vitality and magic which proclaim the master of the form, as may be seen at once in his last three sonatas. This group closes his long series of piano compositions and fittingly contains his finest work. The level of attain-ment rises in each sonata to the heights in the third, in B♭. In the first movements of all three, the development sections show the features already mentioned; the second subjects are many-sectioned and have pic-turesque codas. The slow movements are like richly accompanied songs; they have deeply tranquil opening and closing sections with a dramatic interlude which, in the A major Sonata, has an astonishing complexity and vigour. There is point and significance in the trios of the scherzos, and in the finales an extensive and admirable development of the main theme of the movement. This is especially fine in the finale of the A major Sonata, whose theme is derived, no doubt unconsciously, from the slow movement of the A minor Sonata of 1817 (D537).

Schubert's last great work was the String Quintet in C (D956). It is filled with magnificent moments: the duet for cellos in the first movement; the richness and intriguing instrumentation of the Adagio; the elegiac trio of the third movement (a true pointer to the future); the wonderful rhythmic variants of the finale theme. His subtler blending of the major and minor modes can be seen in the themes of the first and last movements; who, looking at them in isolation, would dream that movements in major keys are being announced? The whole work, as a study of Neapolitan relationships, is without equal.

WORKS

Editions: *F. Schuberts Werke: kritisch durchgesehene Gesamtausgabe*, ed. E. Mandyczewski, J. Brahms and others (Leipzig, 1884–97/*R*1964–9) [SW, ser./vol., p.]

F. Schubert: Neue Ausgabe sämtlicher Werke, ed. W. Dürr, A. Feil, C. Landon and others (Kassel, 1964–) [NSA, ser./vol., p.]

Items are ordered by D number as enumerated in W. Dürr, A. Feil, C. Landon and others: *Franz Schubert: thematisches Verzeichnis seiner Werke in chronologischer Folge von Otto Erich Deutsch*, Neue Ausgabe Sämtlicher Werke, viii/4 (Kassel, 1978); where, exceptionally, numbers have been changed in this edition, a cross-reference is given. Numbers in parentheses following a title refer to separate settings of the same text. Numbers in the right-hand column denote references in the text.

THEATRICAL

D	Title	Genre	Text	Composed	First production	Published	SW; NSA	77ff
11	Der Spiegelritter	Singspiel, 3, only ov. and 1st act complete	A. von Kotzebue	Dec 1811–1812	Swiss Radio, 11 Dec 1949	1893	xxi, 1,; xiv/7, 109; iii/11	5
84	Des Teufels Lustschloss version a version b	opera, 3	Kotzebue	30 Oct 1813–15 May 1814 completed 22 Oct 1814	Vienna, Musikvereinsaal, 12 Dec 1879 (as pubd in 1888)	1888	xv/1; ii/1	6, 77, 78
137	Adrast [see ov., 648]	opera 2, unfinished	J. Mayrhofer	?1817–19	Vienna, Redoutensaal, 13 Dec 1868	1893	xv/7, 317; ii/11	79
190	Der vierjährige Posten	Singspiel, 1	T. Körner	8–19 May 1815	Dresden, 23 Sept 1896	1888	xv/2, 1; ii/2	11, 87
220	Fernando	Singspiel, 1	A. Stadler	27 June–9 July 1815	Vienna, 13 April 1907	1888	xv/2, 111; ii/2	11
239	Claudine von Villa Bella	Singspiel, 3, only ov. and 1st act complete	Goethe	begun 26 July 1815	Vienna, Gemeindehaus Wieden, 26 April 1913	1893	xv/7, 1; ii/12	11
326	Die Freunde von Salamanka	Singspiel, 2	Mayrhofer	18 Nov–31 Dec 1815	Halle, 6 May 1928	1888	xv/2, 171; ii/3	11, 78
435	Die Bürgschaft	opera, 3, 1st and 2nd acts complete	—	begun 2 May 1816	Vienna, 7 March 1908	1893	xv/7, 203; ii/12	11
644	Die Zauberharfe	melodrama, 3	G. von Hofmann	1820	Vienna, Theater an der Wien, 19 Aug 1820	1891	xv/4, 1; ii/4, 3	24, 35, 40, 79

D	Title	Forces	Librettist	Composed	First performance	Published	SW;NSA	
647	Die Zwillingsbrüder	Singspiel, 1	Hofmann	Jan 1819	Vienna, Kärntnertor, 14 June 1820	1889	xv/3, 1; ii/5	24, 79
701	Sakuntala	opera, 3, sketches for 1st and 2nd acts only	J. P. Neumann, after Kalidasa	Oct 1820	Vienna, 12 June 1971	—	—; ii/13	
723	Duet and aria for Hérold's Das Zauberglöckchen (La clochette)	—	E. G. M. Théaulon de Lambert, trans. F. Treitsche	spring 1821	Vienna, Kärntnertor, 20 June 1821	1893	xv/7, 365; ii/14	30
732	Alfonso und Estrella	opera, 3	F. von Schober	20 Sept 1821–27 Feb 1822	Weimar, 24 June 1854	1892	xv/5, 1; ii/6	32, 33, 37, 39, 40, 45, 53, 72, 75, 77, 78, 79, 85
787	Die Verschworenen (Der häusliche Krieg)	Singspiel, 1	I. F. Castelli, after Aristophanes: Lysistrata	March–April 1823	Vienna, Musikvereinssaal. March 1861	1889	xv/3, 115; ii/7	37, 75, 80
791	Rüdiger	opera, sketches for nos.1–2 only	?I. von Mosel	begun May 1823	Vienna, Redouensaal, 5 Jan 1868	1867	—; ii/14	
796	Fierabras	opera, 3	J. Kupelwieser	25 May–2 Oct 1823	Karlsruhe, 9 Feb 1897	1886	xv/6, 1; ii/8	38, 39, 77, 78, 80, 85
797	Rosamunde, Fürstin von Zypern	incidental music to romantic play, 4	H. von Chézy	autumn 1823	Vienna, Theater an der Wien, 20 Dec 1823	1891	xv/4, 345; ii/9	40, 78, 79, 81
918	Der Graf von Gleichen	opera, 2, sketches only	E. von Bauernfeld	begun 19 June 1827	—	—	—; ii/14	50, 51
966	[see 11]	orch interlude to 11/3, frag.						
981	Der Minnesänger	Singspiel, unfinished, lost	—	—	—	—	—	
982	—	opera, sketches, 3 nos. only	—	after 1820	—	—	—; ii/14	

SACRED

82ff

D	Title	Forces	Composed	Published	SW;NSA
24e	Mass, ?F, frag.	SATB, orch, org	?1812	—	—; i/5
27	Salve regina, F	S, orch, org	28 June 1812	1928	—; i/8
31	Kyrie, d	S, T, SATB, orch, org	25 Sept 1812	1888	xiv, 175; i/5
45	Kyrie, B♭	SATB	1 March 1813	1888	xiv, 226; i/5

D	Title	Forces	Composed	Published	SW; NSA	
49	Kyrie, d	S, A, T, B, SATB, orch	April 1813	1888	xiv, 189; i/5	
56	Sanctus, canon with coda, Bb	3vv	21 April 1813	1892	xix, 89; i/8	
66	Kyrie, F	SATB, orch, org	12 May 1813	1888	xiv, 203; i/5	
71a	Alleluja, F, canon	3vv	?July 1813	1956	—; i/8	
105	Mass no.1, F [see also 185]	S, S, A, T, T, B, SATB, orch, org	17 May–22 July 1814	1856	xiii/1, 1; i/1	8, 10, 84
106	Salve regina, Bb	T, orch, org	28 June–1 July 1814	1888	xiv, 47; i/8	
136	Offertory: Totus in corde langueo, C	S/T, cl/vn, orch, org	?1815	1825, op.46	xiv, 1; i/8	10, 84
167	Mass no.2, G	S, T, B, SATB, str, org	2–7 March 1815	1846	xiii/1, 121; i/1	
175	Stabat mater, g	SATB, orch, org	4–6 April 1815	1888	xiv, 101; i/8	
181	Offertory: Tres sunt, a	SATB, orch, org	10–11 April 1815	1888	xiv, 23; i/8	
184	Gradual: Benedictus es, Domine, C	SATB, orch, org	15–17 April 1815	c1843, op.150	xiv, 29; i/8	
185	Dona nobis pacem, F [alternative movt for 105]	B, SATB, orch, org	25–26 April 1815	1887	xiii/1, 931; i/1	
223	Salve regina (Offertorium), F version a	S, orch, org	5 July 1815	—	—; i/8	
	version b		28 Jan 1823	1825, op.47	xiv, 9; i/8	
324	Mass no.3, Bb	S, A, T, B, SATB, orch, org	begun 11 Nov 1815	c1837, op.141	xiii/1, 157; i/2	10, 84
379	Deutsches Salve regina (Hymne an die heilige Mutter Gottes), F	SATB, org	21 Feb 1816	1859	xiv, 215; i/8	
383	Stabat mater, oratorio, F/f	S, T, B, SATB, orch	begun 28 Feb 1816	1888	xiv, 109; i/7	84
386	Salve regina, Bb	SATB	early 1816	1833	xiv, 224; i/8	
452	Mass no.4, C [see also 961]	S, A, T, B, SATB, orch, org	June–July 1816	1825, op.48	xiii/1, 209; i/2	16, 47, 82, 84
453	Requiem, c, frag.	SATB, orch	July 1816	—	—; i/5	
460	Tantum ergo, C	S, SATB, orch, org	Aug 1816	1888	xiv, 39; i/8	
461	Tantum ergo, C	S, A, T, B, SATB, orch	Aug 1816	1935	—; i/8	
486	Magnificat, C	S, A, T, B, SATB, orch, org	15 Sept 1815	1888	xiv, 77; i/8	
488	Auguste jam coelestium, G	S, T, orch	Oct 1816	1888	xiv, 59; i/8	
607	Evangelium Johannis VI, E	1v, bc	1818	1920	—; i/8	
621	Deutsches Requiem (Deutsche Trauermesse), g	S, A, T, B, SATB, org	Aug 1818	1826	—; i/6	21
676	Salve regina (Offertorium), A	S, str	Nov 1819	1845, op.153	xiv, 17; i/8	
678	Mass no.5, Ab	S, A, T, B, SATB, orch, org	Nov 1819–Sept 1822			
	version a			1875	—; i/3	
	version b			1887	xiii/2, 1; i/3	24, 34, 84

D	Title	Forces	Text	Composed	Published	SW: NSA	
34	Te solo adoro	S, A, T, B	Metastasio	5 Nov 1812	1940	—; viii/2	
35	Serbate, o dei custodi	S, A, T, B	Metastasio	Oct 1812	1940	—; viii/2	
	version 1	SATB					
	version 2						
47	Dithyrambe (Der Besuch), frag.	T, B, SATB, pf	Schiller	29 March 1813	—	—; ii	
168	Nun lasst uns den Leib begraben (Begräbnislied)	SATB, pf	F. Klopstock	9 March 1815	1872	xvii, 241; ii	
168a	Osterlied [formerly 987]	SATB, pf	Klopstock	9 March 1815	1872	xvii, 244; ii	
232	Hymne an den Unendlichen	SATB, pf	Schiller	11 July 1815	1829, op.112/3	xvii, 167; ii	
294	Namensfeier für Franz Michael Vierthaler (Gratulations Kantate)	S, T, B, STB, orch		27 Sept 1815	1892	xvii, 142; i	
329a	Das Grab (1), sketch	SATB	J. Salis-Seewis	?28 Dec 1815	—	—; ii	
439	An die Sonne	SATB, pf	J. P. Uz	June 1816	1872	xvii, 218; ii	
440	Chor der Engel	SATB	Goethe	June 1816	1839	xvii, 245; ii	
451	Prometheus, cantata, lost	S, B, chorus, orch	P. Dräxler von Carin	17 June 1816	—	—	15, 22
472	Kantate zu Ehren von Josef Spendou	2S, B, SATB, orch	J. Hoheisel	Sept 1816	1830, op.128	xvii, 109; i	
609	Die Geselligkeit (Lebenslust)	SATB, pf	J. K. Unger	Jan 1818	1872	xvii, 225; ii	
642	Viel tausend Sterne prangen	SATB, pf	A. G. Eberhard	?1812	1937	—; ii	
643a	Das Grab (5)	SATB	Salis-Seewis	1819	1972	—; ii	
665	Im traulichen Kreise [part of 609]						
666	Kantate zum Geburtstag des Sängers Johann Michael Vogl (Der Frühlingsmorgen)	STB, pf	A. Stadler	10 Aug 1819	1849, op.158	xix, 37; ii	
689	Lazarus, oder Die Feier der Auferstehung, oratorio, 3, only 1st act and part of 2nd complete	3S, 2T, SATB, orch	A. H. Niemeyer	Feb 1820	1865	xvii, 1; ii/10	11, 24, 85
748	Am Geburtstag des Kaisers, cantata	S, A, T, B, SATB, orch	J. L. F. von Deinhardstein	Jan 1822	1822; 1849 as op. 157	xvii, 138; ii	
763	Des Tages Weihe	SATB, pf		22 Nov 1822	1842, op. 146	xvii, 212; ii	
815	Gebet	SATB, pf	Fouqué	Sept 1824	1840, op.139	xvii, 198; ii	
826	Der Tanz	SATB, pf	? K. Schnitzer von Meerau	early 1828	1892	xvii, 228; ii	44
875a	Die Allmacht (2), sketch	SATB, pf	J. L. Pyrker von Felsö-Eör	Jan 1826	—	—; ii	

D	Title	Forces	Text	Composed	Published	SW; NSA
920	Ständchen version a [for version b see 'Female or unspecified voices'] [formerly 921]	A, TTBB, pf	Grillparzer	July 1827	1891	xv, 108; iii
930	Der Hochzeitsbraten	S, T, B, pf	Schober	Nov 1827	1829, op.104	xix, 14; ii
936	Kantate für Irene Kiesewetter	2T, 2B, SATB, pf 4 hands	anon. It. text	26 Dec 1827	1892	xvii, 231; ii
942	Mirjams Siegesgesang	S, SATB, pf	Grillparzer	March 1828	c1839, op.136	xvii, 170; ii
953	Der 92. Psalm: Lied für den Sabbath	S, A, T, Bar, B, SATB	Heb. text	July 1828	1841	xvi, 247; ii
954	Glaube, Hoffnung und Liebe	2T, 2B, SATB, wind insts/pf	F. Reil	Aug 1828	1828	xvii, 152; i, ii
985	Gott im Ungewitter	SATB, pf	Uz	?1827	1829, op.112/1	xvii, 156; ii
986	Gott der Weltschöpfer	SATB, pf	Uz	?1827	1829, op.112/2	xvii, 164; ii
987	Osterlied [see 168a]					

MALE VOICES

(NSA nos. refer to vol. and p. in series 3)

D	Title	Forces	Text	Composed	Published	SW; NSA
37	Die Advokaten [based on a previous setting by Anton Fischer]	TTB, pf	Baron Engelhart	25–27 Dec 1812	1827, op.74	xix, 2; iii
38	Totengräberlied (1)	TTB	L. C. H. Hölty	?1813	1892	xix, 76; iv, 3
43	Dreifach ist der Schritt der Zeit (1)	TTB	Schiller	8 July 1813	1897	xxi, 337; iv, 4
51	Unendliche Freude (1)	TTB	Schiller	15 April 1813	1897	xxi, 330; iv, 8
53	Vorüber die stöhnende Klage	TTB	Schiller	18 April 1813	1892	xix, 51; iv, 10
54	Unendliche Freude (2), canon	BBB/TTB	Schiller	19 April 1813	1873	xix, 78; iv, 12
55	Selig durch die Liebe	TTB	Schiller	21 April 1813	1892	xix, 67; iv, 14
57	Hier strecket der wallende Pilger	TTB	Schiller	29 April 1813	1897	xxi, 331; iv, 15
58	Dessen Fahne Donnerstürme wallte	TTB	Schiller	May 1813	1892	xix, 63; iv, 18
60	Hier umarmen sich getreue Gatten	TTB	Schiller	3 Oct 1813	1892	xix, 65; iv, 33
62	Thronend auf erhabnem Sitz	TTB	Schiller	9 May 1813	1956	xxi, 334; iv, 22
63	Wer ist der steile Sternenbahn	TTB	Schiller	10 May 1813	1892	xix, 68; iv, 24
64	Majestätische Sonnenrosse	TTB	Schiller	10 May 1813	1897	xxi, 335; iv, 26
65	Schmerz verzerret ihr Gesicht, canon, sketch	TTB	Schiller	11 May 1813	1892	xix, 54; iv, 180

63, 71

6

D	Title	Forces	Text	Composed	Published	SW; NSA
67	Frisch atmet des Morgens lebendiger Hauch	TTB	Schiller	15 May 1813	1897	xxi, 335; iv, 27
70	Dreifach ist der Schritt der Zeit ('Ewig still steht die Vergangenheit') (3), canon	TTB	Schiller	8 July 1813	1928	—; iv, 177
71	Die zwei Tugendwege	TTB	Schiller	15 July 1813	1892	xix, 69; iv, 32
75	Trinklied ('Freunde, sammelt euch im Kreise')	B, TTB, pf	F. Schäffer	29 Aug 1813	1850	xvi, 128; iii
80	Zur Namensfeier meines Vaters	TTB, gui	F. Schubert	27 Sept 1813	1892	xix, 48; iii
88	Verschwunden sind die Schmerzen, canon	TTB	Schubert	15 Nov 1813	1892	xix, 77; iv, 35
110	Wer ist gross?	B, TTBB, orch		24–5 July 1814	1891	xvi, 205; i
129	Mailied ('Grüner wird die Au') (1)	TTB	Hölty	c1815	1892	xix, 72; iv, 37
132	Lied beim Rundetanz, 1 part only	? TTB/TTBB	J. von Salis-Seewis	1815 or 1816	1974	—; iv, 177
133	Lied im Freien, 1 part only	? TTB/TTBB	Salis-Seewis	1815 or 1816	1974	—; iv, 178
140	Klage um Ali Bey (1)	TTB, ?pf	M. Claudius	1815	1850	xviii, 32
147	Bardengesang	TTB	Ossian, trans. E. de Harold	20 Jan 1816	1892	xix, 70; iv, 42
148	Trinklied ('Brüder! unser Erdenwallen')	T, TTB, pf	I. F. Castelli	Feb 1815	1830, op.131/2	xix, 59; iii
236	Das Abendrot	TTB, pf	L. Kosegarten	20 July 1815	1892	xix, 57; ii
242	Trinklied im Winter	TTB	Hölty	?Aug 1815	1892	xix, 74; iv, 48
243	Frühlingslied ('Die Luft ist blau') (1)	TTB	Hölty	?Aug 1815	1892	xix, 75; iv, 50
267	Trinklied ('Auf! jeder sei nun froh')	TTBB, pf		25 Aug 1815	1872	xvi, 131; iii
268	Bergknappenlied	TTBB, pf		25 Aug 1815	1872	xvi, 133; iii
269	Das Leben version a [for version b see 'Female or unspecified voices']	TBB, pf	J. C. Wannovius	Aug 1815	—	—; iii
277	Punschlied ('Vier Elemente, innig gesellt')	TTB, pf	Schiller	29 Aug 1815	1892	xix, 58; iii
330	Das Grab (2) version b [for version a see 'Songs']	4 vv, pf	Salis-Seewis	28 Dec 1815	1895	xx/3, 231; iii
331	Der Entfernten (1)	TTBB	Salis-Seewis	c1816	1866	xvi, 194; iv, 56
337	Die Einsiedelei (1)	TTBB	Salis-Seewis	c1816	c1860	xvi, 195; iv, 58

No.	Title	Scoring	Poet	Composed	Published	References	
338	An den Frühling (2)	TTBB	Schiller	c1816	1891	xvi, 196; iv, 60	
339	Amors Macht, 1 part only	?TTBB/TTBB	F. von Matthisson	1815 or 1816	1974	—; iv, 178	
340	Badelied, T2 only	?TTBB/TTBB	Matthisson	1815 or 1816	1974	—; iv, 178	
341	Sylphen, T2 only	*TTBB/TTBB	Matthisson	1815 or 1816	1974	—; iv, 179	
356	Trinklied ('Funkelnd im Becher')	TTBB, lost pf acc.		1816	1844	—; iii	
364	Fischerlied (2)	TTBB	Salis-Seewis	c1816–17	1897	xxi, 320; iv, 63	
377	Das Grab (3)	TTBB, pf	Salis-Seewis	11 Feb 1816	1872	xx/4, 6; iii	
387	Die Schlacht (2), sketch	solo vv, chorus, pf	Schiller	March 1816	1897	xxi, 341; ii	
407	Beitrag zur fünfzig jährigen Jubelfeier des Herrn Salieri, [no.1 also in version for TTB, see 441]	T, TTBB, pf	Schubert	by 16 June 1816	1891–2	xvi, 211; iii	
422	Naturgenuss (2)	TTBB, pf	Matthisson	?1822	1823, op.16/2	xvi, 76; iii	
423	Andenken ('Ich denke dein, wenn durch den Hain') (2)	TTB	Matthisson	May 1816	1927	—; iv, 66	
424	Erinnerungen ('Am Seegestad') (2)	TTB	Matthisson	May 1816	1927	—; iv, 68	
425	Lebensbild, lost	TTB		May 1816		—	
426	Trinklied ('Herr Bacchus ist ein braver Mann'), lost	TTB		May 1816		—	
427	Trinklied im Mai	TTB	Hölty	May 1816	1892	xix, 73; iv, 70	
428	Widerhall ('Auf ewig dein')	TTB	Matthisson	May 1816	1927	—; iv, 73	
441	[=TTB version of 407/1]	TTB, pf	Schubert	by 16 June 1816	1892	xix, 53; iii	
494	Der Geistertanz (4)	TTBBB	Matthisson	Nov 1815	1871	xvi, 173; iv, 77	
513	La pastorella al prato (1)	TTBB, pf	C. Goldoni	?1817	1891	xvi, 134; iii	
538	Gesang der Geister über den Wassern (2)	TTBB	Goethe	March 1817	1891	xvi, 175; iv, 81	
569	Das Grab (4)	un.son vv, pf	Salis-Seewis	June 1817	1895	xx/5, 122; iii	
572	Lied im Freien	TTBB	Salis-Seewis	July 1817	1872	xvi, 180; iv, 89	
598	Das Dörfchen version a, sketch	TTBB	G. A. Bürger	Dec 1817	1891	xvi, 223; iii	
	version b [formerly 641]	TTBB, pf		1818	1822, op.11/1	xvi, 41; iii	
		TTBB		c1819	1906–7	—; iv, 97	
635	Leise, leise lasst uns singen	TTBBB					
641	Das Dörfchen [see 598]						
656	Sehnsucht ('Nur wer die Sehnsucht kennt') (4)	TTBB	Goethe	April 1819	1867	xvi, 185; iv, 98	83
657	Ruhe, schönstes Glück der Erde	TTBB, pf		April 1819	1871	xvi, 187; iv, 102	83
704	Gesang der Geister über den Wassern [see 714]						
705	Gesang der Geister über den Wassern (3), sketch	TTBB	Goethe	Dec 1820	1897	xxi, 313; iii	26
709	Frühlingsgesang (1)		F. von Schober	before April 1822	1891	xvi, 169; iv, 106	

D	Title	Forces	Text	Composed	Published	SW, NSA	
710	Im Gegenwärtigen Vergangenes	TTBB, pf	Goethe	?March 1821	1849	xvi, 119; iii	29, 83
714	Gesang der Geister über den Wassern (4)		Goethe				
	version a, sketch [formerly 704]	TTTTBBBB, 2 va, 2 vc, db		Dec 1820	1891	xvi, 215; i	
	version b	TTTTBBBB, 2 va, 2 vc, db		Feb 1821	1858, op.167	xvi, 24; i	
724	Die Nachtigall	TTBB, pf	J. K. Unger	by April 1821	1822, op.11/2	xvi, 50; iii	
740	Frühlingsgesang (2)	TTBB, pf	Schober	Jan–April 1822	1823, op.16/1	xvi, 65; iii	
747	Geist der Liebe ('Der Abend schleiert Flur und Hain') (2)	TTBB, pf	Matthisson	Jan 1822	1822, op.11/3	xvi, 59; iii	
778b	Ich hab in mich gesogen, sketch	TTBB	Rückert	?1823	1978	—; viii/3	
809	Gondelfahrer (2)	TTBB, pf	J. Mayrhofer	March 1824	1824, op.28	xvi, 83; iii	
822	Lied eines Kriegers	B, unison vv, pf		31 Dec 1824	1842	xx/8, 32; iii	
825	Wehmut	TTBB	H. Hüttenbrenner	before summer 1826	1828, op.64/1	xvi, 141; iv, 121	
825a	Ewige Liebe	TTBB	E. Schulze	before summer 1826	1828, op.64/2	xvi, 144; iv, 126	
825b	Flucht	TTBB	K. Lappe	by early 1825	1828, op.64/3	xvi, 148; iv, 133	
835	Bootgesang	TTBB, pf	Scott, trans. D. A. Storck	1825	1826, op.52/3	xvi, 89; iii	
847	Trinklied aus dem 16. Jahrhundert	TTBB	F. Gräffer	July 1825	1849, op.155	xvi, 29; iv, 139	
848	Nachtmusik	TTBB	K. S. von Seckendorff	July 1825	1849, op.156	xvi, 166; iv, 143	
865	Widerspruch version a [for version b see 'Songs']	TTBB, pf	J. G. Seidl	?1826	1828, op.105/1	xvi, 93; iii	
873a	Nachtklänge, sketch	TTBB		?Jan 1826	1974	—; iv, 187	
875	Mondenschein	TTBBBB, pf	Schober	Jan 1826	1831, op.102	xvi, 153; iii	
892	Nachthelle	T, TTBB, pf	Seidl	Sept 1826	1839, op.134	xvi, 98; iii	
893	Grab und Mond	TTBB	Seidl	Sept 1826	1827	xvi, 197; iv, 148	66
901	Wein und Liebe	TTBB	J. C. F. Haug	before June 1827	1827	xvi, 190; iv, 150	51, 83
903	Zur guten Nacht	Bar, TTBB, pf	J. F. Rochlitz	Jan 1827	1827, op.81/3	xvi, 91; iii	51, 83
912	Schlachtlied (2)	TTBB, TTBB	F. G. Klopstock	28 Feb 1827	1844, op.151	xvi, 157; iv, 156	
913	Nachtgesang im Walde	TTBB, 4 hn	Seidl	April 1827	1846, op.139	xvi, 1; i	62
914	Frühlingslied	TTBB	A. Pollak	April 1827	1897	xxi, 321; iv, 166	82
916	Das stille Lied, sketch	TTBB					
941	Hymnus an den Heiligen Geist [see 948]	TTBB	J. G. Seegemund	May 1827	1978	—; iv, 188, viii/3	

D	Title	Forces	Text	Composed	Published	SW; NSA
948	Hymnus an den Heiligen Geist version a [formerly 941] version b [formerly 964]	2T, 2B, TTBB / 2T, 2B, TTBB, wind insts	A. Schmidl	May 1828	1891 / 1849, op.154	xvi, 199; i/8 / xvi, 11; i/8
964	Hymnus an den Heiligen Geist [see 948]					
983	Jünglingswonne	TTBB	Matthisson	?1822	1823, op.17/1	xvi, 137; iv, 112
983a	Liebe	TTBB	Schiller	?1822	1823, op.17/2	xvi, 138; iv, 115
983b	Zum Rundetanz	TTBB	Salis-Seewis	?1822	1823, op.17/3	xvi, 139; iv, 116
983c	Die Nacht	TTBB	? F. W. Krummacher	?1822	1823, op.17/4	xvi, 139; iv, 118
984	Der Wintertag	TTBB, lost pf acc.	?	?	c1865, op.169	—; iii

FEMALE OR UNSPECIFIED VOICES

(NSA nos. refer to vol. and p. in series 3 unless otherwise stated)

D	Title	Forces	Text	Composed	Published	SW; NSA
17	Quell' innocente figlio, version 2	2S	Metastasio	c1812	1940	—; viii/2
33	Entra l'uomo allor che nasce, version 2	S, A	Metastasio	Sept–Oct 1812	1940	—; viii/2
61	Ein jugendlicher Maienschwung	3vv	Schiller	8 May 1813	1897	xxi, 333; iv, 20
69	Dreifach ist der Schritt der Zeit (2)	3vv	Schiller	8 July 1813	1892	xix, 80; iv, 30
130	Der Schnee zerrinnt (1), canon	3vv	Hölty	c1815	1892	xix, 82; iv, 38
131	Lacrimoso son io, canon, 2 versions	3vv		?Aug 1815	1892	xix, 87; iv, 40
169	Trinklied vor der Schlacht	2 unison choruses, pf	T. Körner	12 March 1815	1894	xx/2, 68; iii
170	Schwertlied	1v, unison chorus, pf	Körner	12 March 1815	1873	xx/2, 78; iii
183	Trinklied ('Ihr Freunde und du gold'ner Wein')	1v, unison chorus, pf	A. Zettler	12 April 1815	1887	xx/2, 97; iii
189	An die Freude	1v, unison chorus, pf	Schiller	May 1815	1829, op.111/1	xx/2, 102; iii
199	Mailied ('Grüner wird die Au') (2)	2vv/2 hn	Hölty	24 May 1815	1885	xix, 91; iv, 44
202	Mailied ('Der Schnee zerrinnt') (2)	2vv/2 hn	Hölty	26 May 1815	1885	xix, 91; iv, 44
203	Der Morgenstern (2)	2vv/2 hn	Körner	26 May 1815	1892	xix, 92; iv, 45
204	Jägerlied	2vv/2 hn	Körner	26 May 1815	1892	xix, 92; iv, 46
205	Lützows wilde Jagd	2vv/2 hn	Körner	26 May 1815	1892	xix, 33; iv, 46
244	Willkommen, lieber schöner Mai, canon, 2 versions	3vv	Hölty	?Aug 1815	1892	xix, 85; iv, 51
253	Punschlied: im Norden zu singen	2vv	Schiller	18 Aug 1815	1887	xx/3, 30; iv, 54

D	Title			Composed	Published	SW; NSA	
269	Das Leben / version b [for version a / see 'Male voices']	SSA, pf	Wannovius	25 Aug 1815	1849	xviii, 31; iii	
357	Gold'ner Schein, canon	3vv	Matthisson	May 1816	1892	xix, 81; iv, 64	
442	Das grosse Halleluja / version b [for version a / see 'Songs']	chorus, pf	Klopstock	June 1816	c1847	xx/4, 110; iii	
443	Schlachtlied (I) / version b [for version a / see 'Songs']	chorus, pf	Klopstock	June 1816	1895	xx/4, 112; iii	
521	Jagdlied / version b [for version a / see 'Songs']	unison vv, pf	F. Werner	Jan 1817	1895	xx/5, 3; iii	
706	Der 23. Psalm	SSAA, pf	trans. M. Mendelssohn	Dec 1820	1832, op.132	xviii, 3; iii	26, 84
757	Gott in der Natur	SSAA, pf	E. C. von Kleist	Aug 1822	1839	xviii, 10; iii	
836	Coronach (Totengesang der Frauen und Mädchen)	SSA, pf	Scott, trans. Storck	1825	1826, op.52/4	xviii, 1; iii	
873	Canon, a. sketch	6vv	—	?Jan 1826	1974	—; iv, 187	
920	Ständchen [formerly 921] / version b [for version a / see 'Male voices']	A, SSAA, pf	Grillparzer	July 1827	1840, op.135	xviii, 20; iii	57, 62, 67, 83
988	Liebe säuseln die Blätter, canon	3vv	Hölty	?1815	1873	xix, 83; iv, 172	
988a	—	pf acc. only	—	?after 1820	1969	—; iii	

ORCHESTRAL
(NSA nos. refer to vol. and p. in series 5)

D	Title	Composed	Published	SW; NSA	
2a	Overture, D, frag. [formerly 996]	?1811	—	—; iv	
2b	Symphony, D, frag., 1st movt only [formerly 997]	?1811	—	—; iv	
4	Overture D, for Albrecht's comedy Der Teufel als Hydraulicus	?1812	1886	ii, 1; iv	
12	Overture, D	1811 or 1812	1897	xxi, 23; iv	
26	Overture, D	by 26 June 1812	1886	ii, 13; iv	
39a	3 minuets and trios, lost	1813	—	—; v	
82	Orch frag., D [formerly 966a]	Aug/Sept 1813	1884	i/1, 1; i, 3	6
94a	Orch frag., B♭	c1814	—	—; v	
125	Symphony no.2, B♭	10 Dec 1814–24 March 1815	1884	i/1, 65; i, 71	10
200	Symphony no.3, D	24 May–19 July 1815	1884	i/1, 143; i, 153	10

D	Title	Composed	Published	SW; NSA	
345	Concerto (Concertstück), D, vn, orch	1816	1897	xxi, 46; iv	13
417	Symphony no.4, c, 'Tragic'	by 27 April 1816	1884	i/1, 191; ii	
438	Rondo, A, vn, str	June 1816	1897	xxi, 73; iv	
470	Overture, B♭ [possibly for cantata 472; arr. str qt 601]	Sept 1816	1886	iii, 31; iv	
485	Symphony no.5, B♭	Sept–3 Oct 1816	1885	i/2, 1; ii	15, 76
556	Overture, D	May 1817	1886	i, 47; iv	
580	Polonaise, B♭, vn, orch	Sept 1817	1928	—; iv	
589	Symphony no.6, C	Oct 1817–Feb 1818	1885	i/2, 49; ii	18, 63, 102
590	Overture, D, 'im italienischen Stile' [arr. pf 4 hands, 592]	Nov 1817	1886	ii, 63; iv	18
591	Overture, C, 'im italienischen Stile' [arr. pf 4 hands, 597]	Nov 1817	1865, op.170	ii, 83; iv	18
615	Symphony, D, pf sketches for 2 movts	May 1818		—; v	19
648	Overture, e [possibly for Adrast, 137]	Feb 1819	1886	ii, 101; iv	21
708a	Symphony, D, sketches	after 1820		—; v	
729	Symphony [no.7], E, sketched in score	Aug 1821	1934	—; v	31
759	Symphony [no.7] no.8, b, 'Unfinished'	Oct 1822	1867	i/2, 239; iii	11, 25, 34, 35, 72, 73, 76, 81, 99, 102
849	'Gmunden–Gastein' Symphony [?identical with 944]	June–Sept 1825			48
936a	Symphony, D, sketches	?mid-1828	1978	—; v	
944	Symphony [no.8] no.9, C, 'Great'	?1825–8	1840	i/2, 117; iii	11, 48, 63, 73, 75, 76, 97, 100, 103
966a	Orch frag., D [see 71c]				
966b	Orch sketches, A, frag.	1820 or later		—; v	
996	Overture [see 2a]				
997	Symphony [see 2b]				

117

CHAMBER

(NSA nos. refer to vol. and p. in series 6 unless otherwise stated)

D	Title	Forces	Composed	Published	SW; NSA	
2c	String Quartet, ?d/F, frag. [formerly 998]	2 vn, va, vc	?1811	1978	—; iii	
2d	6 Minuets, C, F, D, C, d, B♭ [formerly 995]	2 ob, 2 cl, 2 hn, 2 bn, trbn	1811	1970	—; ix	4
2f	Trio of a minuet, C, sketch	? wind insts	1811		—; ix	
3	String Quartet, C, frag.	2 vn, va, vc	?summer 1812	1978	—; iii	
8	Overture, c	2 vn, 2 va, vc	29 June 1811	1970	—; ii, 3	
8a	Overture, c [arr. of 8]	2 vn, va, vc	after 12 July 1811	1970	—; iii	
18	String Quartet, g/B♭	2 vn, va, vc	1810 or 1811	1890	v, 1; iii	
19	String Quartet, lost	2 vn, va, vc	1810 or 1811		—	
19a	String Quartet, lost	2 vn, va, vc	1810 or 1811		—	
20	Overture, B♭, lost	2 vn, va, vc	1812		—	
28	Trio (Sonata in 1 movt), B♭	pf, vn, vc	27 July–28 Aug 1812	1923	—; vii, 3	71

D	Title	Forces	Composed	Published	SW;NSA	
32	String Quartet, C movts, 1, 3	2 vn, va, vc	Sept–Oct 1812	1890	v, 11	
	movt 4			1897	Rev. 53	
				1954	—; iii	
36	String Quartet, B♭	2 vn, va, vc	19 Nov 1812–21 Feb 1813	1890	v, 19; iii	
46	String Quartet, C	2 vn, va, vc	3–7 March 1813	1890	v, 37; iii	
68	String Quartet, B♭, 1st movt and finale	2 vn, va, vc	8 June–18 Aug 1813	1890	v, 53; iii	
72	Wind octet, F	2 ob, 2 cl, 2 hn, 2 bn	by 18 Aug 1813	1889	iii, 69; i, 3	
72a	Allegro, F, unfinished	2 ob, 2 cl, 2 hn, 2 bn	1813	1897	Rev, 41; i, 151	
74	String Quartet, D	2 vn, va, vc	22 Aug–Sept 1813	1890	v, 71; iv	
79	Wind nonet, e♭, 'Franz Schuberts Begräbnis-Feyer' (Eine kleine Trauermusik)	2 cl, 2 bn, dbn, 2 hn, 2 trbn	19 Sept 1813	1889	iii, 81; i, 25	5
86	Minuet, D	2 vn, va, vc	?Nov 1813	1886	ii, 154; ix	
87	String Quartet, E♭	2 vn, va, vc	Nov 1813	1840, op.125/1	v, 147; iv	5
87a	Andante, C	?2 vn, va, vc	Nov 1813	—	—; iv	
89	5 minuets and 6 trios, C, F, d, G, C	2 vn, va, vc	19 Nov 1813	1886	ii, 141; ix	5
90	5 Deutsche and 7 trios with coda. C, G, D, F, C	2 vn, va, vc	19 Nov 1813	1886	ii, 147; ix	
94	String Quartet, D	2 vn, va, vc	? 1811 or 1812	1871	v, 93; iii	
94b	5 minuets and 6 Deutsche with trios, lost	2 vn, va, vc, 2 hn	1814	—	—	
96	Trio, G, added to Schubert's arr. of W. Matiegka's Notturno op.21 [replaces orig. 2nd trio]	fl, va, vc, gui	Feb 1814	1926	—; viii/2	7
103	String Quartet, c, frags., Grave and Allegro	2 vn, va, vc	23 April 1814	1939	—; iv	
111a	String Trio, B♭, frag., lost [? sketch for 112]	vn, va, vc	5–13 Sept 1814	—	—	
112	String Quartet, B♭	2 vn, va, vc	5–13 Sept 1814	1863, op.168	v, 109; iv	8
173	String Quartet, g	2 vn, va, vc	25 March–1 April 1815	1871	v, 129; iv	
353	String Quartet, E	2 vn, va, vc	1816	1840, op.125/2	v, 165; iv	16
354	4 komische Ländler, D	2 vn	Jan 1816	1930	—; ix	
355	8 Ländler, f♯	?vn	Jan 1816	1928	—; ix	
370	9 Ländler, D	?vn	Jan 1816	1930	—; ix	
374	11 Ländler, B♭	vn	?Feb 1816	1902	—; ix	
384	Sonata (Sonatina), D	vn, pf	March 1816	1836, op.137/1	viii, 26; viii, 3	16
385	Sonata (Sonatina), a	vn, pf	March 1816	1836, op.137/2	viii, 40; viii, 17	16
408	Sonata (Sonatina), g	vn, pf	April 1816	1836, op.137/3	viii, 56; viii, 33	16

D	Title and remarks		Composed	Published	SW; NSA	
471	String Trio, B♭, 1st movt and frag. of 2nd	vn, va, vc	Sept 1816	1890–97	vi, 1, Rev, 84; vi	
487	Adagio and Rondo concertante, F	vn, va, vc, pf	Oct 1816	1865	vii²/1, 52; vii, 157	
574	Sonata (Duo), A	vn, pf	Aug 1817	1851, op.162	vii, 100; viii, 47	18
581	String Trio, B♭	vn, va, vc	Sept 1817	1897	xxi, 93; vi	18
597a	Variations, A, sketches, lost	vn	Dec 1817	—	—	
601	Overture, B♭, frag. [arr. of orch ov 470]	2 vn, va, vc	c1816	—	—	
667	Piano Quintet, A, 'Die Forelle'	pf, vn, va, vc, db	?autumn 1819	1829, op.114	vii²/1, 52; vii, 185	23, 27, 75, 98
703	String Quartet, c (Quartettsatz), with frag. 2nd movt	2 vn, va, vc	Dec 1820	1870–97	v, 183, Rev, 76; v	26, 98
802	Introduction and variations (on Trockne Blumen from Die schöne Müllerin), e/E	fl, pf	Jan 1824	1850, op.160	vii, 120; viii, 67	41
803	Octet, F movts 1–3, 6 movts 1–6	cl, hn, bn, 2 vn, va, vc, db	Feb–1 March 1824	1853, op.166 1889	iii, 1; i, 27	41, 72, 75, 99, 100
804	String Quartet, a	2 vn, va, vc	Feb–March 1824	1824, op.29/1	v, 191; v	41, 99, 100, 101
810	String Quartet, d, 'Der Tod und das Mädchen'	2 vn, va, vc	March 1824	1831	v, 215; v	41, 49, 99, 100
821	Sonata, a, 'Arpeggione'	arpeggione, pf	Nov 1824	1871	viii, 142; viii, 89	45
887	String Quartet, G	2 vn, va, vc	20–30 June 1826	1851, op.161	v, 251; v	51. 72, 100, *101*
895	Rondo, b (Rondo brillant)	vn, pf	Oct 1826	1827, op.70	viii, 1; viii, 107	**60**
897	Piano Trio movt, E♭, 'Notturno'	pf, vn, vc	?1828	1846, op.148	vii/2, 106; vii, 143	59, 75, 101, 102
898	Piano Trio, B♭	pf, vn, vc	?1828	1836, op.99	vii/2, 2; vii, 91	
929	Piano Trio, E♭	pf, vn, vc	begun Nov 1827	1828, op.100	vii/2, 46; vii, 17	59, 62, 75, 97, 102
934	Fantasy, C	vn, pf	Dec 1827	1850, op.159	viii, 70; viii, 131	60, 62
956	String Quintet, C	2 vn, va, 2 vc	?Sept 1828	1853, op.163	iv, 1; ii, 19	68. 72, 97, 105
995	6 Minuets [see 2d]					
998	String Quartet [see 2c]					
AI/3	Fugue, C, frag, va part only	?2 vn, va, vc	?1812	—	—; viii/1	

SONATAS, FANTASIES AND SHORTER WORKS FOR PIANO
(NSA nos. refer to vol. in series 7/ii unless otherwise stated)

D	Title and remarks	Composed	Published	SW; NSA
2e	Fantasie, c [formerly 993]	1811	—	—; iv
13	Fugue, d	c1812	—	—; iv
14	Overture, sketch, lost	c1812	—	—
21	6 variations, E♭, lost	1812	—	—
24	7 variations, F, frag, lost	?summer 1812	—	—

D	Title and remarks	Composed	Published	SW; NSA	
24a	Fugue, C, ? for org	?summer 1812	1978	—; iv	
24b	Fugue, G, ? for org	?summer 1812	1978	—; iv	
24c	Fugue, d, ? for org	?summer 1812	1978	—; iv	
24d	Fugue, C, frag.	?summer 1812	1978	—; iv	
25c	Fugue, F, frag.	?summer 1812	—	—; viii/2	
29	Andante, C [arr. of Str Qt, 3]	9 Sept 1812	1888	xi, 136; iv	
37a	fugal sketches, Bb [formerly 967]	?1813	—	—; iv	
41a	Fugue, e, frag.	1813	—	—; iv	
71b	Fugue, e, frag.	July 1813	—	—; iv	
154	Allegro, E [sketch of 157]	11 Feb 1815	1897	xxi, 136; i	
156	10 variations, F	15 Feb 1815	1887	xi, 112; iv	
157	Sonata, E, inc.	begun Feb 1815	1888	x, 2; i	
178	Adagio, G, 2 versions [2nd version frag.]	8 April 1815	1897	xxi, 244; iv	18
279	Sonata, C [minuet = 277a with alternative trio; ? finale = 346]	Sept 1815	1888	x, 16; i	18, 104
346	Allegretto, C, frag. [? finale of 279]	?1816	1897	xxi, 222; iv	
347	Allegretto moderato, C, frag.	?1813	1897	xxi, 230; iv	
348	Andantino, C, frag.	?1816	1897	xxi, 233; iv	
349	Adagio, C, frag.	?1816	1897	xxi, 242; iv	
459	Sonata, E, frag. (nos.1, 2 of 'Fünf Klavierstücke')	Aug 1816	1843	xi, 170; i	
459a	'Fünf Klavierstücke', C, A, E (nos.3–5)	?1816	1843	xi, 178; iv	
505	Adagio, Db [orig. slow movt of 625; adapted (? by publisher) as introduction to 506]	?Sept 1818	1897	Rev, 4; iv	18
506	Rondo, E [? finale of 566]	?June 1817	1848, op.145	xi, 105; iv	
537	Sonata, a	March 1817	c1852, op.164	x, 60; i	
557	Sonata, Ab	May 1817	1888	x, 30; i	
566	Sonata, e [? finale = 506]	June 1817			
	Moderato		1888	x, 40; i	
	Allegretto		1907	—; i	
	Scherzo		1928–9	—; i	18
567	Sonata, Db, inc. [1st version of 568]	June 1817	1897	xxi, 140; i	
568	Sonata, Eb	?June 1817	1829, op.122	x, 74; i	18
570	Scherzo, D, Allegro f#, inc. [? intended as movts 3–4 of 571]	?July 1817	1897	xxi, 236; i	
571	Sonata, f#, frag. of 1st movt only	July 1817	1897	xxi, 160; i	18
575	Sonata, B	Aug 1817	1846, op.147	x, 44; i	
576	13 variations on a theme by Anselm Hüttenbrenner, a	Aug 1817	1867	xi, 124; iv	
593	2 scherzos, Bb, Db	Nov 1817	1871	xi, 190; iv	
604	Andante, A [? slow movt of 570/571]	1816 or July 1817	1888	xi, 138; iv	
605	Fantasia, C, frag.	1821–3	1897	xxi, 214; iv	
605a	Fantasy, C, 'Grazer Fantasie'	?1818	1969	—; iv	
606	March, E	?1818	1840	xi, 198; iv	

D	Title and remarks	Composed	Published	SW; NSA	
612	Adagio, E [? slow movt of 613]	April 1818	1869	xi, 142; iv	19
613	Sonata, C, 2 movts, frag. [? slow movt = 612]	April 1818	1897	xxi, 164; ii	21
625	Sonata, f, 2 movts, frag. [slow movt = 505]	Sept 1818	1897	xxi, 172; ii	
655	Sonata, c♯, frag. of 1st movt	April 1819	1897	xxi, 186; ii	
664	Sonata, A	1819 or 1825	1829, op.120	x, 134; ii	
718	Variation on a waltz by Diabelli, c	March 1821	1824	xi, 134; iv	
759a	Overture to Alfonso und Estrella, D [arr. from 732]	Nov 1822	c1839, op.69	—; iv	34, 37
760	Fantasy, C, 'Wandererfantasie'	Nov 1822	1823, op.15	xi, 2; v	
769a	Sonata, e, frag. [formerly 994]	c1823	1958	—; i	
780	6 Momens musicals [sic] C, A♭, f, c♯, f, A♭	1823–8	1828, op.94	xi, 88; v	59, 64
784	Sonata, a	Feb 1823	1839, op.143	x, 94; ii	37, 100
817	Ungarische Melodie, b [? 1st version of pf duet, 818]	2 Sept 1824	1928	—; v	
840	Sonata, C, 'Reliquie', movts 3–4 inc.	April 1825	1861	xxi, 190; ii	47
845	Sonata, a	before end May 1825	1826, op.42	x, 110; ii	47, 49, 50, 59, 100
850	Sonata, D	Aug 1825	1826, op.53	x, 146; ii	48, 50, 59
894	Sonata, G (formerly known as Fantasie, Andante, Menuetto und Allegretto)	Oct 1826	1827, op.78	x, 178; iii	50, 55, 100
899	4 Impromptus, c, E♭, G♭, A♭ nos.1–2 / nos.3–4	? summer–autumn 1827	1827, op.90/1–2 / 1857, op.90/3–4	xi, 28; v	59, 100, 103
900	Allegretto, c, frag.	? after 1820	1897	xxi, 220; v	
915	Allegretto, c	26 April 1827	1870	xi, 146; v	
916b	Piano piece, C, sketch	? summer–autumn 1827	1978	—; v	
916c	Piano piece, c, sketch	? summer–autumn 1827	1978	—; v	
935	4 Impromptus, f, A♭, B♭, f	Dec 1827	1833, op.142	xi, 58; v	103
946	3 Klavierstücke, e♭, E♭, C	May 1828	1863	xi, 150; v	64, 103
958	Sonata, c	Sept 1828	1839	x, 204; iii	67
959	Sonata, A	Sept 1828	1839	x, 232; iii	67
960	Sonata, B♭	Sept 1828	1839	x, 264; iii	67, 76
967	fugal sketches [see 37a]				
980f	March, G	?		—; vi	
993	Fantasie [see 2e]				
994	Sonata [see 769a]				

DANCES FOR PIANO
(NSA nos. refer to vol. and p. in series 7/ii)

D	Title and remarks	Composed	Published	SW; NSA
19b	Waltzes and march, lost	? 1812 or 1813	—	—
22	12 minuets with trios, lost	1812	—	—
41	30 minuets with trios, 10 lost	1813	1889	xii, 137; vi
91	2 minuets, D, A, each with 2 trios, 2 other minuets lost	22 Nov 1813	1956	—; vi

D	Title and remarks	Composed	Published	SW; NSA	
128	12 Wiener Deutsche	?1812	1897	xxi, 248: vi	
135	Deutscher, E, with trio [see 146]	1815	1930	—; vi	
139	Deutscher, C♯, with trio	1815	1930	—; vi	
145	12 Waltzes [no.7 = no.2 of 970], 17 Ländler, 9 Ecossaises [no.5 = no.1 of 421; no.6 = no.5 of 697], incl. 3 Atzenbrugger Tänze (nos.1–3)	1815–July 1821	1823, op.18	xii, 14; vii	31
146	20 Waltzes (Letzte Walzer) [no.3 = 135 with new trio]	1815	1830, op.127	xii, 66; vii	
	nos.1, 3–11	1815			
	nos.2, 12–20	Feb 1823			
158	Ecossaise, d/F	21 Feb 1815	1889	xii, 136; vi	
277a	Minuet, a [used in Sonata, 279], with trio	?Sept 1815	1925	—; iv	
299	12 Ecossaises [no.1 = Ecossaise no.1 from 145]	3 Oct 1815			
	nos.1–8		1897	xxi, 264; vi	
	nos.9–12		1912	—; vi	
334	Minuet, A, with trio	c1815	1897	xxi, 256; iv	
335	Minuet, E, with 2 trios	c1813	1897	xxi, 258; vi	
365	36 Originaltänze (Erste Walzer), incl. Trauerwalzer (no.2) and 3 Atzenbrugger Tänze (nos.29–31)	1816–July 1821	1821, op.9	xii, 2; vii	31, 32
366	17 Ländler [no.17 arr. from 814 no.1]	1816–Nov 1824			
	nos.6 and 17		1824	xii, 88; vi	
	nos.1–17		1869		
378	8 Ländler, B♭	13 Feb 1816	1889	xii, 102; vi	
380	3 minuets, E, A, C, each with 2 trios, 2nd trio of 3rd minuet lost	22 Feb 1816	1889		
	nos.1 and 2		1897	xxi, 262; vi	
	no.3		1956	—; vi	
420	12 Deutsche	1816	1871	xii, 94; vii	
421	6 Ecossaises, A♭, f, E♭, B♭, E♭, A♭ [no. 1 = Ecossaise no.5 of 145]	May 1816	1889	xii, 132; vi	
511	Ecossaise, E♭	c1817	1889	—; vi	
529	8 Ecossaises	Feb 1817	1924	xii, 134; vi	
	nos.1–3, 6, 8, D, D, D, G, D, D				
	nos.4, 5, 7, D		1871	xxi, 267; vi	
600	Minuet, c♯ [? trio = 610]	?1814	1897	xxi, 261; iv	
610	Trio, E [? minuet = 600]	Feb 1818	1897	xii, 157; vi	
640	2 dances [see 980a]		1889		
643	Deutscher, c♯, and Ecossaise, D♭	1819	1889	xii, 117; vi	
679	2 Ländler [see 980b]				
680	2 Ländler [see 980c]				
681	12 Ländler, nos.1–4 lost	c1815	1930	—; vi	
697	6 Ecossaises, A♭	May 1820			
	nos.1–4, 6		1889	xii, 134; vi	
	no.5 = no.6 of 145		1823	—; vi	
722	Deutscher, G♭	8 March 1821	1889	xii, 115; vii	

734	16 Ländler and 2 Ecossaises (Wiener-Damen Ländler)		1826, op.67		**xii, 48; vii**
735	Galop and 8 Ecossaises		1825, op.49		**xii, 119; vii**
769	2 Deutsche				**xii, 114; vi**
	no.1, A		1889		
	no.2, D	by Dec 1823	1823		
779	34 Valses sentimentales	Jan 1824	1825, op.50		xii, 34; vii
781	12 Ecossaises	c1823			xii, 125; vii
	no.1 [= Ecossaise no.2 of 783]	Jan 1823	1825, op.33		
	nos.4, 7		1824		
	nos.2–3, 5–6, 8–12		1889		
782	Ecossaise, D	c1823	1824		—; vii
783	16 Deutsche and 2 Ecossaises [no.2 = no.1 of 781]	Jan 1823–July 1824	1825, op.33		xii, 28; vii
790	12 Deutsche (Ländler)	May 1823	1864, op.171		xii, 82; vi
816	3 Ecossaises, D, D, Bb	Sept 1824	1956		—; v
820	6 Deutsche, Ab, Ab, Ab, Bb, Bb, Bb	Oct 1824	1931		—; v
841	2 Deutsche, F, G	April 1825	1930		—; v
844	Waltz, G (Albumblatt)	16 April 1825	1897		xxi, 268; vi
924	12 Grazer Walzer	?Sept 1827	1828, op.91	58	xi; 60; vii
925	Grazer Galopp, C	?Sept 1827	1828	58	xii, 123; vii
944a	Deutscher, lost	1 March 1828	—		—
969	12 Waitzes (Valses nobles)	by end 1826	1827, op.77	55.	xii, 54; vii
970	6 Ländler, Eb, Eb, Ab, Ab, Db, Db [no.2 = no.7 of 145]	?	1889		xii, 106; vii
971	3 Deutsche, a, A, E		1823		xii, 108; vii
972	3 Deutsche, Db, Ab, A	by end 1822	1889		xii, 110; vi
973	3 Deutsche, E, E, Ab	?	1889		xii, 111; vi
974	2 Deutsche, Db	?	1889		xii, 113; vi
975	Deutscher, Db	?	1889		xii, 116; vi
976	Cotillon, Eb	by end 1825	1825		xii, 118; vi
977	8 Ecossaises	?	1889		xii, 129; vi
978	Waltz, Ab	by end 1825	1825		—; vii
979	Waltz, G	by end 1826	1826		—; vii
980	2 waltzs, G, b	by end 1826	1826		—; vii
980a	2 dances, A, E, sketches [formerly 640]	?	1956		—; v
980b	2 Ländler, Eb [formerly 679]	?	1925		—; v
980c	2 Ländler, Db, frag. [formerly 680]	?	1930		—; vii
980d	Waltz, C	by end 1827	1828		—; vii
980e	2 dances, g, F, sketches [? for pf]	?	—		—; vi

PIANO FOUR HANDS

(NSA nos. refer to vol. and p. in series 7/i)

D	Title and remarks	Composed	Published	SW: NSA	
1	Fantasie, G	8 April–1 May 1810	1888	ix/3, 189; i	4
1b	Fantasie, G, frag.	1810 or 1811	—	—; i	
1c	Sonata, F, frag., 1st movt only	1810 or 1811	—	—; i	
9	Fantasie, g	20 Sept 1811	1888	ix/3, 224; i	
48	Fantasie, c (Grande sonate)	April–10 June 1813			
	1st version [without finale]		1871	ix/3, 234; i	
	2nd version [complete]		1888	—; i	
592	Overture, D, 'im italienischen Stile' [arr. of orch ov., 590]	Dec 1817	1872	ix/2, 26; v	19
597	Overture, C, 'im italienischen Stile' [arr. of orch ov., 591]	Nov or Dec 1817	1872	ix/2, 14; v	19, 20
599	4 polonaises, d, Bb, E, F	July 1818	1827, op.75	ix/3, 160; iv, 126	20
602	3 marches héroïques, b, C, D	1818 or 1824	1824, op.27	ix/1, 2; iv, 3	
603	Introduction, 4 variations on an original theme and finale [see 968a]				
608	Rondo, D				19
	version a	Jan 1818	—	—; i	
	version b (Notre amitié est invariable)	c1818	1835, op.138	ix/2, 136; i	
617	Sonata, Bb	summer–autumn 1818	1823, op.30	ix/2, 40; i	20
618	Deutscher, G, with 2 trios and 2 Ländler, E	summer–autumn 1818	1909	—; iv, 167	
618a	Polonaise and trio, sketch [trio used in 599]	July 1818	1972	—; iv, 180	20, 33
624	8 variations on a French song, e	Sept 1818	1822, op.10	ix/2, 150; i	
668	Overture, g	Oct 1819	1897	xxi, 106; v	
675	Overture, F	?Nov 1819	1825, op.34	ix/2, 2; v	
733	3 marches militaires, D, G, Eb	? summer–autumn 1818	1826, op.51	ix/1, 56; iv, 20	50
773	Overture to Alfonso und Estrella [arr. from 732]	1823	1826; 1830 as op.69	—; v	50
798	Overture to Fierabras [arr. from 796]	late 1823	1897	xxi, 120; v	
812	Sonata, C, 'Grand Duo'	June 1824	1838, op.140	ix/2, 66; ii, 5	43, 100
813	8 variations on an original theme, Ab	summer 1824	1825, op.35	ix/2, 168; ii, 27	43, 47
814	4 Ländler, Eb, Ab, c, C [no.1 arr. as 366 no.17]	July 1824	1869	ix/3, 172; iv, 176	
818	Divertissement à l'hongroise, g	?autumn 1824	1826, op.54	ix/3, 2; ii, 38	43, 50
819	6 grandes marches, Eb, g, b, D, eb, E	?autumn 1824	1825, op.40	ix/1, 20; iv, 33	
823	Divertissement sur des motifs originaux français, e	c1825		ix/3, 38; ii, 621	50
	1 Marche brillante		1826, op.63/1		
	2 Andantino varié		1827, op.84/1		
	3 Rondeau brillant		1827, op.84/2		

D	Title	Composed	Published	SW/NSA	
824	6 polonaises, d, F, B♭, D, A, E	1826		ix/3, 136; iv, 140	
859	Grande marche funèbre, c, on the death of Alexander I of Russia	Dec 1825		ix/1, 70; iv, 74	
885	Grande marche héroïque, a, for the coronation of Nicholas I of Russia	1826		ix/1, 78; iv, 82	
886	2 marches caractéristiques [see 968b]				
908	8 variations on a theme from Hérold's Marie, C	Feb 1827	op.82/1	ix/2, 194; iii	58
928	March, G, 'Kindermarsch'	12 Oct 1827	1870	ix/1, 116; iv, 124	63
940	Fantasie, f	Jan–April 1828	1829, op.103	ix/3, 112; iii	64
947	Allegro, a, 'Lebensstürme'	May 1828	1840, op.144	ix/3, 88; iii	64
951	Rondo, A	June 1828	1828, op.107	ix/2, 118; iii	64
952	Fugue, e, pf/org	3 June 1828	1848, op.152	ix/3, 176; iii	
968	Allegro moderato, C, and Andante, a (Sonatine)	?1818	1888	ix/3, 180; i	
968a	Introduction, 4 variations on an original theme and finale, B♭ [formerly 603]	?1824	1860, op.82/2	ix/2, 216; i	
968b	2 marches caractéristiques, C [formerly 886]	?1826	1830, op.121	ix/?, 94; i	86ff

SONGS

The following list includes duets, melodramas and works for or with unison chorus or incorporating brief passages for four-part chorus; all with pf acc. unless otherwise stated. SW nos. refer to vol. and p. in series 20, and NSA nos. to vol. and p. in series 4, unless otherwise stated. Incipits given where different from title.

D	Title	Incipit	Text	Key	Composed	Published	SW; NSA	
1a	Song sketch (no text)		—	c	?1810	1969	—; vi, 157	
5	Hagars Klage	Hier am Hügel heissen Sandes	C. A. Schücking	c	30 March 1811	1894	i, 1; vi, 3	4
6	Des Mädchens Klage (1)	Der Eichwald brauset	Schiller	d	1811 or 1812	1894	i, 16; iii	5
7	Leichenfantasie	Mit erstorbnem Scheinen	Schiller	d	c1811	1894	i, 22; vi, 22	5
10	Der Vatermörder	Ein Vater starb von des Sohnes Hand	G. C. Pfeffel	c	26 Dec 1811	1894	i, 40; vi, 46	
15	Der Geistertanz (1), frag.	Die breiterne Kammer der Toten erbebt	Matthisson	c	c1812	1895	x, 92; vii, 188	
15a	Der Geistertanz (2), frag.	Die breiterne Kammer der Toten erbebt	Matthisson	f	c1812	1895	x, 94; vii, 190	
17	Quell' innocente figlio version 1		Metastasio	F	c1812	1940	—; viii/2	
23	Klaglied	Meine Ruh' ist dahin	F. Rochlitz	g	1812	1830, op.131/3	i, 52; vi, 56	
30	Der Jüngling am Bache (1)	An der Quelle sass der Knabe	Schiller	F	24 Sept 1812	1894	i, 48; iv	
33	Entra l'uomo allor che nasce version 1		Metastasio	e	Sept–Oct 1812	1940	—; viii/2	
35	Serbate, o dei custodi version 3		Metastasio	C	10 Dec 1812	1940	—; viii/2	

D	Title	Incipit	Text	Key	Composed	Published	SW; NSA
39	Lebenstraum	Ich sass an einer Tempelhalle	G. von Baumberg	C	c1810	1969	—; vi, 171
42	Misero pargoletto (1)		Metastasio		?1813		
	version a, inc.			g		1969	—; vi, 180
	version b, inc.			g		1969	—; vi, 181
	Misero pargoletto (2)			g		1895	x, 31; vi, 60
44	Totengräberlied (2)	Grabe, Spaten, grabe!	Hölty	e	19 Jan 1813	1894	i, 54; vi, 64
50	Die Schatten	Freunde, deren Grüfte	Matthisson	A	12 April 1813	1894	i, 58; vi, 68
52	Sehnsucht (1)	Ach, aus dieses Tales Gründen	Schiller	d	15–17 April 1813	1868	i, 62; ii, 241
59	Verklärung	Lebensfunke, vom Himmel entglüht	A. Pope, trans. J. G. von Herder	a	4 May 1813	1832	i, 68; vi, 73
73	Thekla: eine Geisterstimme (1)	Wo ich sei, und wo mich hingewendet	Schiller	G	22–3 Aug 1813	1868	i, 70; iv
76	Pensa, che questo istante		Metastasio		7 Sept 1813		
	version a			D		1969	—; vi, 184
	version b			D	13 Sept 1813	1871	x, 34; vi, 76
77	Der Taucher	Wer wagt es, Rittersmann	Schiller		17 Sept 1813–5 April 1814		
	version a			d		1831	i, 73; vi, 78
	version b [formerly 111]			d	by 1815	1894	i, 102; vi, 114
78	Son fra l'onde	Verschwunden sind die Schmerzen	Metastasio	c	18 Sept 1813	1895	x, 36; vi, 150
81	Auf den Sieg der Deutschen, with 2 vn, vc	Des Phöbus Strahlen	?Schubert	F	autumn 1813	1895	x, 74; xiv
83	Zur Namensfeier des Herrn Andreas Siller, with vn, harp			G	28 Oct–4 Nov 1813	1895	x, 72; xiv
93	Don Gayseros	Einsam wandelt dein Freund	F. de la Motte Fouqué		c1815	1894	
	1 Don Gayseros, Don Gayseros			F			i, 132; vii, 167
	2 Nächtens klang die süsse Laute	Lehnst du deine bleichgehärmte Wange		F			i, 137; vii, 173
	3 An dem jungen Morgenhimmel			E♭			i, 141; vii, 177
95	Adelaide		Matthisson	A♭	1814	1848	i, 169; vii, 3
97	Trost: an Elisa		Matthisson	a	1814	1894	i, 154; vii, 6
98	Erinnerungen (1)	Am Seegestad	Matthisson				
	version a			B♭	autumn 1814	1968	—; vii, 167
	version b			B♭	c1814	1894	i, 166; vii, 8
99	Andenken (1)	Ich denke dein	Matthisson	F	April 1814	1894	i, 144; vii, 11

No.	Title	Incipit	Key	Poet	Date	Pub.	References	
100	Geisternähe	Der Dämmrung Schein	E♭	Matthisson	April 1814	1894	i, 147; vii, 14	
101	Erinnerung	Kein Rosenschimmer leuchtet	e	Matthisson	April 1814	1894	i, 151; vii, 18	
102	Die Betende	Laura betet	B	Matthisson	autumn 1814	1840	i, 156; vii, 21	
104	Die Befreier Europas in Paris	Sie sind in Paris!		J. C. Mikan				
	version a		G		May 1814	1968	—; vii, 180	
	version b		G		May 1814	1968	—; vii, 182	
	version c		G		16 May 1814	1895	x, 76; vii, 24	
107	Lied aus der Ferne	Wenn in des Abends letztem Scheine		Matthisson				
	version a		E		July 1814	1894	i, 158; vii, 26	
	version b		D		?July 1814	1968	—; vii, 29	
108	Der Abend	Purpur malt die Tannenhügel	d	Matthisson	July 1814	1894	i, 161; vii, 31	
109	Lied der Liebe	Durch Fichten am Hügel	B♭	Matthisson	July 1814	1894	i, 163; vii, 33	
111	Der Taucher [see 77]							
113	An Emma	Weit in nebelgrauer Ferne		Schiller				
	version a		F		17 Sept 1814	1894	i, 172; iii	
	version b		F		c1814	1821	i, 174; iii	
	version c		F		c1814	1826, op.58/2	i, 176; iii	
114	Romanze	Ein Fräulein klagt' im finstern Turm		Matthisson				
	version a		g		Sept 1814	1902	—; vii, 36	
	version b		g		29 Sept 1814	1868	i, 178; vii, 42	
115	An Laura, als sie Klopstocks Auferstehungslied sang	Herzen, die gen Himmel sich erheben	E	Matthisson	2–7 Oct 1814	1840	i, 183; vii, 48	
116	Der Geistertanz (3)	Die bretterne Kammer der Toten erbebt	c	Matthisson	14 Oct 1814	1840	i, 186; vii, 52	
117	Das Mädchen aus der Fremde (1)	In einem Tal bei armen Hirten	A	Schiller	16 Oct 1814	1894	i, 189; viii	
118	Gretchen am Spinnrade	Meine Ruh' ist hin	d	Goethe	19 Oct 1814	1821, op.2	i, 191; i, 10	8, 30, 78, 86
119	Nachtgesang	O gib vom weichem Pfühle	A♭	Goethe	30 Nov 1814	1850	i, 197; vii, 55	
120	Trost in Tränen	Wie kommt's dass du so traurig bist	F	Goethe	30 Nov 1814	1835	i, 198; vii, 56	
121	Schäfers Klagelied	Da droben auf jenem Berge		Goethe				8, 22
	version a		e		Nov 1814	1894	i, 203; i, 194	
	version b		c		30 Nov 1814	1821, op.3/1	i, 200; i, 20	
122	Ammenlied	Am hohen, hohen Turm	g	M. Lubi	Dec 18 4	1872	i, 224; vii, 59	
123	Sehnsucht	Was zieht mir das Herz so?	G	Goethe	3 Dec 1814	1842	i, 206; vii, 60	

D	Title	Incipit	Text	Key	Composed	Published	SW; NSA	
124	Am See							9, 10
	version a	Sitz' ich im Gras	Mayrhofer	g	Dec 1814	1968	—; vii, 194	
	version b			g	7 Dec 1814	1885	i, 210; vii, 65	
126	Szene aus Goethes Faust (Dom), with 4vv	Wie anders, Gretchen, war dir's	Goethe					9
	version a			c	Dec 1814	1873	i, 215; vii, 196	
	version b			c	12 Dec 1814	1832	i, 219; vii, 71	
134	Ballade	Ein Fräulein schaut vom hohen Turm	J. Kenner	g	c1815	1830, op.126	ii, 198; vii, 77	
138	Rastlose Liebe	Dem Schnee, dem Regen	Goethe					12, 30
	version a			E	19 May 1815	1821, op.51	iii, 198; i, 35	
	version b			D	1821	1970	—; i, 208	
141	Der Mondabend	Rein und freundlich lacht der Himmel	J. G. Kumpf	A	1815	1830, op.131/1	ii, 20; vii, 86	
142	Geistes-Gruss	Hoch auf dem alten Turme	Goethe		1815 or 1816			
	version a			Eb/Gb		1895	iii, 189; v	
	version b			Eb/Gb		1885	iii, 190; v	
	version c			D/F		—	—; v	
	version d			Eb/Gb		1895	iii, 191; v	
	version e			Eb/Gb		—	—; v	
	version f			E/G	rev. ?1828	1828, op.92/3	iii, 192; v	
143	Genügsamkeit	Dort raget ein Berg	F. von Schober	c#	1815	1829, op.109/2	iii, 230; vii, 88	
144	Romanze, unfinished	In der Väter Hallen ruhte	F. Graf zu Stolberg-Stolberg	E	April 1816	1897	Rev. 46; vii, 201	
149	Der Sänger	Was hör' ich draussen vor dem Tor	Goethe					
	version a			D	Feb 1815	1894	ii, 41; vii, 90	
	version b			D	1815	1829, op.117	ii, 33; vii, 97	
150	Lodas Gespenst	Der bleiche, kalte Mond	Ossian, trans. E. Baron de Harold	g/Bb	17 Jan 1816	1830	ii, 21; vii, 105	
151	Auf einen Kirchhof	Sei gegrüsst, geweihte Stille	F. von Schlechta	A	2 Feb 1815	c1850	ii, 1; vii, 119	
152	Minona	Wie treiben die Wolken so finster	F. A. Bertrand	a	8 Feb 1815	1894	ii, 6; vii, 124	
153	Als ich sie erröten sah	All' mein Wirken	B. A. Ehrlich	G	10 Feb 1815	1845	ii, 15; vii, 135	

No.	Title	Incipit	Poet	Key	Date	Pub.	Refs
155	Das Bild	Ein Mädchen ist's		F	11 Feb 1815	1862, op.165/3	ii, 19; vii, 140
159	Die Erwartung	Hör' ich das Pförtchen	Schiller				
	version a			B♭	May 1816	1968	—; vii, 141
	version b			B♭	1816	1829, op.116	ii, 47; vii, 153
160	Am Flusse (1)	Verfliesset, vielgeliebte Lieder	Goethe	d	27 Feb 1815	1894	i, 58; xiii
161	An Mignon	Über Tal und Fluss getragen	Goethe		27 Feb 1815		
	version a			g♯	27 Feb 1815	1894	ii, 59; i, 249
	version b			g	1815	1825, op.19/2	ii, 60; i, 129
162	Nähe des Geliebten	Ich denke dein	Goethe		27 Feb 1815		
	version a			G♭		1894	ii, 62; i, 276
	version b			G♭		1821, op.5/2	ii, 63; i, 40
163	Sängers Morgenlied (1)	Süsses Licht! aus goldenen Pforten	Körner	G	27 Feb 1815	1894	ii, 64; viii
164	Liebesrausch (1), frag.	... Gianz des Guten	Körner	G	March 1815	1928	—; viii
165	Sängers Morgenlied (2)	Süsses Licht! aus goldenen Pforten	Körner	C	1 March 1815	1872	ii, 66; viii
166	Amphiaraos	Vor Thebens siebenfach gähnenden Toren	Körner	g	1 March 1815	1894	ii 68; viii
169	Trinklied vor der Schlacht, for 2 unison choruses	Schlacht, du brichst an!	Körner	C	12 March 1815	1894	ii, 76; iii/3
170	Schwertlied, with unison chorus	Du Schwert an meiner Linken	Körner	C	12 March 1815	1873	ii, 78; iii/3
171	Gebet während der Schlacht	Vater, ich rufe dich!	Körner	B♭	12 March 1815	1831	ii, 80; viii
172	Der Morgenstern (1), frag.	Stern der Liebe	Körner	G♭	12 March 1815	—	—; viii
174	Das war ich	Jüngst träumte mir	Körner				
	version a			G	26 March 1815	c1842	ii, 84; viii
	version b, frag.			D	cJune 1816	1897	Rev, 16; viii
176	Die Sterne	Was funkelt ihr so mild mich an?	J. G. Fellinger	A♭	6 April 1815	1872	ii, 36; viii
177	Vergebliche Liebe	Ja, ich weiss es	J. K. Bernard	c	6 April 1815	1867, op.173/3	ii, 38; viii
179	Liebesrausch (2)	Dir, Mädchen, schlägt	Körner	G	8 April 1815	1872	ii, 90; viii
180	Sehnsucht der Liebe	Wie die Nacht mit heiligem Beben	Körner				
	version a			G	8 April 1815	1894	ii, 92; viii
	version b, frag., lost			G	July 1815	—	—
182	Die erste Liebe	Die erste Liebe füllt das Herz	Fellinger	C	12 April 1815	1842	ii, 94; viii

D	Title	Incipit	Text	Key	Composed	Published	SW; NSA
183	Trinklied, with unison chorus	Ihr Freunde und du gold'ner Wein	A. Zettler	G	12 April 1815	1887	ii, 97; iii/3
186	Die Sterbende	Heil! dies ist die letzte Zähre	Matthisson	A♭	May 1815	1894	ii, 100; viii
187	Stimme der Liebe (1)	Abendgewölke schweben hell	Matthisson	F	May 1815	1894	ii, 98; viii
188	Naturgenuss (1)	Im Abendschimmer wallt der Quell	Matthisson	B♭	May 1815	1887	ii, 99; viii
189	An die Freude, with unison chorus	Freude, schöner Götterfunken	Schiller	E	May 1815	1829, op.111/1	ii, 102; iii/3
191	Des Mädchens Klage (2) version a version b	Der Eichwald brauset	Schiller	c c	15 May 1815 1815	1894 1826, op.58/3	ii, 104; iii ii, 106; iii
192	Der Jüngling am Bache (2)	An der Quelle sass der Knabe	Schiller	f	15 May 1815	1887	ii, 108; iv
193	An den Mond	Geuss, lieber Mond	Hölty	f	17 May 1815	1826, op.57/3	ii, 110; iii
194	Die Mainacht	Wann der silberne Mond	Hölty	d	17 May 1815	1894	ii, 112; viii
195	Amalia	Schön wie Engel	Schiller	A	19 May 1815	1867, op.173/1	ii, 113; viii
196	An die Nachtigall	Geuss nicht so laut	Hölty	f♯	22 May 1815	1865, op.172/3	ii, 116; viii
197	An die Apfelbäume, wo ich Julien erblickte	Ein heilig Säuseln	Hölty	A	22 May 1815	1850	ii, 117; viii
198	Seufzer	Die Nachtigall singt überall	Hölty	g	22 May 1815	1894	ii, 120; viii
201	Auf den Tod einer Nachtigall (1), frag.	Sie ist dahin	Hölty	f♯	25 May 1815	1970	—; x
204a	Das Traumbild, lost		Hölty	—	May 1815	—	
206	Liebeständelei	Süsses Liebchen, komm zu mir!	Körner	E♭	26 May 1815	1872	ii, 122; viii
207	Der Liebende	Beglückt, beglückt, wer dich erblickt	Hölty	B♭	29 May 1815	1894	ii, 123; viii
208	Die Nonne version a, frag. version b [formerly 212]	Es liebt' in Welschland	Hölty	A♭ A♭	29 May 1815 16 June 1815	1897 1895	Rev, 19; viii ii, 124; viii
209	Der Liedler	Gib, Schwester, mir die Harf herab	Kenner	a	Jan 1815	1825, op.38	ii, 184; ii, 144
210	Die Liebe (Klärchens Lied)	Freudvoll und leidvoll	Goethe	B♭	3 June 1815	1838	ii, 130; viii
211	Adelwold und Emma	Hoch, und ehern schier von Dauer	Bertrand	F	5–14 June 1815	1894	ii, 132; viii
212	Die Nonne [see 208]						
213	Der Traum	Mir träumt', ich war ein Vögelein	Hölty	A	17 June 1815	1865, op.172/1	ii, 158; viii

214	Die Laube	Nimmer werd' ich, nimmer dein vergessen	Hölty	Ab	17 June 1815	1865, op.172/2	ii, 159; viii	
215	Jägers Abendlied (1)	Im Felde schleich' ich still und wild	Goethe	F	20 June 1815	1907	—; i, 198	
215a	Meerestille (1)	Tiefe Stille herrscht im Wasser	Goethe	C	20 June 1815	1952	—; i, 197	
216	Meerestille (2)	Tiefe Stille herrscht im Wasser	Goethe	C	21 June 1815	1821, op.3/2	ii, 160; i, 23	12, 88
217	Kolmas Klage	Rund um mich Nacht	Ossian, trans. Kenner	c	22 June 1815	1830	ii, 161; viii	
218	Grablied	Er fiel den Tod fürs Vaterland	L. Kosegarten	f	24 June 1815	1848	ii, 166; viii	
219	Das Finden	Ich hab' ein Mädchen funden	Kosegarten	Bb	25 June 1815	1848	ii, 167; viii	
221	Der Abend	Der Abend blüht	Kosegarten	B	15 July 1815	1829, op.118/2	ii, 178; viii	
222	Lieb Minna	Schwüler Hauch weht mir herüber	A. Stadler	f	2 July 1815	1885	ii, 168; viii	
224	Wandrers Nachtlied	Der du von dem Himmel bist	Goethe	Gb	5 July 1815	1821, op.4/3	ii, 170; i, 34	
225	Der Fischer version a	Das Wasser rauscht	Goethe	Bb	5 July 1815	1970	—; i, 208	
	version b			Bb	c1815	1821, op.5/3	ii, 171; i, 42	
226	Erster Verlust	Ach, wer bringt die schönen Tage	Goethe	f	5 July 1815	1821, op.5/4	ii, 172; i, 44	12
227	Idens Nachtgesang	Vernimm es, Nacht	Kosegarten	Bb	7 July 1815	1885	ii, 173; viii	
228	Von Ida	Der Morgen blüht	Kosegarten	f	7 July 1815	1894	ii, 174; viii	
229	Die Erscheinung	Ich lag auf grünen Matten	Kosegarten	E	7 July 1815	1829, op.108/3	ii, 175; v	
230	Die Täuschung	Im Erlenbusch, im Tannenhain	Kosegarten	E	7 July 1815	1862, op.165/4	ii, 176; viii	
231	Das Sehnen	Wehmut, die mich hüllt	Kosegarten	a	8 July 1815	1865, op.172/4	ii, 177; viii	
233	Geist der Liebe	Wer bist du, Geist der Liebe	Kosegarten	E	15 July 1815	1829, op.118/1	ii, 180; viii	
234	Tischlied	Mich ergreift, ich weiss nicht wie	Goethe	C	15 July 1815	1829, op 118/3	ii, 182; viii	
235	Abends unter der Linde (1)	Woher, o namenloses Sehnen	Kosegarten	F	24 July 1815	1894	ii, 204; viii	
237	Abends unter der Linde (2)	Woher, o namenloses Sehnen	Kosegarten	F	25 July 1815	1872	ii, 206; viii	
238	Die Mondnacht	Siehe, wie die Mondesstrahlen	Kosegarten	F#	25 July 1815	1894	ii, 208; viii	
240	Huldigung	Ganz verloren, ganz versunken	Kosegarten	E	27 July 1815	1894	ii, 210; viii	
241	Alles um Liebe	Was ist es, das die Seele füllt?	Kosegarten	E	27 July 1815	1894	ii, 212; viii	
245	An den Frühling [see 587b]							
246	Die Bürgschaft	Zu Dionys, dem Tyrannen	Schiller	g	Aug 1815	1830	iii, 11; viii	

D	Title	Incipit	Text	Key	Composed	Published	SW; NSA
247	Die Spinnerin	Als ich still und ruhig spann	Goethe	b	Aug 1815	1829, op.118/6	iii, 44; viii
248	Lob des Tokayer	O köstlicher Tokayer	Baumberg	B♭	Aug 1815	1829, op.118/4	iii, 66; viii
249 250	Die Schlacht (1), frag. Das Geheimnis (1)	Sie konnte mir kein Wörtchen sagen	Schiller Schiller	b A♭	1 Aug 1815 7 Aug 1815	1872	—; iii/2 iii, 2; xiii
251	Hoffnung (1)	Es reden und träumen die Menschen	Schiller	G♭	7 Aug 1815	1872	iii, 4; iv
252	Das Mädchen aus der Fremde (2)	In einem Tal bei armen Hirten	Schiller	F	12 Aug 1815	1887	iii, 10; viii
253	Punschlied: im Norden zu singen	Auf der Berge freien Höhen	Schiller	B♭	18 Aug 1815	1887	iii, 30; viii
254 255	Der Gott und die Bajadere Der Rattenfänger	Mahadöh, der Herr der Erde Ich bin der wohlbekannte Sänger	Goethe Goethe	E♭ G	18 Aug 1815 19 Aug 1815	1887 c1850	iii, 32; viii iii, 34; viii
256	Der Schatzgräber	Arm am Beutel, krank am Herzen	Goethe	d	19 Aug 1815	1887	iii, 35; viii
257	Heidenröslein	Sah ein Knab' ein Röslein stehn	Goethe	G	19 Aug 1815	1821, op.3/3	iii, 37; i, 24
258	Bundeslied	In allen guten Stunden	Goethe	B♭	4 or 19 Aug 1815	1887	iii, 38; viii
259 260	An den Mond (1) Wonne der Wehmut	Füllest wieder Busch und Tal Trocknet nicht, trocknet nicht	Goethe Goethe	E♭ c	19 Aug 1815 20 Aug 1815	c1850 1829, op.115/2	iii, 40; ix iii, 42; viii
261 262	Wer kauft Liebesgötter? Die Fröhlichkeit	Von allen schönen Waren Wes' Adern leichtes Blut durchspringt	Goethe M. J. Prandstetter	C E	21 Aug 1815 22 Aug 1815	c1850 1895	iii, 43; viii iii, 64; ix
263	Cora an die Sonne	Nach so vielen trüben Tagen	Baumberg	E♭	22 Aug 1815	1848	iii, 50; ix
264	Der Morgenkuss version a version b	Durch eine ganze Nacht	Baumberg Baumberg	E♭ C	22 Aug 1815 c1815	1872 1850	iii, 51; ix —; ix
265 266 270	Abendständchen: An Lina Morgenlied An die Sonne	Sei sanft wie ihre Seele Willkommen, rotes Morgenlicht Sinke, liebe Sonne	Baumberg Stolberg Baumberg	B♭ F E♭	23 Aug 1815 24 Aug 1815 25 Aug 1815	1895 1895 1829, op.118/5	iii, 52; ix iii, 54; ix iii, 56; ix
271	Der Weiberfreund	Noch fand von Evens Töchterscharen	A. Cowley, trans. J. F. von Ratschky	A	25 Aug 1815	1895	iii, 57; ix
272	An die Sonne	Königliche Morgensonne	C. A. Tiedge	E♭	25 Aug 1815	1872	iii, 58; ix

12, 30

No.	Title	Incipit	Poet	Key	Date	Pub.	Reference
273	Lilla an die Morgenröte	Wie schön bist du, du güldne Morgenröte		D	25 Aug 1815	1895	iii, 59; ix
274	Tischlerlied	Mein Handwerk geht durch alle Welt		C	25 Aug 1815	1850	ii, 60; ix
275	Totenkranz für ein Kind	Sanft wehn, im Hauch der Abendluft	Matthisson	g	25 Aug 1815	1895	iii, 61; ix
276	Abendlied	Gross und rotentflammet	Stolberg	A	28 Aug 1815	1895	iii, 62; ix
278	Ossians Lied nach dem Falle Nathos	Beugt euch aus euren Wolken nieder	Ossian, trans. Harold		?Sept 1815		
	version a			E		1897	Rev, 34; ix
	version b			E		1830	ii, 108; ix
280	Das Rosenband	Im Frühlingsgarten fand ich sie	F. G. Klopstock	Ab	Sept 1815	1837	ii, 72; ix
281	Das Mädchen von Inistore	Mädchen Inistores	Ossian, trans. Harold	c	Sept 1815	1830	ii, 110; ix
282	Cronnan	Ich sitz' bei der moosigten Quelle	Ossian, trans. Harold	c	5 Sept 1815	1830	iv, 21; ix
283	An den Frühling (1)	Willkommen, schöner Jüngling!	Schiller	F	6 Sept 1815	1865, op.172/5	iii, 68; xi
284	Lied	Es ist so angenehm	?Schiller	G	6 Sept 1815	1895	iii, 69; ix
285	Furcht der Geliebten (An Cidli)	Cidli, du weinest	Klopstock				
	version a			Ab	12 Sept 1815	1895	ii, 70; ix
	version b			Ab	c1815	1885	ii, 71; ix
286	Selma und Selmar	Weine du nicht	Klopstock				
	version a			F	c1815	1895	iii, 74; ix
	version b			F	14 Sept 1815	1837	iii, 75; ix
287	Vaterlandslied	Ich bin ein deutsches Mädchen	Klopstock				
	version a			C	14 Sept 1815	1895	iii, 76; ix
	version b			C	c1815	1895	iii, 77; ix
288	An Sie	Zeit, Verkündigerin der besten Freuden	Klopstock	Ab	14 Sept 1815	1895	iii, 78; ix
289	Die Sommernacht	Wenn der Schimmer von dem Monde	Klopstock				
	version a			C	14 Sept 1815	1895	iii, 80; ix
	version b			C	c1815	1895	iii, 82; ix
290	Die frühen Gräber	Willkommen, o silberner Mond	Klopstock	a	14 Sep 1815	1837	iii, 84; ix
291	Dem Unendlichen	Wie erhebt sich das Herz	Klopstock				
	version a			F	15 Sep 1815	1895	iii, 85; ix
	version b			F	c1815	1831	iii, 90; ix
	version c			G	c1815	1895	iii, 95; ix
292	Klage [see 371]						

90

D	Title	Incipit	Text	Key	Composed	Published	SW; NSA
293	Shilric und Vinvela	Mein Geliebter ist ein Sohn des Hügels	Ossian, trans. Harold	B♭	20 Sept 1815	1830	iii, 100; ix
295	Hoffnung	Schaff, das Tagwerk meiner Hände	Goethe		c1816		
	version a			F		1872	iii, 193; ix
	version b			E		1895	iii, 194; ix
296	An den Mond (2)	Füllest wieder Busch und Tal	Goethe	A♭	c1816	1868	iii, 195; ix
297	Augenlied	Süsse Augen, klare Bronnen!	Mayrhofer		?1817		
	version a			F		1895	iii, 168; ix
	version b			F		1850	—; ix
298	Liane	Hast du Lianen nicht geschen?	Mayrhofer	C	Oct 1815	1895	iii, 165; ix
300	Der Jüngling an der Quelle	Leise, rieselnder Quell	J. G. von Salis-Seewis	A	c1817	1842	vi, 208; ix
301	Lambertine	O Liebe, die mein Herz erfüllet	J. L. Stoll	E♭	12 Oct 1815	1842	iii, 112; ix
302	Labetrank der Liebe	Wenn im Spiele leiser Töne	Stoll	F	15 Oct 1815	1895	iii, 114; ix
303	An die Geliebte	O, dass ich dir vom stillen Auge	Stoll	G	15 Oct 1815	1887	iii, 116; ix
304	Wiegenlied	Schlumm're sanft!	Körner	F	15 Oct 1815	1895	iii, 117; ix
305	Mein Gruss an den Mai	Sei mir gegrüsst, o Mai	Kumpf	B♭	15 Oct 1815	1895	iii, 118; ix
306	Skolie	Lasst im Morgenstrahl des Mai'n	J. L. von Deinhardstein	B♭	15 Oct 1815	1895	iii, 120; ix
307	Die Sternewelten	Oben drehen sich die grossen	U. Jarnik, trans. Fellinger	F	15 Oct 1815	1895	iii, 121; ix
308	Die Macht der Liebe	Überall, wohin mein Auge blicket	J. N. von Kalchberg	B♭	15 Oct 1815	1895	iii, 123; ix
309	Das gestörte Glück	Ich hab' ein heisses junges Blut	Körner	F	15 Oct 1815	1872	iii, 124; ix
310	Sehnsucht (1)	Nur wer die Sehnsucht kennt	Goethe		18 Oct 1815		
	version a			A♭		1895	iii, 126; iii
	version b			F		1895	iii, 128; iii
311	An den Mond, frag.			A	19 Oct 1815	—	—; ix
312	Hektors Abschied	Will sich Hektor ewig von mir wenden	Schiller				
	version a			f	19 Oct 1815	1895	iii, 130; iii
	version b			f	c1815	1826, op.58/1	iii, 36; iii
313	Die Sterne	Wie wohl ist mir im Dunkeln	Kosegarten	B♭	19 Oct 1815	1895	iii, 142; ix
314	Nachtgesang	Tiefe Feier schauert um die Welt	Kosegarten	E♭	19 Oct 1815	1887	iii, 144; ix
315	An Rosa I	Warum bist du nicht hier	Kosegarten	A♭	19 Oct 1815	1895	iii, 145; ix

No.	Title	Incipit	Author	Key	Composed	Published	References	
316	An Rosa II	Rosa, denkst du an mich?	Kosegarten					
	version a			Ab	19 Oct 1815	1895	iii, 146; ix	
	version b			Ab	c1815	1895	iii, 147; ix	
317	Idens Schwanenlied	Wie schaust du aus dem Nebelflor	Kosegarten					
	version a			f		—	—; ix	
	version b			f	c1815	1895	iii, 148; ix	
318	Schwangesang	Endlich stehn die Pforten offen	Kosegarten	f	19 Oct 1815	1895	iii, 150; ix	
319	Luisens Antwort	Wohl weinen Gottes Engel	Kosegarten	bb	19 Oct 1815	1895	iii, 152; ix	
320	Der Zufriedene	Zwar schuf das Glück hin eden	C. L. Reissig	A	23 Oct 1815	1895	iii, 154; ix	
321	Mignon	Kennst du das Land	Goethe	A	23 Oct 1815	1895	iii, 155; ix	
322	Hermann und Thusnelda	Ha, dort kömmt er	Klopstock	Eb	27 Oct 1815	1837	iii, 159; ix	
323	Klage der Ceres	Ist der holde Lenz erschienen?	Schiller	G	9 Nov 1815–June 1816	1895	iii, 171; ix	
325	Harfenspieler (1)	Wer sich der Einsamkeit ergibt	Goethe	a	13 Nov 1815	1895	iii, 187; i, 218	
327	Lorma (1), frag.	Lorma sass in der Halle von Aldo	Ossian, trans. Harold	a	28 Nov 1815	1928	—; x	
328	Erlkönig	Wer reitet so spät	Goethe					12, 13, 16, 17, 26, 29, 30, 46, 87
	version a			g	?Oct 1815	1895	iii, 202; i, 173	
	version b			g	1815	1868	iii, 214; i, 180	
	version c			g	1815	1895	iii, 208; i, 187	
	version d			g	1815	1821, op.1	iii, 219; i, 3	
329	Die drei Sänger, frag.	Der König sass beim frohen Mahle	F. Bobrik	A	23 Dec 1815	1895	x, 97; ix	
330	Das Grab (2) version a [for version b see 'Male voices']	Das Grab ist tief und stille	Salis-Seewis	c	28 Dec 1815	1895	iii, 231; iii/3	
342	An mein Klavier	Sanftes Klavier	C. F. D. Schubart	A	c1816	1885	iv, 138; x	
343	Am Tage aller Seelen (Litanei auf das Fest aller Seelen)	Ruhn in Frieden alle Seelen	J. G. Jacobi		Aug 1816			
	version a			Eb		1831	v, 126; x	
	version b			Eb		—	—; x	
344	Am ersten Maimorgen	Heute will ich fröhlich, fröhlich sein	Claudius	G	c1816	—	—; x	
350	Der Entfernten (2)	Wohl denk' ich allenthalben	Salis-Seewis	Eb	?1816	1885	iv, 69; x	
351	Fischerlied (1)	Das Fischergewerbe gibt rüstigen Mut!	Salis-Seewis	D	?1816	1895	iv, 70; xi	
352	Licht und Liebe (Nachtgesang). S. T	Liebe ist ein süsses Licht	M. von Collin	G	?1816	c1847	iv, 253; iii/2	

D	Title	Incipit	Text	Key	Composed	Published	SW, NSA	
358	Die Nacht	Du verstörst uns nicht, o Nacht!	J. P. Uz	A♭	1816	c1849	iv, 127; x	
359	Sehnsucht (2)	Nur wer die Sehnsucht kennt	Goethe	d	1816	1872	iv, 200; iii	
360	Lied eines Schiffers an die Dioskuren	Dioskuren, Zwillingsterne	Mayrhofer	A♭	1816	1826, op.65/1	iv, 221; iii	
361	Am Bach im Frühlinge	Du brachst sie nun, die kalte Rinde	Schober	D♭	1816	1829, op.109/1	iv, 230; x	
362	Zufriedenheit (1)	Ich bin vergnügt	Claudius	A	1815 or 1816	1895	iv, 244; xi	
363	An Chloen, frag.	Die Munterkeit ist meinen Wangen	Uz	G	1816	—	—; x	
367	Der König in Thule	Es war ein König in Thule	Goethe	d	early 1816	1821, op.5/5	iv, 202; i, 45	
368	Jägers Abendlied (2)	Im Felde schleich' ich still und wild	Goethe	D♭	?early 1816	1821, op.3/4	iv, 203; i, 25	
369	An Schwager Kronos	Spude dich, Kronos!	Goethe	d	1816	1825, op.19/1	iv, 204; i, 121	16, 47, 88
371	Klage	Trauer umfliesst mein Leben	Stolberg-Stolberg	b	Jan 1816	1872	iv, 5; x	
372	An die Natur	Süsse, heilige Natur		F	15 Jan 1816	1895	iv, 2; x	
373	Lied	Mutter geht durch ihre Kammern	Fouqué	g	?15 Jan 1816	1895	iv, 3; x	
375	Der Tod Oskars	Warum öffnest du wieder	Ossian, trans. Harold	c	Feb 1816	1830	iv, 7; x	
376	Lorma (2), frag.	Lorma sass in der Halle von Aldo	Ossian, trans. Harold	a	10 Feb 1816	1895	x, 102; x	
381	Morgenlied	Die frohe neubelebte Flur		C	24 Feb 1816	1895	iv, 29; x	
382	Abendlied	Sanft glänzt die Abendsonne		F	24 Feb 1816	1895	iv, 30; x	
388	Laura am Klavier	Wenn dein Finger durch die Saiten meistert	Schiller					
	version a			E	March 1816		iv, 41; x	
	version b			A	c1816		iv, 46; x	
389	Des Mädchens Klage (3)	Der Eichwald braust	Schiller	c	March 1816	1873	iv, 52; iii	
390	Entzückung an Laura (1)	Laura, über diese Welt	Schiller	A	March 1816	1895	iv, 54; x	
391	Die vier Weltalter	Wohl perlet im Glase	Schiller	G	March 1816	1829, op.111/3	iv, 56; x	
392	Pflügerlied	Arbeitsam und wacker	Salis-Seewis	C	March 1816	1895	iv, 58; x	
393	Die Einsiedelei (2)	Es rieselt, klar und wehend	Salis-Seewis	A	March 1816	c1845	iv, 60; xi	
394	An die Harmonie	Schöpferin beseelter Töne!	Salis-Seewis	A	March 1816	1895	iv, 62; x	
395	Lebensmelodien	Auf dem Wasser wohnt mein stilles Leben	A. W. von Schlegel	G	March 1816	1829, op.111/2	iv, 72; x	
396	Gruppe aus dem Tartarus (1), frag.	Horch, wie Murmeln des empörten Meeres	Schiller	c	March 1816	1975	—; ii, 171	26

No.	Title	First line	Poet	Key	Date	Pub.	Ref.
397	Ritter Toggenburg	Ritter, treue Schwesterliebe	Schiller	F	13 March 1816	1832	iv, 31; x
398	Frühlingslied (2)	Die Luft ist blau	Hölty	G	13 May 1816	1887	iv, 97; x
399	Auf den Tod einer Nachtigall (2)	Sie ist dahin	Hölty	a	13 May 1816	1895	iv, 98; x
400	Die Knabenzeit	Wie glücklich, wem das Knabenkleid	Hölty	A	13 May 1816	1895	iv, 100; x
401	Winterlied	Keine Blumen blühn	Hölty	a	13 May 1816	1895	iv, 102; x
402	Der Flüchtling	Frisch atmet des Morgens lebendiger Hauch	Schiller	B♭	18 March 1816	1872	iv, 35; x
403	Lied	Ins stille Land	Salis-Seewis				
	version a			g	27 March 1816	1845	iv, 66; x
	version b			a	April 1816	1895	iv, 67; x
	version c			a	March 1816	—	—; x
	version d			a	Aug 1823	—	—; x
404	Die Herbstnacht	Mit leisen Harfentönen	Salis-Seewis	F	March 1816	1885	iv, 61; x
405	Der Herbstabend	Abendglockenhalle zittern	Salis-Seewis				
	version a			f	April 1816	1895	iv, 68; x
	version b			f	1816	—	—; x
406	Abschied von der Harfe	Noch einmal tön, o Harfe	Salis-Seewis	e	March 1816	1887	iv, 80; x
409	Die verfehlte Stunde	Quälend ungestilltes Sehnen	A. W. von Schlegel	f	April 1816	1872	iv, 70; x
410	Sprache der Liebe	Lass dich mit gelinden Schlägen	A. W. von Schlegel	E	April 1816	1829, op.115/3	iv, 78; x
411	Daphne am Bach	Ich hab' ein Bächlein funden	Stolberg-Stolberg	D	April 1816	1887	iv, 81; x
412	Stimme der Liebe	Meine Selinde	Stolberg-Stolberg				
	version a			E	1816	—	—; x
	version b			D	c1816	1838	iv, 82; x
413	Entzückung	Tag voll Himmel	Matthisson	C	April 1816	1895	iv, 84; x
414	Geist der Liebe (1)	Der Abend schleiert Flur und Hain	Matthisson	G	April 1816	1895	iv, 87; x
415	Klage	Die Sonne steigt	Matthisson	C	April 1816	1895	iv, 88; x
416	Lied in der Abwesenheit, frag.	Ach, mir ist das Herz so schwer	Stolberg-Stolberg	b	April 1816	1925	—; x
418	Stimme der Liebe (2)	Abendgewölke schweben hell	Matthisson	G	29 April 1816	1895	iv, 90; x
419	Julius an Theone	Nimmer, nimmer darf ich dir gestehen	Matthisson	g	30 April 1816	1895	iv, 95; x
429	Minnelied	Holder klingt der Vogelsang	Hölty	E	May 1816	1885	iv, 103; x
430	Die frühe Liebe	Schon im bunten Knabenkleide	Hölty				
	version a			E	May 1816	1895	iv, 104; x
	version b, lost			E	c1816	—	—

D	Title	Incipit	Text	Key	Composed	Published	SW; NSA	
431	Blumenlied	Es ist ein halbes Himmelreich	Hölty	E	May 1816	1887	iv, 105; x	81
432	Der Leidende version a version b	Nimmer trag' ich länger		b b	May 1816	1850 1895	iv, 106; x iv, 107; x	
433	Seligkeit	Freuden sonder Zahl	Hölty	E	May 1816	1895	iv, 108; x	
434	Erntelied	Sicheln schallen, Ähren fallen	Hölty	E	May 1816	1850	iv, 109; x	
436	Klage version a version b [formerly 437]	Dein Silber schien	Hölty	F F	12 May 1816 1816	1850 —	iv, 95; x —; x	
437	Klage [see 436]							
442	Das grosse Halleluja version a [for version b see 'Female or unspecified voices']	Ehre sei dem Hocherhabnen	Klopstock	E	June 1816	c1847	iv, 110; x	
443	Schlachtlied (1) version a [for version b see 'Female or unspecified voices']	Mit unserm Arm ist nichts getan	Klopstock	E	June 1816	1895	iv, 112; x	
444	Die Gestirne	Es tönet sein Lob	Klopstock	F	June 1816	1831	iv, 114; x	
445	Edone	Dein süsses Bild, Edone	Klopstock	E♭	June 1816	1837	iv, 116; x	
446	Die Liebesgötter	Cypris, meiner Phyllis gleich	Uz	C	June 1816	1887	iv, 118; x	
447	An den Schlaf	Komm, und senke die umflorten Schwingen	Uz	A	June 1816	1895	iv, 120; x	
448	Gott im Frühlinge	In seinem schimmernden Gewand	Uz		June 1816	1887	iv, 121; x	
	version a version b			E E	June 1816 cJune 1816	— 1872	—; x iv, 124; x	
449	Der gute Hirt	Was sorgest du?	Uz	E	June 1816			62
450	Fragment aus dem Aeschylus	So wird der Mann, der sonder Zwang	Aeschylus, trans. Mayrhofer	E	June 1816			
	version a version b			A♭ A♭		1895 1832	iv, 128; x iv, 131; x	
454	Grablied auf einen Soldaten	Zieh hin, du braver Krieger du!	C. F. D. Schubart	c	July 1816	1872	iv, 140; x	
455	Freude der Kinderjahre	Freude, die im frühen Lenze	F. von Köpken	C	July 1816	1887	iv, 142; x	
456	Das Heimweh	Oft in einsam stillen Stunden	K. G. T. Winkler	F	July 1816	1887	iv, 144; x	
457	An die untergehende Sonne	Sonne, du sinkst	Kosegarten	E♭	July 1816– May 1817	1827, op.44	iv, 134; iii	

No.	Title	Incipit	Text	Key	Date	Pub.	Refs	
458	Aus Diego Manazares (Ilmerine)	Wo irrst du durch einsame Schatten	F. von Schlechta	Ab	30 July 1816	1872	iv, 146; x	
462	An Chloen	Bei der Liebe reinsten Flammen	Jacobi	Ab	Aug 1816	1895	iv, 149; x	
463	Hochzeit-Lied	Will singen euch im alten Ton	Jacobi	Eb	Aug 1816	1895	iv, 150; x	
464	In der Mitternacht	Tocesstille deckt das Tal	Jacobi	c	Aug 1816	1895	iv, 151; x	
465	Trauer der Liebe	Wo die Taub in stillen Buchen	Jacobi					
	version a			Ab	Aug 1816	1885	iv, 152; x	
	version b			Ab	c1816	—	—; x	
466	Die Perle	Es ging ein Mann zur Frühlingszeit	Jacobi	d	Aug 1816	1872	iv, 153; x	
467	Pflicht und Liebe	Du, der ewig um mich trauert	F. W. Gotter	c	Aug 1816	1885	x, 104; x	
468	An den Mond	Was schaust du so hell und klar	Hölty	A	7 Aug 1816	1895	iv, 148; x	
469	Mignon (1), 2 frags.	So lässt mich scheinen	Goethe	Ab	Sept 1816	1897	Rev, 86; iii	
473	Liedesend	Auf seinem goldnen Throne	Mayrhofer					
	version a			c	Sept 1816	1895	iv, 154; x	
	version b			c		1833	iv, 159; x	
474	Lied des Orpheus, als er in die Hölle ging	Wälze dich hinweg	Jacobi					
	version a, inc.			Gb	Sept 1816	1895	iv, 164; x	
	version b			Gb	1816	1832	iv, 170; x	
475	Abschied (nach einer Wallfahrtsarie)	Über die Berge zieht ihr fort	Mayrhofer	G	Sept 1816	1885	iv, 176; xi	
476	Rückweg	Zum Donaustrom, zur Kaiserstadt	Mayrhofer	d	Sept 1816	1872	iv, 178; xi	
477	Alte Liebe rostet nie		Mayrhofer	B	Sept 816	1895	iv, 180; xi	
478	Harfenspieler I (Gesänge des Harfners no.1) (2)	Wer sich der Einsamkeit ergibt	Goethe					16, 34, 89
	version a			a	Sept 1816	1895	iv, 181; i, 220	
	version b			a	1822	1822, op.12/1	iv, 189; i, 85	
479	Harfenspieler II (Gesänge des Harfners no.3)	An die Türen will ich schleichen	Goethe					16, 34
	version a			a	Sept 1816	1895	iv, 184; i, 224	
	version b			a	1822	1822, op.12/3	iv, 196; i, 93	
480	Harfenspieler III (Gesänge des Harfners no.2) (1, 2, 3)	Wer nie sein Brot mit Tränen ass	Goethe					16, 34
	version a			a	Sept 1816	1895	iv, 186; i, 291	
	version b			a	Sept 1816	1895	iv, 187; i, 226	
	version c			a	1822	1822,	iv, 192; i, 89	

D	Title	Incipit	Text	Key	Composed	Published	SW; NSA
481	Sehnsucht (3)	Nur wer die Sehnsucht kennt	Goethe	a	Sept 1816	op.12/2 1895	iv, 198; iii
482	Der Sänger am Felsen	Klage, meine Flöte	C. Pichler	e	Sept 1816	1895	iv, 200; xi
483	Lied	Ferne von der grossen Stadt	Pichler	E	Sept 1816	1895	iv, 212; xi
484	Gesang der Geister über den Wassern (1), frag.	.. dann zur Tiefe nieder	Goethe	G	Sept 1816	1895	x, 594; xi
489	Der Wanderer	Ich komme von Gebirge her	G. P. Schmidt von Lübeck				16, 30, 87, 99
	version a			c♯	Oct 1816	1895	iv, 214; i, 200
	version b [formerly 493b]			b	c1816	1970	—; i, 204
	version c [formerly 493a]			c♯	c1816	1821, op.4/1	iv, 217; i, 26
490	Der Hirt	Du Turm! zu meinem Leide	Mayrhofer	F	Oct 1816	1895	iv, 220; xi
491	Geheimnis	Sag an, wer lehrt dich Lieder	Mayrhofer	B♭	Oct 1816	1887	iv, 223; xi
492	Zum Punsche	Woget brausend, Harmonien	Mayrhofer	d	Oct 1816	1849	iv, 226; xi
493	Der Wanderer [see 489b–c]						
495	Abendlied der Fürstin	Der Abend rötet nun das Tal	Mayrhofer	F	Nov 1816	1868	iv, 227; xi
496	Bei dem Grabe meines Vaters	Friede sei um diesen Grabstein	M. Claudius	E♭	Nov 1816	1885	iv, 234; xi
496a	Klage um Ali Bey	Lasst mich! lasst mich! ich will klagen	Claudius	e♭	Nov 1816	1968	—; vii, 84
497	An die Nachtigall	Er liegt und schläft	Claudius	G	Nov 1816	1829, op.98/1	iv, 238; v
498	Wiegenlied	Schlafe, schlafe, holder süsser Knabe		A♭	Nov 1816	1829, op.98/2	iv, 239; v
499	Abendlied	Der Mond ist aufgegangen	Claudius	B♭	Nov 1816	1885	iv, 240; xi
500	Phidile	Ich war erst sechzehn Sommer alt	Claudius	G♭	Nov 1816	1895	iv, 242; xi
501	Zufriedenheit (2)	Ich bin vergnügt	Claudius				
	version a			E	Nov 1816	1895	iv, 246; xi
	version b			G		—	—; xi
502	Herbstlied	Bunt sind schon die Wälder	Salis-Seewis	G	Nov 1816	1872	iv, 248; xi
503	Mailied (3)	Grüner wird die Au	Hölty	G	Nov 1816	—	—; xi
504	Am Grabe Anselmos	Dass ich dich verloren habe	Claudius				
	version a			e♭	4 Nov 1816	1821, op.6/3	iv, 236; i, 56
	version b			e♭	c1816	1970	—; i, 216
507	Skolie	Mädchen entsiegelten	Matthisson	G	Dec 1816	1895	iv, 249; xi
508	Lebenslied	Kommen und Scheiden	Matthisson	C	Dec 1816	1845	iv, 250; xi

		First line	Poet	Composed	Key	Published	Reference
509	Leiden der Trennung	Vom Meere trennt sich die Welle	Metastasio, trans. H. von Collin	Dec 1816			
	version a, frag.				g	—	—; xi
	version b				g	1872	iv, 251; xi
510	Vedi quanto adoro		Metastasio	Dec 1816	E♭	1895	x, 40; xi
513a	Nur wer die Liebe kennt, sketch		Werner	?1817	A♭	1974	—; xi
514	Die abgeblühte Linde	Wirst du halten, was du schwurst	L. von Széchényi	?1817	a	1821, op.7/1	v, 29; i, 59
515	Der Flug der Zeit	Es floh die Zeit im Wirbelfluge	Széchényi	?1817	A	1821, op.7/2	v, 33; i, 63
516	Sehnsucht	Der Lerche wolkennahe Lieder	Mayrhofer	?1816	C	1822, op.8/2	vi, 386; i, 73
517	Der Schäfer und der Reiter	Ein Schäfer sass im Grünen	Fouqué	April 1817			
	version a				E	1972	—; i, 191
	version b				E	1822, op.13/1	v, 6; i, 95
518	An den Tod	Tod, du Schrecken der Natur	Schubart	1816 or 1817	B	1824	v, 130; v
519	Die Blumensprache	Es deuten die Blumen	? E. Platner	?1817	B♭	1867, op.173/5	v, 25; xi
520	Frohsinn	Ich bin von lockerem Schlage	Castelli	Jan 1817			
	version a			Jan 1817	F	1895	v, 2; xi
	version b			c1817	F	1850	—; xi
521	Jagdlied	Trarah! Trarah! wir kehren daheim	Werner	Jan 1817	F	1855	v, 3; xi
	version a [for version b see 'Female and unspecified voices']						
522	Die Liebe	Wo weht der Liebe hoher Geist?	G. Leon	Jan 1817	G	1895	v, 4; xi
523	Trost	Nimmer lange weil' ich hier		Jan 1817	c♯	1885	v, 5; xi
524	Der Alpenjäger	Auf hohen Bergesrücken	Mayrhofer	Jan 1817			
	version a				E	1895	v, 12; i, 233
	version b				D	1970	—; i, 236
	version c				F	1822, op.13/3	v, 16; i, 104
525	Wie Ulfru fischt	Der Angel zuckt	Mayrhofer	Jan 1817			
	version a				d	1970	—; i, 269
	version b				d	1823, op.21/3	v, 18; i, 158
526	Fahrt zum Hades	Der Nachen dröhnt	Mayrhofer	Jan 1817	d	1832	v, 20; xi

D	Title	Incipit	Text	Key	Composed	Published	SW; NSA	
527	Schlaflied (Abendlied; Schlummerlied)	Es mahnt der Wald	Mayrhofer		Jan 1817			
	version a			F		1975	—; ii, 193	
	version b			F		1823,	v, 24; ii, 20	
528	La pastorella al prato (2)	Du kleine grünumwachs'ne Quelle	C. Goldoni	G	Jan 1817	1872	x, 46; xi	
530	An eine Quelle	Vorüber, ach vorüber	Claudius	A	Feb 1817	1829, op.109/3	iv, 232; xi	19, 30, 41
531	Der Tod und das Mädchen	Vorüber, ach vorüber	Claudius	d	Feb 1817	1821, op.7/3	v, 35; i, 66	
532	Das Lied vom Reifen, frag.	Seht meine lieben Bäume an	Claudius	A♭	Feb 1817	1895	v, 36; xi	
533	Täglich zu singen	Ich danke Gott und freue mich	Claudius	F	Feb 1817	1895	v, 38; xi	
534	Die Nacht	Die Nacht ist dumpfig und finster	Ossian, trans. Harold	g	Feb 1817	1830	v, 39; xi	
535	Lied, with small orch	Brüder, schrecklich brennt die Träne		g	Feb 1817	1895	x, 78; iii/1	
536	Der Schiffer	Im Winde, im Sturme	Mayrhofer		?March 1817			
	version a			E♭		1970	—; i, 263	
	version b			E♭		1823, op.21/2	v, 24; i, 152	
539	Am Strome	Ist mir's doch, als sei mein Leben	Mayrhofer	B	March 1817	1822, op.8/4	v, 54; i, 82	
540	Philoktet	Da sitz' ich ohne Bogen	Mayrhofer	b	March 1817	1831	v, 56; xi	
541	Memnon	Den Tag hindurch nur einmal	Mayrhofer	D♭	March 1817	1821, op.6/1	v, 59; i, 46	19
542	Antigone und Oedip	Ihr hohen Himmlischen	Mayrhofer	C	March 1817	1821, op.6/2	v, 62; i, 50	
543	Auf dem See	Und frische Nahrung	Goethe		March 1817			
	version a			E		1895	v, 66; v	
	version b			E♭		1828, op.92/2	v, 70; v	
544	Ganymed	Wie im Morgenglanze	Goethe	A♭	March 1817	1825, op.19/3	v, 75; i, 132	17, 47, 90
545	Der Jüngling und der Tod	Die Sonne sinkt, o könnt ich	J. von Spaun		March 1817			
	version a			c♯		1895	v, 80; xi	
	version b			c♯		1872	v, 82; xi	
546	Trost im Liede	Braust des Unglücks Sturm empor	Schober	d	March 1817	1827; 1828 as op.101/3	v, 84; v	

D	Title		First line	Poet	Key	Composed	Published	Reference	
547	An die Musik		Du holde Kunst	Schober					19, 88
		version a			D	March 1817	1895	v, 86; iv	
		version b			D	c1817	1827 cp.88/4	v, 87; iv	
548	Orest auf Tauris		Ist dies Tauris	Mayrhofer	Eb	March 1817	1831	vi, 118; xi	
549	Mahomets Gesang (1), frag		Seht den Felsenquell	Goethe	c#	March 1817	1895	x, 110; xiii	19
550	Die Forelle		In einem Bächlein helle	Schubart					
		version a			Db	c1817	1855	v, 132; ii, 194	
		version b			Db	c1817	1855	v, 135; ii, 202	
		version c			Db	Feb 1818	1895	v, 138; ii, 198	
		version d			Db	c1820	1820, 1827 as op.32	v, 141; ii, 109	
		version e			Db	Oct 1821	1975	—; ii, 206	
551	Pax vobiscum		Der Friede sei mit euch!	Schober	F	April 1817	1831	v, 88; xi	70
552	Hänflings Liebeswerbung		Ahidi! ich liebe	F. Kind					
		version a			A	April 1817	1970	—; i, 260	
		version b			A	c1817	1823, op.20/3	v, 90; i, 145	
553	Auf der Donau		Auf der Wellen Spiegel	Mayrhofer	Eb	April 1817	1823, op.21/1	v, 92; i, 148	
554	Uraniens Flucht		Lasst uns, ihr Himmlischen	Mayrhofer	D	April 1817	1895	v, 99; xi	
555	Song sketch (no text)		—	—	a	?May 1817	1934	—; xi	
558	Liebhaber in allen Gestalten		Ich wollt', ich wär' ein Fisch	Goethe	A	May 1817	1887	iii, 46; xi	
559	Schweizerlied		Uf'm Bergli bin i g'sässe	Goethe	F	May 1817	1885	iii, 48; xi	
560	Der Goldschmiedsgesell		Es ist doch meine Nachbarin	Goethe	F	May 1817	1850	iii, 49; xi	
561	Nach einem Gewitter		Auf den Blumen	Mayrhofer	F	May 1817	1872	v, 116; xi	
562	Fischerlied (3)		Das Fischergewerbe gibt rüstigen Mut!	Salis-Seewis	F	May 1817	1895	v, 118; xi	
563	Die Einsiedelei (3)		Es rieselt, klar und wehend	Salis-Seewis	C	May 1817	1887	v, 120; xi	
564	Gretchen im Zwinger (Gretchen; Gretchens Bitte), frag.		Ach neige; du Schmerzensreiche	Goethe	bb	May 1817	1838	x, 116; xi	
565	Der Strom		Mein Leben wälzt sich murrend fort		d	?June 1817	1876	v, 123; xi	
569	Das Grab (4), for unison chorus		Das G'rab ist tief und stille	Salis-Seewis	c#	June 1817	1895	v, 122; iii/3	
573	Iphigenia		Blüht denn hier an Tauris Strande	Mayrhofer	Gb	July 1817	1829, op.98/3	v, 127; v	
577	Entzückung an Laura (2)		Laura, Laura, über diese Welt	Schiller					
		frag. a			A	Aug 1817	1873	x, 119; x	
		frag. b		Amoretten seh ich		Db		1895	x, 120; x	

D	Title	Incipit	Text	Key	Composed	Published	SW; NSA	
578	Abschied	Lebe wohl! lebe wohl!	Schubert	b	24 Aug 1817	1838	x, 80; xi	
579	Der Knabe in der Wiege (Wiegenlied)	Er schläft so süss	A. Ottenwalt					
	version a			C	autumn 1817	1872	v, 180; xi	
	version b, frag.			A♭	Nov 1817	1897	Rev, 70; xi	
579a	Vollendung [formerly 989]	Wenn ich einst das Ziel errungen habe	Matthisson	A	?Sept–Oct 1817	1970	—; xi	
579b	Die Erde [formerly 989a]	Wenn sanft entzückt	Matthisson	E	?Sept–Oct 1817	1970	—; xi	
582	Augenblicke im Elysium [see 990b]							
583	Gruppe aus dem Tartarus (2)	Horch, wie Murmeln des empörten Meeres	Schiller	C	Sept 1817	1823, op.24/1	v, 144; ii, 13	19, 26, 92
584	Elysium	Vorüber die stöhnende Klage!	Schiller	E	Sept 1817	1830	v, 149; xi	
585	Atys	Der Knabe seufzt	Mayrhofer	a	Sept 1817	1833	v, 159; xi	
586	Erlafsee	Mir ist so wohl, so weh'	Mayrhofer	F	Sept 1817	1818; 1822 as op.8/3	v, 164; i, 78	19
587	An den Frühling (3) version a	Willkommen schöner Jungling!	Schiller	A	Oct 1817	1885	iii, 8; xi	
	version b [formerly 245]			B♭	c1817	1895	iii, 6; xi	
588	Der Alpenjäger	Willst du nicht das Lämmlein huten	Schiller					
	version a, frag.			E♭	Oct 1817	1897	Rev, 66; ii, 236	
	version b			C	c1817	1825, op.37/2	v, 168; ii, 138	
594	Der Kampf	Nein, länger werd' ich diesen Kampf	Schiller	d	Nov 1817	1829, op.110	v, 171; xi	
595	Thekla: eine Geisterstimme (2)	Wo ich sei, und wo mich hingewendet	Schiller					
	version a			c♯	Nov 1817	1895	v, 177; iv	
	version b			c	c1817	1827, op.88/2	v, 178; iv	
596	Lied eines Kindes, frag.	Lauter Freude fühl' ich		B♭	Nov 1817	1895	x, 122; xi	
611	Auf der Riesenkoppe	Hoch auf dem Gipfel deiner Gebirge	Körner	d	March 1818	c1850	v, 184; xii	
614	An den Mond in einer Herbstnacht	Freundlich ist dein Antlitz	A. Schreiber	A	April 1818	1832	v, 188; xii	
616	Grablied für die Mutter	Hauche milder, Abendluft	—	b	June 1818	1838	v, 194; xii	
619	Vocal exercise, 2vv, figured bass (no text)		—	C	July 1818	1892	ser. xix, 95; viii/2	

			Poet	Key	Composed	Published	Reference
620	Einsamkeit	Gib mir die Fülle der Einsamkeit!	Mayrhofer	B♭	July 1818	1840	v, 196; xii
622	Der Blumenbrief	Euch Blümlein will ich senden	Schreiber	D	Aug 1818	1833	v, 213; xii
623	Das Marienbild	Sei gegrüsst, du Frau der Huld	Schreiber	C	Aug 1818	1831	v, 214; xii
626	Blondel zu Marien	In düstrer Nacht	Schreiber	c?	Sept 1818	1842	v, 218; xii
627	Das Abendrot	Du heilig, glühend Abendrot!	Schreiber	E	Nov 1818	1867, op.173/6	v, 220; xii
628	Sonett I	Apollo, lebet noch	Petrarch, trans. A. W. von Schlegel	B♭	Nov 1818	1895	v, 225; xii
629	Sonett II	Allein, nachdenklich, wie gelähmt	Petrarch, trans. A. W. von Schlegel	g	Nov 1818	1895	v, 228; xii
630	Sonett III	Nunmehr, da Himmel, Erde	Petrarch, trans. J. D. Gries	C	Dec 1818	1895	v, 234; xii
631	Blanka (Das Mädchen)	Wenn mich einsam Lüfte fächeln	F. von Schlegel	a	Dec 1818	1885	v, 236; xii
632	Vom Mitleiden Mariä	Als bei dem Kreuz Maria stand	F. von Schlegel	g	Dec 1818	1831	v, 238; xii
633	Der Schmetterling	Wie soll ich nicht tanzen	F. von Schlegel	F	c1819	1826, op.57/1	iii, 225; iii
634	Die Berge	Sieht uns der Blick gehoben	F. von Schlegel	G	c1819	1826, op.57/2	ii, 227; iii
636	Sehnsucht (2)	Ach, aus dieses Tales Gründen	Schiller		c1821		
	version a			b		1975	—; ii, 250
	version b			b		1895	vi, 23; ii, 258
	version c			b		1826, op. 39	vi, 29; ii, 165
637	Hoffnung (2)	Es reden und träumen die Menschen	Schiller	B♭	c1819	1827, op.87/2	vi, 36; iv
638	Der Jüngling am Bache (3)	An der Quelle sass der Knabe	Schiller				
	version a			d	April 1819	1895	vi, 40; iv
	version b			c	c1819	1827, op.87/3	vi, 36; iv
639	Widerschein	Fischer harrt am Brückenbogen	Schlechta	D	c1819	1820	—; v
	version a						
	version b [formerly 949]	Tom lehnt harrend auf der Brücke		B♭		1832	ix, 130; v
645	Abend. frag.	Wie ist es denn	L. Tieck	g	?Jan 1819	—	—; xii
646	Die Gebüsche	Es wehet kühl und leise	F. von Schlegel	G	Jan 1819	1885	vi, 1; xii

D	Title	Incipit	Text	Key	Composed	Published	SW; NSA	
649	Der Wanderer	Wie deutlich des Mondes Licht	F. von Schlegel	D	Feb 1819	1826, op.65/2	vi, 5; iii	
650	Abendbilder	Still beginnt's im Hain zu tauen	J. P. Silbert	a	Feb 1819	1831	vi, 7; xii	
651	Himmelsfunken	Der Odem Gottes weht	Silbert	G	Feb 1819	1831	vi, 14; xii	
652	Das Mädchen	Wie so innig, möcht ich sagen	F. von Schlegel					
	version a			A	Feb 1819	1842	vi, 16; xii	
	version b			A	cFeb 1819	—	—; xii	
653	Bertas Lied in der Nacht	Nacht umhüllt mit wehendem Flügel	Grillparzer	e♭	Feb 1819	c1842	vi, 18; xii	
654	An die Freunde	Im Wald, im Wald da grabt mich ein	Mayrhofer	a	March 1819	c1842	vi, 20; xii	
658	Marie	Ich sehe dich in tausend Bildern	Novalis	D	?May 1819	1895	vi, 53; xii	
659	Hymne I	Wenige wissen das Geheimnis	Novalis	a	May 1819	1872	vi, 42; xii	
660	Hymne II	Wenn ich ihn nur habe	Novalis	b♭	May 1819	1872	vi, 49; xii	
661	Hymne III	Wenn alle untreu werden	Novalis	b♭	May 1819	1872	vi, 50; xii	
662	Hymne IV	Ich sag' es jedem	Novalis	A	May 1819	1872	vi, 52; xii	
663	Der 13. Psalm, frag.	Ach, Herr, wie lange	trans. M. Mendelssohn	D♭	June 1819	1927	—; xii	
669	Beim Winde	Es träumen die Wolken	Mayrhofer	g	Oct 1819	1829	vi, 54; xii	
670	Die Sternennächte	In mondenhellten Nächten	Mayrhofer	D♭	Oct 1819	1862	vi, 56; xii	
671	Trost	Hörnerklagen rufen klagend	Mayrhofer	E♭	Oct 1819	1849 op.165/2	vi, 60; xii	
672	Nachtstück		Mayrhofer					24
	version a	Wenn über Bergen der Nebel sich breitet		c♯	Oct 1819	1975	—; ii, 225	
	version b	Wenn über Berge sich der Nebel breitet		c	c1819	1825, op.36/2	vi, 62; ii, 125	
673	Die Liebende schreibt	Ein Blick von deinen Augen	Goethe	B♭	Oct 1819	1832; 1862 as op.165/1	vi, 68; xii	
674	Prometheus	Bedecke deinen Himmel, Zeus	Goethe	g	Oct 1819	1850	vi, 70; xii	24, 34
677	Strophe aus Die Götter Griechenlands	Schöne Welt, wo bist du?	Schiller		Nov 1819			24
	version a			a/A		1895	vi, 76; xii	
	version b			a/A		1848	vi, 78; xii	
682	Über allen Zauber Liebe, frag.	Sie hüpfte mit mir auf grünem Plan	Mayrhofer	G	c1820	1895	x, 123; xii	
684	Die Sterne	Du staunest, o Mensch	F. von Schlegel	E♭	1820	1850	vi, 102; xii	
685	Morgenlied	Eh' die Sonne früh aufersteht	Werner	a	1820	1821, op.4/2	vi, 104; i, 30	

D	Title / version	First line	Author	Key	Composed	Published	Ref	
686	Frühlingsglaube	Die linden Lüfte sind erwacht	Uhland					
	version a			Bb	Sept 1820	1970	—; i, 252	
	version b			Bb	1820	1970	—; i, 256	
	version c			Ab	Nov 1822	1823, op.20/2	vi, 108; i, 141	
687	Nachthymne	Hinüber wall' ich	Novalis	D	Jan 1820	1872	vi, 372; xii	
688	Vier Canzonen				Jan 1820	1871		
		1 Non t'accostar all'urna	J. A. Vitorelli	C			x, 48; xii	
		2 Guarda, che bianca lur a	Vitorelli	G			x, 50; xii	
		3 Da quel sembiante appresi	Metastasio	Bb			x, 52; xii	
		4 Mio ben ricordati	Metastasio	bb			x, 53; xii	
690	Abendröte	Tiefer sinket schon die Senne	F. von Schlegel	A	March 1823	1830	vi, 94; xii	
691	Die Vögel	Wie lieblich und fröhlich	F. von Schlegel	A	March 1820	1865, op.172/6	vi, 86; xii	
692	Der Knabe	Wenn ich nur ein Vöglein wäre	F. von Schlegel	A	March 1820	1872	vi, 88; xii	
693	Der Fluss	Wie rein Gesang sich windet	F. von Schlegel	B	March 1820	1872	vi, 91; xii	
694	Der Schiffer	Friedlich lieg' ich hingegessen	F. von Schlegel	D	March 1820	1842	vi, 98; xii	
695	Namenstagslied	Vater, schenk' mir diese Stunde	A. Stadler	A	March 1820	1895	x, 81; xii	
698	Des Fräuleins Liebeslauschen (Liebeslauschen)	Da unten steht ein Ritter	Schlechta	A	Sept 1820	1832	vi, 113; xii	
699	Der entsühnte Orest	Zu meinen Füssen bricht du dich	Mayrhofer	C	Sept 1820	1831	vi, 121; xii	
700	Freiwilliges Versinken	Wohin? O Helios!	Mayrhofer	d	Sept 1820	1831	vi, 124; xii	
702	Der Jüngling auf dem Hügel	Ein Jüngling auf dem Hügel	H. Hüttenbrenner	G	Nov 1820	1822, op.8/1	vi, 126; i, 68	26
707	Der zürnenden Diana	Ja, spanne nur den Bogen	Mayrhofer		Dec 1820			46
	version a			A		1895	vi, 133; ii, 210	
	version b			Ab		1825, op.36/1	vi, 141; ii, 113	
708	Im Walde (Waldesnacht)	Windes Rauschen, Gottes Flügel	F. von Schlegel	c#	Dec 1320	1832	vi, 149; xii	26
711	Lob der Tränen	Laue Lüfte, Blumendüfte	A. W. von Schlegel		1818			
	version a			D		1970	—; i, 229	
	version b			D		1822, op.13/2	v, 10; i, 100	
712	Die gefangenen Sänger	Hörst du von den Nachtigallen	A. W. von Schlegel	G	Jan 1821	1842	vi, 164; xiii	
713	Der Unglückliche	Die Nacht bricht an	Pichler		Jan 1821			
	version a			b		1895	vi, 168; iv	
	version b			b		1827, op.37/1	vi, 173; iv	

D	Title	Incipit	Text	Key	Composed	Published	SW; NSA	
715	Versunken	Voll Locken kraus ein Haupt	Goethe	A♭	Feb 1821	1845	vi, 178; xiii	100
716	Grenzen der Menschheit	Wenn der uralte heilige Vater	Goethe	E	March 1821	1832	vi, 185; xiii	29, 55, 92
717	Suleika II	Ach um deine feuchten Schwingen	? M. von Willemer	B♭	?March 1821	1825, op.31	vi, 201; ii, 97	46
719	Geheimes	Über meines Liebchens Äugeln	Goethe	A♭	March 1821	1822, op.14/2	vi, 183; i, 118	29, 34
720	Suleika I version a	Was bedeutet die Bewegung?	?Willemer	b	March 1821	1970	—; i, 239	
	version b			b	c1821	1822, op.14/1	vi, 194; i, 108	
721	Mahomets Gesang (2), frag.	Seht den Felsenquell	Goethe	c♯	March 1821	1895	x, 125; xiii	
725	Linde Lüfte wehen, Mez, T, frag.			b	April 1821	1929	—; iii/2	
726	Mignon I (1)	Heiss mich nicht reden	Goethe	b	April 1821	1870	vi, 189; iii	
727	Mignon II (2)	So lasst mich scheinen	Goethe	b	April 1821	1850	vi, 191; iii	
728	Johanna Sebus, frag.	Der Damm zerreisst	Goethe	d	April 1821	1895	x, 128; xiii	
731	Der Blumen Schmerz	Wie tönt es mir so schaurig	J. Mayláth	e	Sept 1821	1821; 1867 as op.173/4	vi, 210; v	
736	Ihr Grab	Dort ist ihr Grab	K. A. Engelhardt	E♭	?1822	1842	vii, 4; xiii	
737	An die Leier	Ich will von Atreus Söhnen	F. S. Ritter von Bruchmann, after Anacreon	E♭	? 1822 or 1823	1826, op.56/2	vii, 42; iii	
738	Im Haine	Sonnenstrahlen durch die Tannen	Bruchmann	A	? 1822 or 1823	1826, op.56/3	vii, 46; iii	
741	Sei mir gegrüsst	O du Entrissne mir	F. Rückert	B♭	between end 1821 and autumn 1822	1823, op.20/1	vi, 214; i, 137	32, 37, 60
742	Der Wachtelschlag	Ach! mir schallt's dorten	S. F. Sauter	A	1822	1822; 1827 as op.68	vii, 2; iii	
743	Selige Welt	Ich treibe auf des Lebens Meer	J. C. Senn	A♭	?autumn 1822	1823, op.23/2	vii, 14; ii, 6	
744	Schwanengesang	Wie klag ich's aus	Senn	A♭	?autumn 1822	1823, op.23/3	vii, 16; ii, 8	
745	Die Rose version a	Es lockte schöne Wärme	F. von Schlegel	G	1822	1822; 1827 as op.73	vii, 18; iii	
	version b					1895	vii, 21; iii	
746	Am See	In des Sees Wogenspiele	Bruchmann	E♭	? 1822 or 1823	1831	vii, 74; xiii	

D	Title / first line	Poet	Key	Composed	Published	Refs	
749	Herrn Josef Spaun, Assessor in Linz (Sendschreiben an den Assessor Spaun in Linz) — Und nimmer schreibst du?	M. von Collin	c	Jan 1822	1850	x, 84; xiii	
751	Die Liebe hat gelogen	A. von Platen-Hallermünde	c	by 7 April 1822	1823, op.23/1	vii, 28; ii, 4	34
752	Nachtviolen	Mayrhofer	C	April 1822	1872	vii, 6; xiii	
753	Heliopolis I	Mayrhofer	e	April 1822	1826, op.65/3	vii, 10; iii	
754	Heliopolis II — Fels auf Felsen hingewälzet	Mayrhofer	c	April 1822	1842	vii, 14; xiii	
756	Du liebst mich nicht — Mein Herz ist zerrissen	Platen-Hallermünde		July 1822			
	version a		g#		1895	vii, 24; iii	
	version b		a		1826, op.59/1	vii, 26; iii	
758	Todesmusik — In des Todes Feierstunde	Schober	Gb	Sept 1822	1829, op.108/2	vii, 30; v	
761	Schatzgräbers Begehr — In tiefster Erde ruht ein alt Gesetz	Schober		Nov 1822			
	version a		d		1823, op.23/4	vii, 35; ii, 10	
	version b		d		1895	vii, 187; ii, 189	
762	Schwestergruss — Im Mondenschein wall' ich auf und ab	Bruchmann	f#	Nov 1822	1833	vii, 38; xiii	
764	Der Musensohn — Durch Feld und Wald zu schweifen	Goethe		Dec 1822			34
	version a		Ab		1895	vii, 48; v	
	version b		G	c1822	1828, op.92/1	vii, 51; v	
765	An die Entfernte — So hab' ich wirklich dich verloren?	Goethe	G	Dec 1822	1868	vii, 54; xiii	92
766	Am Flusse (2) — Verfliesset, vielgeliebte Lieder	Goethe	D	Dec 1822	1872	vii, 56; xiii	34
767	Willkommen und Abschied — Es schlug mein Herz	Goethe		Dec 1822			
	version a		D		1895	vii, 58; iii	
	version b		C	c1822	1826	vii, 64; iii	
768	Wandrers Nachtlied — Über allen Gipfeln ist Ruh	Goethe	Bb	by July 1824	1827; 1828 as op.96/1	vii, 70; v	
770	Drang in die Ferne — Vater, du glaubst es nicht	K. G. von Leitner	a/A	early 1823	1823; 1827 as op.71	vii, 91; iii	

D	Title	Incipit	Text	Key	Composed	Published	SW; NSA	
771	Der Zwerg	Im trüben Licht verschwinden schon die Berge	M. von Collin	a	? 1822 or 1823	1823, op.22/1	vii, 95; i, 160	86
772	Wehmut	Wenn ich durch Wald und Fluren geh'	M. von Collin	d	? 1822 or 1823	1823, op.22/2	vii, 102; i, 168	
774	Auf dem Wasser zu singen	Mitten im Schimmer der spiegelnden Wellen	Stolberg-Stolberg	Ab	1823	1823; 1827 as op.72	vii, 106; iii	
775	Dass sie hier gewesen	Dass der Ostwind Düfte	Rückert	C	?1823	1826, op.59/2	viii, 2; iii	39, 92
776	Du bist die Ruh		Rückert	Eb	1823	1826, op.59/3	viii, 4; iii	39, 91, 97
777	Lachen und Weinen		Rückert	Ab	?1823	1826, op.59/4	viii, 7; iii	87
778	Greisengesang version a version b	Der Frost hat mir bereifet	Rückert	b b	by June 1823	— 1826, op.60/1	—; iii viii, 10; iii	
778a	Die Wallfahrt	Meine Tränen im Bussgewand	Rückert	f	?1823	1969	—; xiii	
785	Der zürnende Barde	Wer wagt's, wer wagt's	Bruchmann	g	Feb 1823	1831	vii, 71; xiii	
786	Viola	Schneeglöcklein, o Schneeglöcklein	Schober	Ab	March 1823	1830, op.123	vii, 76; xiii	93
788	Lied (Die Mutter Erde)	Des Lebens Tag ist schwer	Stolberg-Stolberg	a/A	April 1823	1838	vii, 104; xiii	
789	Pilgerweise	Ich bin ein Waller auf der Erde	Schober	f#	April 1823	1832	vii, 108; xiii	
792	Vergissmeinnicht	Als der Frühling sich vom Herzen	Schober	Ab	May 1823	1833	vii, 114; xiii	
793	Das Geheimnis (2)	Sie konnte mir kein Wörtchen sagen	Schiller	G	May 1823	1867, op.173/2	vii, 125; xiii	
794	Der Pilgrim version a version b	Noch in meines Lebens Lenze	Schiller	E D	May 1823 c1823	1895 1825, op.37/1	vii, 130; ii, 229 —; ii, 132	
795	Die schöne Müllerin		W. Müller		Oct–Nov 1823	1824, op.25		38, 39, 41, 54, 55, 93ff
1	Das Wandern	Das Wandern ist des Müllers Lust		Bb			vii, 134; ii, 21	88
2	Wohin?	Ich hört' ein Bächlein rauschen		G			vii, 136; ii, 23	86
3	Halt!	Eine Mühle seh' ich blinken		C			vii, 140; ii, 29	
4	Danksagung an den Bach	War es also gemeint		G			vii, 143; ii, 34	
5	Am Feierabend	Hätt' ich tausend Arme zu rühren		a			vii, 147; ii, 36	94
6	Der Neugierige	Ich frage keine Blume		B			vii, 149; ii, 42	94
7	Ungeduld	Ich schnitt es gern in alle Rinden ein		A			vii, 152; ii, 46	89
8	Morgengruss	Guten Morgen, schöne Müllerin		C			vii, 154; ii, 50	

No.	Title	Incipit	Key	Author	Composed	Published	References	
9	Des Müllers Blumen	Am Bach viel kleine Blumen stehn	A				vii, 155; ii, 52	
10	Tränenregen	Wir sassen so traulich beisammen	A				vii, 156; ii, 54	
11	Mein!	Bächlein, lass dein Rauschen sein	D				vii, 158; ii, 57	
12	Pause	Meine Laute hab' ich gehängt	B♭				vii, 162; ii, 63	94
13	Mit dem grünen Lautenbande	Schad' um das schöne grüne Band	B♭				vii, 165; ii, 68	94
14	Der Jäger	Was sucht denn der Jäger	c				vii, 166; ii, 70	
15	Eifersucht und Stolz	Wohin so schnell	g				vii, 168; ii, 72	94
16	Die liebe Farbe	Ir Grün will ich mich kleiden	b				vii, 172; ii, 76	
17	Die böse Farbe	Ich möchte ziehn in die Welt hinaus	B				vii, 174; ii, 78	
18	Trockne Blumen	Ihr Blümlein alle, die sie mir gab	e				vii, 178; ii, 83	
19	Der Müller und der Bach	Wo ein treues Herze in Liebe vergeht	g				vii, 181; ii, 87	94
20	Des Baches Wiegenlied	Gute Ruh', gute Ruh'	E				vii, 184; ii, 90	
797	Romanze zum Drama Rosamunde (3b)	Der Vollmond strahlt auf Bergeshöhn	H. von Chézy	f			—; ii, 94	
799	Im Abendrot	O, wie schön ist deine Welt	K. Lappe	A♭	autumn 1823	1824, op.26	viii, 30; xiii	88, 97
800	Der Einsame	Wann meine Grillen schwirren	Lappe		1824 or Feb 1825	1832		88
	version a		G		early 1825	1825	viii, 36; —	
	version b		G		c1825	1827, op.41	viii, 41; ii, 172	
801	Dithyrambe	Nimmer, das glaub mir	Schiller	A	by June 1826	1826, op.60/2	viii, 14; iii	
805	Der Sieg	O unbewölktes Leben!	Mayrhofer	F	March 1824	1833	viii, 16; iii	
806	Abendstern	Was weilst du einsam an dem Himmel	Mayrhofer	a	March 1824	1833	viii, 18; xiii	
807	Auflösung	Verbirg dich, Sonne	Mayrhofer	G	March 1824	1842	viii, 20; xiii	
808	Gondelfahrer (1)	Es tanzen Mond und Sterne	Mayrhofer	C	March 1824	1872	viii, 26; xiii	
822	Lied eines Kriegers, with unison chorus	Des stolzen Männerlebens schönste Zeichen		A	31 Dec 1824	1842	viii, 32; iii/3	87, 90
827	Nacht und Träume	Heil'ge Nacht, du sinkest nieder	M. von Collin		by June 1823			88, 89
	version a		B			1975	—; ii, 267	
	version b		B			1825, op.43/2	viii, 32; ii, 184	
828	Die junge Nonne	Wie braust durch die Wipfel	J. N. Craigher de Jachelutta	f	early 1825	1825, op.43/1	viii, 62; ii, 178	46, 47, 55, 87
829	Abschied, melodrama	Leb wohl, du schöne Erde	A. von Pratobevera	F	Feb 1826	1873	x, 136; xiii	
830	Lied der Anne Lyle	Wärst du bei mir im Lebenstal	A. MacDonald, trans. ? S. May	c	?early 1825	1828, op.85/1	ix, 78; iv	64

D	Title	Incipit	Text	Key	Composed	Published	SW; NSA	
831	Gesang der Norna	Mich führt mein Weg	Scott, trans. S. H. Spiker	f	early 1825	1828, op.85/2	ix, 82; iv	64
832	Des Sängers Habe	Schlagt mein ganzes Glück	Schlechta	Bb	Feb 1825	1830	viii, 46; xiii	
833	Der blinde Knabe	O sagt, ihr Lieben, mir einmal	C. Cibber, trans. Craigher					
	version a			Bb	April 1825	1895	viii, 54; v	
	version b			Bb	April 1825	1827, 1828 as op.101/2	viii, 58; v	
834	Im Walde	Ich wandre über Berg und Tal	E. Schulze	g	March 1825	1835, op.93/1	—; v	61
	version a							
	version b			bb	c1825	1828, op.90/1	viii, 96; v	
837	Ellens Gesang I	Raste, Krieger, Krieg ist aus	Scott, trans. D. A. Storck	Db	April–July 1825	1826, op.52/1	viii, 70; iii	
838	Ellens Gesang II	Jäger, ruhe von der Jagd!	Scott, trans. Storck	Eb	April–July 1825	1826, op.52/2	viii, 78; iii	
839	Ellens Gesang III (Hymne an die Jungfrau)	Ave Maria! Jungfrau mild!	Scott, trans. Storck	Bb	April 1825	1826, op.52/6	viii, 90; iii	48
842	Totengräbers Heimwehe	O Menschheit, o Leben	Craigher	f	April 1825	1833	viii, 50; xiii	
843	Lied des gefangenen Jägers	Mein Ross so müd in dem Stalle	Scott, trans. Storck	d	April 1825	1826, op.52/7	viii, 92; iii	
846	Normans Gesang	Die Nacht bricht bald herein	Scott, trans. Storck	c	April 1825	1826, op.52/5	viii, 82; iii	
851	Das Heimweh	Ach, der Gebirgssohn	J. L. Pyrker von Felsö-Eör					49
	version a			a	Aug 1825	1895	viii, 112; iii	
	version b			a		1827, op.79/1	viii, 120; iii	
852	Die Allmacht (1)	Gross ist Jehovah, der Herr	Pyrker		Aug 1825			49, 55, 62
	version a			A		—	—; iii	
	version b			C		1827, op.79/2	viii, 120; iii	
853	Auf der Bruck	Frisch trabe sonder Ruh	Schulze					61
	version a			G	March or Aug 1825	1835, op.93/2	—; iii	
	version b			Ab	c1825	1828, op.90/2	viii, 106; iii	
854	Fülle der Liebe	Ein sehnend Streben	F. von Schlegel	Ab	Aug 1825	1830	viii, 132; iii	
855	Wiedersehn	Der Frühlingssonne holdes Lächeln	A. W. von Schlegel	G	Sept 1825	1842	viii, 136; xiii	
856	Abendlied für die Entfernte	Hinaus, mein Blick!	A. W. von Schlegel	F	Sept 1825	1827, op.88/1	viii, 138; iv	88

D	Title	First line	Poet	Key	Composed	Published	Edition	Pages
857	Zwei Szenen aus dem Schauspiel Lacrimas		C. W. von Schütz		Sept 1825	1829, op.124		
	1 Lied der Delphine	Ach, was soll ich beginnen		A			viii, 146; xiii	
	2 Lied des Florio	Nun, da Schatten niedergleiten		E			viii, 143; xiii	
860	An mein Herz	O Herz, sei endlich stille	Schulze	a	Dec 1825	1832	viii, 154; xiii	
861	Der liebliche Stern	Ihr Sternlein, still in der Höhe	Schulze	G	Dec 1825	1832	viii, 160; xiii	
862	Um Mitternacht	Keine Stimme hör ich schallen	Schulze		Dec 1825			
	version a			B♭		—	—; iv	
	version b			B♭	?March 1826	1827, op.88/3	viii, 212; iv	
863	An Gott, lost		C. C. Hohlfeld	—	by 1827	—	—	
864	Das Totenhemdchen, lost		E. von Bauernfeld	—	after 1824	—	—	
865	Widerspruch	Wenn ich durch Busch und Zweig	J. G. Seidl	D	?1826	1828, op.105/1	ser. xvi, 93; v	
	version b [for version a see 'Male voices']							
866	Vier Refrainlieder		Seidl					51, 64
	1 Die Unterscheidung	Die Mutter hat mich jüngst gescholten		G	?summer 1828	1828, op.95	viii, 240; v	
	2 Bei dir allein	Du sagtest mir es, Mutter		A♭			viii, 243; v	
	3 Die Männer sind méchant			a			viii, 248; v	
	4 Irdisches Glück	So mancher sieht mit finstrer Miene		d			viii, 250; v	
867	Wiegenlied	Wie sich der Äuglein kindlicher Himmel	Seidl	A♭	?1826	1828, op.105/2	viii, 252; v	
868	Das Echo [see 990c]							
869	Totengräber-Weise	Nicht so düster und so bleich	Schlechta	f♯	1826	1832	viii, 198; xiv	
870	Der Wanderer an den Mond	Ich auf der Erd', am Himmel du	Seidl	g/G	1826	1827, op.80/1	viii, 234; iv	
871	Das Zügenglöcklein	Kling die Nacht durch, klinge	Seidl		1826			51, 87
	version a			A♭		1979	—; iv	
	version b			A♭		1827, op.80/2	viii, 237; iv	
874	O Quell, was strömst du rasch und wild, frag.		Schulze	G	?Jan 1826	1974	—; xiv	
876	Im Jänner 1817 (Tiefes Leid)	Ich bin von aller Ruh geschieden	Schulze	e	Jan 1826	1838	viii, 164; xiv	

D	Title	Incipit	Text	Key	Composed	Published	SW; NSA	
877	Gesänge aus Wilhelm Meister		Goethe		Jan 1826	1827, op.62		49, 55, 56
	1 Mignon und der Harfner (5), S,T	Nur wer die Sehnsucht kennt		b			viii, 166; iii	
	2 Lied der Mignon (2)	Heiss mich nicht reden		e			viii, 169; iii	
	3 Lied der Mignon (3)	So lasst mich scheinen		B			viii, 172; iii	
	4 Lied der Mignon (6)	Nur wer die Sehnsucht kennt		a			viii, 174; iii	
878	Am Fenster	Ihr lieben Mauern hold und traut	Seidl	F	March 1826	1828, op.105/3	viii, 176; v	
879	Sehnsucht	Die Scheibe friert	Seidl	d	March 1826	1828, op.105/4	viii, 179; v	
880	Im Freien	Draussen in der weiten Nacht	Seidl	E♭	March 1826	1827, op.80/3	viii, 184; iv	
881	Fischerweise version a version b	Den Fischer fechten Sorgen	Schlechta	D D	March 1826	1895 1828, op.96/4	viii, 190; v viii, 194; v	62
882	Im Frühling	Still sitz' ich an des Hügels Hang	Schulze	G	March 1826	1828, op.101/1	viii, 202; v	51
883	Lebensmut	O wie dringt das junge Leben	Schulze	B♭	March 1826	1832	viii, 206; xiv	
884	Über Wildemann	Die Winde sausen am Tannenhang	Schulze	d	March 1826	1829, op.108/1	viii, 216; v	51
888	Trinklied (Come, thou monarch of the vine)	Bacchus, feister Fürst	Shakespeare, trans. F. M. von Grünbühel and Bauernfeld	C	July 1826	1850	viii, 227; xiv	51
889	Standchen (Hark, hark the lark)	Horch, horch! die Lerch	Shakespeare, trans. A. W. von Schlegel	C	July 1826	1830	viii, 228; xiv	51
890	Hippolits Lied	Lasst mich, ob ich auch still verglüh	F. von Gerstenberg	a	July 1826	1830	viii, 230; xiv	
891	Gesang (An Sylvia; Who is Sylvia?)	Was ist Silvia	Shakespeare, trans. Bauernfeld	A	July 1826	1828, op.106/4	viii, 232; v	51, 58, 89
896	Fröhliches Scheiden, sketch	Gar fröhlich kann ich scheiden	Leitner	F	autumn 1827–early 1828	1920	—; xiv	
896a	Sie in jedem Liede, sketch	Nehm ich die Harfe	Leitner	B♭	autumn 1827–early 1828	—	—; xiv	
896b	Wolke und Quelle, sketch	Auf meinen heimischen Bergen	Leitner	C	autumn 1827–early 1828	—	—; xiv	

	Title	Incipit	Poet	Key	Composed	Published	References
902	Drei Gesänge				1827		64
1	L'incanto degli occhi (Die Macht der Augen) (2)	Da voi, cari lumi (Nur euch, schöne Sterne)	Metastasio	C		1827, op.83	x, 54; iv
2	Il traditor deluso (Der getäuschte Verräter) (2)	Ahimè, io tremo! (Weh mir, ich bebe)	Metastasio	e			x, 58; iv
3	Il modo di prender moglie (Die Art, ein Weib zu nehmen)	Or sù! non ci pensiamo (Wohlan! und ohne Zagen)		C			x, 65; iv
904	Alinde	Die Sonne sinkt ins tiefe Meer	Rochlitz	A	Jan 1827	1827, op.81/1	iv, 257; iv
905	An die Laute	Leiser, leiser, kleine Laute	Rochlitz	D	Jan 1827	1827, op.81/2	iv, 262; iv	88
906	Der Vater mit dem Kind	Dem Vater liegt das Kind im Arm	Bauernfeld	D	Jan 1827	1832	viii, 261; xiv
907	Romanze des Richard Löwenherz	Grosse Taten tat der Ritter	Scott, trans. K. L. M. Müller		?March 1826			64
	version a			b		1979	—; iv
	version b			b		1828, op.86	viii, 220; iv
909	Jägers Liebeslied	Ich schiess' den Hirsch	Schober	D	Feb 1827	1828, op.96/2	viii, 264; v
910	Schiffers Scheidelied	Die Wogen am Gestade schwellen	Schober	e	Feb 1827	1833	viii, 267; xiv
911	Winterreise		Müller		Feb–spring 1827	1823, op.89	54, 59, 64, 69, 79, 80, 81, 84, 93ff, 102
	Book 1:						
1	Gute Nacht	Fremd bin ich eingezogen		d			ix, 2; iv	97
2	Die Wetterfahne	Der Wind spielt mit der Wetterfahne		a			ix, 6; iv
3	Gefrorne Tränen	Gefrorne Tropfen fallen		f			ix, 8; iv	86
4	Erstarrung	Ich such im Schnee vergebens		c			ix, 10; iv	97
5	Der Lindenbaum	Am Brunnen vor dem Tore		E			ix, 16; iv	59, 97
6	Wasserflut	Manche Trän' aus meinen Augen		f♯				
	version a			e			ix, 20; iv
	version b			e			—; iv
7	Auf dem Flusse	Der du so lustig rauschtest		e			ix, 22; iv
8	Rückblick	Es brennt mir unter beiden Sohlen		g			ix, 26; iv
9	Irrlicht	In die tiefsten Felsengründe		b			ix, 30; iv

155

D	Title	Incipit	Text	Key	Composed	Published	SW; NSA	
10	Rast	Nun merk ich erst						
	version a			c			ix, 32; iv	
	version b			d		1895	ix, 34; iv	
11	Frühlingstraum	Ich träumte von bunten Blumen		A/a			ix, 36; iv	95
12	Einsamkeit	Wie eine trübe Wolke						
	version a			b			ix, 40; iv	
	version b			d		1895	ix, 42; iv	
	Book 2:							
13	Die Post	Von der Strasse her ein Posthorn klingt		E♭	begun Oct 1827		ix, 44; iv	
14	Der greise Kopf	Der Reif hat einen weissen Schein		c			ix, 48; iv	88
15	Die Krähe	Eine Krähe war mit mir		c			ix, 50; iv	
16	Letzte Hoffnung	Hie und da ist an den Bäumen		E♭			ix, 53; iv	
17	Im Dorfe	Es bellen die Hunde		D			ix, 56; iv	97
18	Der stürmische Morgen	Wie hat der Sturm zerrissen		d			ix, 60; iv	
19	Täuschung	Ein Licht tanzt freundlich		A			ix, 62; iv	80
20	Der Wegweiser	Was vermeid ich denn die Wege		g			ix, 64; iv	97
21	Das Wirthaus	Auf einen Totenacker		F			ix, 68; iv	
22	Mut	Fliegt der Schnee mir ins Gesicht						
	version a			a		—	—; iv	
	version b			g			ix, 70; iv	
23	Die Nebensonnen	Drei Sonnen sah ich						
	version a			A		—	—; iv	
	version b			A			ix, 72; iv	
24	Der Leiermann	Drüben hinterm Dorfe						
	version a			a		1895	ix, 74; iv	
	version b			b			ix, 76; iv	
916a	Song sketch (no text)			C	?May 1827	—	—; xiv	
917	Das Lied im Grünen	Ins Grüne, ins Grüne	J. A. F. Reil	A	June 1827	1829, op.115/1	ix,85; xiv	57
919	Frühlingslied (2)	Geöffnet sind des Winters Riegel	A. Pollak	A♭	?early 1827	1897	ser. xxi, 325; xiv	
922	Heimliches Lieben	O du, wenn deine Lippen	K. L. von Klenke					58
	version a			B♭	Sept 1827	1895	ix, 92; v	
	version b			B♭	c1827	1828, op.106/1	ix, 97; v	

D	Title	Incipit	Poet	Key	Composed	Published	Reference	
923	Eine altschottische Ballade	Dein Schwert, wie ist's von Blut so rot	anon. Eng., trans. Herder	g	Sept 1827	1862, cp.165/5	ix, 104; xiv	58
	version a, 2vv							
	version b			g	c1827	1895	ix, 402; xiv	
	version c, 2vv			g	c1827	1971	—; xiv	
926	Das Weinen	Gar tröstlich kommt geronnen	Leitner	D	autumn 1827–early 1828	1828, cp.106/2	ix, 106; v	
927	Vor meiner Wiege	Das also, das ist der enge Schrein	Leitner	b	autumn 1827–early 1828	1828, cp.106/3	ix, 108; v	
931	Der Wallensteiner Lanzknecht beim Trunk	Hei! schenket mir im Helme ein!	Leitner	g	Nov 1827	1835	ix, 112; xiv	
932	Der Kreuzzug	Ein Münich steht in seiner Zell	Leitner	D	Nov 1827	1832	ix, 114; xiv	62
933	Des Fischers Liebesglück	Dort blinket durch Weiden	Leitner	a	Nov 1827	1835	ix, 116; xiv	
937	Lebensmut, frag.	Fröhlicher Lebensmut	L. Rellstab	Bb	?summer 1828	1872	x, 134; xiv	
938	Der Winterabend	Es ist so still	Leitner	Bb	Jan 1828	1835	ix, 118; xiv	62
939	Die Sterne	Wie blitzen die Sterne	Leitner	Eb	Jan 1828	1828, op.96/1	ix, 125; v	
943	Auf dem Strom, with hn/vc obbl	Nimm die letzten Abschiedsküsse	Rellstab	E	March 1828	1829, op.119	x, 2; xiv	62
945	Herbst	Es rauschen die Winde	Rellstab	e	April 1828	1895	x, 90; xiv	
949	Widerschein [see 639b]							
955	Glaube, Hoffnung und Liebe	Glaube, hoffe, liebe!	C. Kuffner	Eb	Aug 1828	1828, op.97	viii, 28; v	
957	Schwanengesang				Aug–Oct 1828	1829		
	Book 1:							
	1 Liebesbotschaft	Rauschendes Bächlein, so silbern	Rellstab	G	Aug 1828		ix, 134; xiv	67, 68
	2 Kriegers Ahnung	In tiefer Ruh liegt um mich her	Rellstab	c			ix, 139, xiv	87
	3 Frühlingssehnsucht	Säuselnde Lüfte wehend so mild	Rellstab	Bb			ix, 144; xiv	
	4 Ständchen	Leise flehen meine Lieder	Rellstab	d			ix, 148; xiv	
	5 Aufenthalt	Rauschender Strom, brausender Wald	Rellstab	e			ix, 151; xiv	
	6 In der Ferne	Wehe dem Fliehenden	Rellstab	b			ix, 156; xiv	

158

D	Title	Incipit	Text	Key	Composed	Published	SW; NSA	
Book 2:								
7	Abschied	Ade! du muntre, du fröhliche Stadt	Rellstab	E♭			ix, 160; xiv	
8	Der Atlas	Ich unglückselger Atlas	Heine	g			ix, 167; xiv	
9	Ihr Bild	Ich stand in dunklen Träumen	Heine	b♭			ix, 170; xiv	
10	Das Fischermädchen	Du schönes Fischermädchen	Heine	A♭			ix, 172; xiv	67, 89, 90
11	Die Stadt	Am fernen Horizonte	Heine	c			ix, 175; xiv	
12	Am Meer	Das Meer erglänzte weit hinaus	Heine	C			ix, 178; xiv	91
13	Der Doppelgänger	Still ist die Nacht	Heine	b			ix, 180; xiv	67, 87, 90 91
14	Die Taubenpost	Ich hab' eine Brieftaub	Seidl	G	Oct 1828		ix, 182; xiv	68
965	Der Hirt auf dem Felsen, with cl obbl	Wenn auf dem höchsten Fels	Müller, ?H. von Chézy	B♭	Oct 1828	1830, op.129	x, 16; xiv	68
965a	Die Taubenpost [see 957/14]							
989	Vollendung [see 579a]							
989a	Die Erde [see 579b]							
990	Der Graf von Habsburg	Zu Aachen in seiner Kaiserspracht	Schiller	G	?1815	1853	—; xiv	67
990a	Kaiser Maximilian auf der Martinswand	Hinauf! hinauf! in Sprung und Lauf	H. von Collin	B♭	?1815	1853	—; xiv	
990b	Augenblicke in Elysium, lost [formerly 582]		Schober		?		—	
990c	Das Echo [formerly 868]	Herzliebe gute Mutter	Castelli	B♭	?	1830, op.130	viii, 258; xiv	
990d	Die Schiffende, lost	Sie wankt dahin!	Hölty	—	?	—	—; iv	
990e	L'incanto degli occhi (1) ?frag.	Da voi, cari lumi	Metastasio	B♭	?	1933	—; iv	
990f	Il traditor deluso (1), ?frag., lost	Ahimè! io tremo!	Metastasio	—	?	—	—	
991	[part of 323]							
A1/30	Mein Frieden	Ferne, ferne flammenhelle Sterne	Heine	E♭	?1815	1840	—	

1: Die verfehlte Stunde, 409; Die vier Weltalter, 391; Die Vögel, 691; Die Wallfahrt,778a; Die Wetterfahre, 911/2; 'Die Winde sausen am Tannenhang', 884

'Die Wogen am Gestade schwellen', 910; 'Dioskuren, Zwillingssterne', 360; 'Dir, Mädchen, schlägt', 179; Dithyrambe, 801; Dom, 126a-b; Don Gayseros, 93/1; 'Dort blinket durch Weiden', 933; 'Dort ist ihr Grab', 736; 'Dort raget ein Berg', 143; Drang in die Ferne, 770; 'Draussen in der weiten Nacht', 880; Drei Gesänge, 902; 'Drei Sonnen sah ich', 911/23a-b; 'Drüben hinterm Dorfe', 911/24a-b; Du bist die Ruh, 776; 'Du brachst sie run, die kalte Rinde', 361

'Du, der ewig um much trauert', 467; 'Du heilig, glühend Abendrot!', 627; 'Du holde Kunst', 547a-b; 'Du kleine grünumwachs'ne Quelle', 530; Du liebst mich nicht, 756a-b; 'Durch eine ganze Nacht', 264a-b; 'Durch Feld und Wald zu schweifen', 764a-b; 'Durch Fichten am Hügel', 109; 'Du sagtest mir es, Mutter', 866/3; 'Du schönes Fischermädchen', 957/10; 'Du Schwert an meiner Linken', 170; 'Du staunest, o Mensch', 684; 'Du Turm! zu meinem Leide', 490; 'Du verstörst uns nicht, o Nacht!', 358; Edone, 445

'Eh die Sonne früh aufersteht', 685; 'Ehre sei dem Hocherhabnen', 442; Eifersucht und Stolz, 795/15; 'Ein Blick von deinen Augen', 673; Eine altschottische Ballade, 923a-c; 'Eine Krähe war mit mir', 911/15; 'Eine Mühle seh' ich blinken', 795/3; 'Ein Fräulein klagt' im finstern Turm', 114a-b; 'Ein Fräulein schaut vom hohen Turm', 134; 'Einheilig Säuseln', 197; 'Ein Jüngling auf dem Hügel', 702; 'Ein Licht tanzt freundlich', 911/19; 'Ein Mädchen ist's', 155; 'Ein Münich steht in seiner Zell', 932

Einsamkeit, 620, 911/12a-b; 'Einsam wandelt dein Freund', 95; 'Ein Schäfer sass im Grünen', 517a-b; 'Ein sehnend Streben', 854; 'Ein Vater starb von des Sohnes Hand', 10; Ellens Gesang, 837, 838, 839; Elysium, 584; 'Endlich stehn die Pforten offen', 318; Entra l'uomo allor che nasce, 33; Entzückung, 413; Entzückung an Laura, 390, 577a-b; 'Er fiel den Tod fürs Vater and', 218; Erinnerung, 101; Erinnerungen, 98; Erlafsee, 586; 'Er liegt und schläft', 497; Erlkönig, 328a-d; Erntelied, 434; 'Er schläft so süss', 579a-b; Erstarrung, 911/4

Erster Verlust, 226; 'Es bellen die Hunde', 911/17; 'Es brennt mir unter beiden Sohlen', 911/8; 'Es deuten die Blumen', 519; 'Es floh die Zeit im Wirbelfluge', 515; 'Es ging ein Mann zur Frühlingszeit', 466; 'Es ist doch meine Nachbarin', 560; 'Es ist ein halbes Himmelreich', 431; 'Es ist so angenehm', 284; 'Es ist so still', 938; 'Es liebt' in Welschland', 208a-b; 'Es lockte schöne Wärme', 745a-b; 'Es mahnt der Wald', 527a-b; 'Es rauschen die Winde', 945; 'Es reden und träumen die Menschen', 251, 637; 'Es rieselt, klar und wehend', 393, 563

'Es schlug mein Herz', 767a-b; 'Es tanzen Mond und Sterne', 808; 'Es tönet sein Lob', 444; 'Es träumen die Wolken', 669; 'Es war ein König in Thule', 367; 'Es wehet kühl und leise', 646; 'Euch Blümlein will ich senden', 622; 'Fahrt zum Hades, 526; 'Fels auf Felsen hingewälzet', 754; 'Ferne, ferne flammen'zelle Sterne', Al/30; 'Ferne von der grossen Stadt', 483; 'Fischer harrt am Brückenbogen', 639a; Fischerlied, 351, 562; Fischerweise, 881a-b; 'Fliegt der Schnee mir ins Gesicht', 911/22a-b; Fragment aus dem Aeschylus, 450a-b

Freiwilliges Versinken, 700; 'Fremd bin ich eingezogen', 911/1; Freude der Kinderjahre, 455; 'Freude, die im frühen Lenze', 455; 'Freuden sonder Zahl', 433; 'Freude, schöner Götterfunken', 189; 'Freudvoll und leidvoll', 210; 'Freunde, deren Grüfte', 50; 'Freundlich ist dein Antlitz', 614; 'Friede sei um diesen Grabstein', 496; 'Friedlich lieg' ich hingegossen', 694; 'Frisch atmet des Morgens lebendiger Hauch' 402

'Frisch trabe sonder Ruh', 852a-b; 'Fröhlicher Lebensmut', 937; Fröhliches Scheiden, 896; Frohsinn, 520a-b; Frühlingsglaube, 686a-c; Frühlingslied, 398, 919; Frühlingssehnsucht 957/3; Frühlingstraum, 911/11; Fülle der Liebe, 854; 'Füllest wieder Busch und Tal', 259, 296; Furcht der Geliebten, 285a-b; Ganymed, 544; 'Ganz verloren, ganz versunken', 240; 'Gar fröhlich kann ich scheiden', 896; 'Gar tröstlich kommt geronnen', 926; Gebet während der Schlacht, 171; Gefrorne Tränen, 911/3; 'Gefrorne Tropfen fallen', 911/3

Geheimnis, 491; Geist der Liebe, 233, 414; Geistesnähe, 100; Geistes-Gruss, 142a-f. Genügsamkeit, 143; 'Geöffnet sind des Winters Riegel', 919; Gesang, 891; Gesang der Geister über dem Wassern, 484; Gesang des Harfners, 478a-b, 479a-b, 480a-c; 'Geuss, lieber Mond', 193; 'Geuss nicht so laut', 196; 'Gib mir die Fülle der Einsamkeit', 620; 'Gib, Schwester, mir die Harf herab', 209; '... Glanz des Guten', 164; 'Glaube, hoffe, liebe', 955

Glaube, Hoffnung und Liebe, 955; Gondelfahrer, 808; Gott im Frühlinge, 448a-b; 'Grabe, Spaten, grabe!', 44; Grablied, 218; Grablied auf einen Soldaten, 454; Grablied für die Mutter, 616; Greisengesang, 778a-b; Grenzen der Menschheit, 716; Gretchen, 564; Gretchen am Spinnrade, 118; Gretchen im Zwinger, 564; Gretchens Bitte, 564; 'Grosse Taten tat der Ritter', 907a-b; 'Gross ist Jehovah, der Herr', 852a-b

'Gross und rotentflammet', 276; 'Grüner wird die Au', 503; Gruppe aus dem Tartarus, 396, 583; 'Guarda, che bianca luna', 688/2; Gute Nacht, 911/1; 'Guten Morgen, schöne Müllerin', 795/8; 'Gute Ruh', gute Ruh', 795/20; 'Ha, dort kömmt er', 322; Hagars Klage, 5; Halt', 795/3; Hänflings Liebeswerbung, 552a-b; Harfenspieler,

MISCELLANEOUS
(published in NSA viii/1–2 unless otherwise stated)

D		
16	7 contrapuntal studies, nos.1–4, g, nos.3–7, a, ?vv, ?1823, ed. in Orel (1940/R1977)	
25	2 contrapuntal studies, a 2–4, frags., begun 18 June 1812	
25a	2 contrapuntal studies, a 4, frags., ?sum. 1812	
25b	15 contrapuntal studies, a 3, frags., ?sum. 1812 (part facs. in Landon, 1969)	
AI/3	Fugue, C, str qt, frag., va only, ?1812	
AI/14	Waltz, 'Kupelwieser-Walzer', G, pf, 17 Sept 1826 (Vienna, 1970)	53
AI/23	Lebenslied, TTB/TTBB, 2nd T only, 1815 or 1816 (Kassel, 1974) [? part of los: Lebensbild, 425]	
AI/28	Klage, song, c1817 [formerly 512]	
AI/32	Figured bass exercises, before 1812 [formerly 598a]	
AII/1	arr. of ov. to Gluck's Iphigenie en Aulide, pf 4 hands, frag., ?early 1810	
AII/2	arr. of W. Matiegka's Notturno op.21, fl, va, vc, gui, 26 Feb 1814 (Munich, 1926) [see also 96]	
AII/3	arr. of 2 arias from Gluck's Echo et Narcisse, 1v, pf, March 1816	
AII/4	arr. of M. Stadler's Psalm viii, S, 2 ob, 2 cl, str, timp, org, 29 Aug 1823 (Vienna, 1960)	

DOUBTFUL AND SPURIOUS WORKS

D		
AI/4	Str qt, G, frag., by A. Stadler [formerly 2]	
AI/7	March, 2 pf 8 hands, Nov 1825, lost [formerly 858]	
AI/12	7 leichte Variationen, G, pf, ?1810	
AI/15	Minuet and trio, D, pf [formerly 336]	
AI/17	Tantum ergo, Bb, frag., S only	
AI/25	Drum Schwester und Brüder, 1v, chorus, insts, frag., Oct 1819	
AI/26	Sturmbeschworung, ? trio/qt, mixed vv, frag., S only	
AI/29	Kaiser Ferdinand II, song	
AIII/6	Offertory: Clamavi ad te, frag., ?Nov 1813, by J. Preindl [formerly 85]	
AIII/11	Lass immer in der Jugend Glanz, canon, 2vv, after Mozart [formerly 92]	
AIII/12	Selig alle, die im Herrn entschliefen, canon, 2vv, after Mozart [formerly 127]	

Bibliography

BIBLIOGRAPHIES

O. E. Deutsch, ed.: *Franz Schubert: die Dokumente seines Lebens und Schaffens*, ii/1: *Die Dokumente seines Lebens* (Munich, 1914, enlarged 2/1964, Neue Ausgabe sämtlicher Werke, viii/5, with a selective list of Deutsch's writings on Schubert, p. 616; Eng. trans., 1946/ R1977, as *Schubert: a Documentary Biography*)

W. Kahl: *Verzeichnis des Schrifttums über Franz Schubert: 1828–1928* (Regensburg, 1938)

A. H. King: 'Bibliography', *Schubert: a Symposium*, ed. G. Abraham (London, 1946/R1969, 2/1952)

CATALOGUES

G. Nottebohm: *Thematisches Verzeichnis der im Druck erschienenen Werke von Franz Schubert* (Vienna, 1874)

O. E. Deutsch with D. R. Wakeling: *Schubert: a Thematic Catalogue of his Works* (London, 1951) [preface, p. ix, lists and discusses all previous catalogues; corrections and addns to catalogue in *ML*, xxxiv (1953), 25]; Ger. trans., rev., enlarged, by W. Dürr, A. Feil, C. Landon and others, Neue Ausgabe sämtlicher Werke, viii/4, as *Franz Schubert: thematisches Verzeichnis seiner Werke in chronologischer Folge von Otto Erich Deutsch* (Kassel, 1978) [reviews: R. Klein: 'Der neue "Deutsch" und andere Schubert-Publikationen', *ÖMz*, xxxiii (1978), 573; E. Sams: 'Schubert and OED2', *MT*, cxx (1979), 577]

R. van Hoorickx: 'Thematic Catalogue of Schubert's Works: New Additions, Corrections and Notes', *RBM*, xxviii–xxx (1974–6), 136

DOCUMENTS

O. E. Deutsch, ed.: *Franz Schubert: die Dokumente seines Lebens und Schaffens*, ii/1: *Die Dokumente seines Lebens* (Munich, 1914, enlarged 2/1964, Neue Ausgabe sämtlicher Werke, viii/5; Eng. trans., 1946/ R1977, as *Schubert: a Documentary Biography*)

——: *Franz Schuberts Briefe und Schriften* (Munich, 1919, 4/1954; Eng. trans., 1928/R1970)

——: *Franz Schuberts Tagebuch* (Vienna, 1928; Eng. trans., 1928) [facs. and transcr.]

H. Werlé, ed.: *Franz Schubert in seinen Briefen und Aufzeichnungen* (Leipzig, 1948, 4/1955)

H. Müller von Asow: 'Unbekannte Briefe der Familie Schubert', *ÖMz*, xiii (1958), 317

R. Klein: *Schubert-Stätten* (Vienna, 1972)

C. Landon: 'Ein neuer Schubert-Brief', *ÖMz*, xxxii (1977), 545

R. van Hoorickx: 'An Unknown Schubert Letter', *MT*, cxxii (1981), 291

ICONOGRAPHY

A. Trost: 'Franz Schuberts Bildnisse', *Berichte und Mittheilungen des Alterthums-Vereines zu Wien*, xxxiii/2 (1898), 85

O. E. Deutsch, ed.: *Franz Schubert: die Dokumente seines Lebens und Schaffens*, iii: *Sein Leben in Bildern* (Munich, 1913)

O. E. Deutsch: *Die historischen Bildnisse Franz Schuberts in getreuen Nachbildungen* (Vienna, 1922)

A. Orel: *Franz Schubert, 1797–1828: sein Leben in Bildern* (Leipzig, 1939)

R. Petzoldt: *Franz Schubert: sein Leben in Bildern* (Leipzig, 1953)

O. E. Deutsch: 'Rieders Schubert-Bildnis', *ÖMz*, xiv (1959), 1

F. Novotny: 'Zu einem Bildnis Franz Schuberts', *Musica*, xv (1961), 57

E. Hilmar and O. Brusatti, eds.: *Franz Schubert* (Vienna, 1978) [exhibition catalogue]

E. Badura-Skoda: 'A Schubert Life Mask', *MT*, cxx (1979), 575

MANUSCRIPTS, SOURCES

M. Friedlaender: 'Fälschungen in Schuberts Liedern', *VMw*, ix (1893), 166

E. Mandyczewski, ed.: *Revisionsbericht*, Franz Schuberts Werke: kritisch durchgesehene Gesamtausgabe (Leipzig, 1897/*R*1969)

J. Mantuani: 'Schubertiana: ein Beitrag zur Schubertforschung', *Die Musik*, i (1901–2), 1374 [Schubert autographs found in St Peter's, Vienna]

E. Decsey: 'Aus Josef Hüttenbrenner's Schubert-Nachlass', *Die Musik*, xi (1911–12), 297

R. Lachmann: 'Die Schubert-Autographen der Staatsbibliothek zu Berlin', *ZMw*, xi (1928), 109

J. G. Prod'homme: 'Les manuscrits de Schubert à la Bibliothèque du Conservatoire de Paris', *ReM*, xii (1928), 209

Internationaler Kongress für Schubertforschung: Wien 1928 [contains essays by R. Haas, J. Wolf, G. Kinsky, M. Friedlaender, on Schubert collections and source material]

M. J. E. Brown: 'Recent Schubert Discoveries', *ML*, xxxii (1951), 349

F. Racek: 'Von den Schuberthandschriften der Stadtbibliothek', *Festschrift zum hundertjährigen Bestehen der Wiener Stadtbibliothek, 1856–1956* (Vienna, 1956), 98

M. J. E. Brown: 'New, Old and Rediscovered Schubert Manuscripts', *ML*, xxxvii (1957), 359

——: 'Schubert's Manuscripts: some Chronological Issues', *MR*, xix (1958), 180

——: 'Schubert: Discoveries of the Last Decade', *MQ*, xlvii (1961), 293

W. Suppan: 'Schubert-Autographe im Nachlass Weis-Ostborn', *SM*, vi (1964), 131

M. J. E. Brown: 'Two Schubert Discoveries', *MT*, cix (1968), 801 [Albumleaf, 1821; *Die Wallfahrt* D778a]

A. Feil and W. Dürr: 'Kritisch revidierte Gesamtausgaben von Werken Franz Schuberts im 19. Jahrhundert', *Musik und Verlag: Karl Vötterle zum 65. Geburtstag* (Kassel, 1968), 268

O. E. Deutsch: 'Eine merkwürdige Schubert-Handschrift', *Musa–mens–musici: im Gedenken an Walther Vetter* (Leipzig, 1969), 283 [Schubert's arr. for voice and orch of Stadler's Psalm viii, AII/4]

A. Feil and W. Dürr: 'Die neue Schubert-Ausgabe: über einige Probleme des Herausgabens von Musik', *ÖMz*, xxiv (1969), 553

R. van Hoorickx: 'About some Early Schubert Manuscripts', *MR*, xxx (1969), 118

I. Kecskeméti: 'Neu entdeckte Schubert-Autographe', *ÖMz*, xxiv (1969), 564

C. Landon: 'Neue Schubert-Funde', *ÖMz*, xxiv (1969), 299; Eng. trans., *MR*, xxxi (1970), 200

A. Orel: 'Schubertiana in Schweden', *Musa–mens–musici: im Gedenken an Walther Vetter* (Leipzig, 1969), 297

R. van Hoorickx: 'Two Essays on Schubert, I: Schubert's Variations, op.10, II: Ferdinand and Franz Schubert', *RBM*, xxiv (1970), 81

M. J. E. Brown: 'Schubert: Discoveries of the Last Decade', *MQ*, lvii (1971), 351

A. Weinmann: 'Zwei neue Schubert-Funde', *ÖMz*, xxvii (1972), 75 [version *a* of *Mut* D911, no.22; 4th setting of *Das Grab* D569 for chorus]

R. van Hoorickx: 'The Schubert Manuscript D.966', *ML*, liv (1973), 385
——: 'A Schubert Manuscript Identified', *MT*, cxv (1974), 127 [D966]
——: 'Un manuscrit inconnu de Schubert', *RBM*, xxviii–xxx (1974–6), 260 [*Über Wildemann* D884]

F. G. Zeileis: 'Bemerkungen zur Erstveröffentlichung einer bisher ungedruckten Komposition aus Franz Schuberts Studienzeit', *Beiträge zur Musikdokumentation: Franz Grasberger zum 60. Geburtstag* (Tutzing, 1975), 493

R. van Hoorickx: 'Some Unknown Schubert Manuscripts', *MT*, cxviii (1977), 1001

O. Biba: 'Einige neue und wichtige Schubertiana im Archiv der Gesellschaft der Musikfreunde', *ÖMz*, xxxiii (1978), 604

G. Brosche: 'Der Schubert-Autographen der Österreichischen National-Bibliothek', *ÖMz*, xxxiii (1978), 611

E. Hilmar: *Verzeichnis der Schubert-Handschriften in der Musiksammlung der Wiener Stadt- und Landesbibliothek* (Kassel, 1978)

R. Winter: 'Schubert's Undated Works, a New Chronology', *MT*, cxix (1978), 498

CONTEMPORARY ACCOUNTS

R. Bright: *Travels from Vienna through Lower Hungary, with some Remarks on the State of Vienna during the Congress in the year 1814* (Edinburgh, 1818)

J. C. von Zedlitz: 'Nachruf an Schubert', *Wiener Zeitschrift für Kunst und Literatur* (25 Nov 1828)

J. Mayrhofer: 'Erinnerungen an Franz Schubert', *Neues Archiv für Geschichte, Staatenkunde, Literatur und Kunst*, i/16 (1829), 23

L. von Sonnleithner: 'Biographie des Franz Schuberts', *Monatsberichte der Gesellschaft der Musikfreunde des österreichischen Kaiserstaates*, i/2 (1829), 19

J. Mailáth, ed.: *Leben der Sophie Müller* (Vienna, 1832) [diary references]

A. Schindler: 'Erinnerungen an Franz Schubert', *Niederrheinische Musikzeitung für Kunstfreunde und Künstler*, v (1857), 73, 81

H. von Chézy: *Unvergessenes: Denkwürdigkeiten aus dem Leben, von ihr selbst erzählt* (Leipzig, 1858), 259ff

I. F. Castelli: *Memoiren meines Lebens*, iv (Vienna, 1861), 123f

H. Hoffmann von Fallersleben: *Mein Leben: Aufzeichnungen und Erinnerungen*, ii (Hanover, 1868), 50ff

E. von Bauernfeld: 'Einiges von Franz Schubert', *Signale für die musikalische Welt*, xxvii (1869), 977, 993, 1009, 1025; Eng. trans., *Musical World* (15 Jan, 19 Feb 1870)

A. Fareanu: 'Leopold Sonnleithner: Erinnerungen an Franz Schubert', *ZMw*, i (1918–19), 466

J. von Spaun: *Neues um Franz Schubert: einige Bemerkungen über die Biographie Schuberts von Herrn Ritter v. Kreissle-Hellborn* [1865] (Vienna, 1934)

G. Schünemann, ed.: *Erinnerungen an Schubert: Josef von Spauns erste Lebensbeschreibung* [1829] (Berlin and Zurich, 1936)

O. E. Deutsch, ed.: *Schubert: die Erinnerungen seiner Freunde* (Leipzig, 1957, 3/1974; Eng. trans., 1958)

BIOGRAPHY

C. G. von Leitner: *Anselm Hüttenbrenner* (Graz, 1868)

C. von Würzbach: 'Schubert', *Biographisches Lexikon des Kaiserthums Oesterreich*, pt.32 (Vienna, 1876), 30–110

G. Grove: 'Schubert, Franz', *Grove 1*; repr. in *Beethoven, Schubert, Mendelssohn* (London, 1951)

L. Herbeck: *Johann Herbeck: ein Lebensbild von seinem Sohne* (Vienna, 1885), 162ff

M. Friedlaender: *Beiträge zur Biographie Franz Schuberts* (Berlin, 1887; Leipzig, 1928, as *Franz Schubert: Skizze seines Lebens und Wirkens*)

O. E. Deutsch: *Schubert-Brevier* (Berlin, 1905)

M. Vancsa: 'Schubert und seine Verleger', *Jahresbericht des Schubertbundes Vienna, 1905*, 47

E. Mandyczewski: *Geschichte der k. k. Gesellschaft der Musikfreunde*, suppl. (Vienna, 1912)

R. Schmekal: 'Grillparzer und die Gesellschaft der Musikfreunde in Wien', *Der Merker*, v (1915), 447

W. Schweisheimer: 'Der kranke Schubert', *ZMw*, iii (1921), 552

N. Flower: *Franz Schubert: the Man and his Circle* (London, 1928, 2/1949)

K. Kobald: *Franz Schubert und seine Zeit* (Zurich, Leipzig and Vienna, 1928; Eng. trans., 1928)

A. Orel: *Der junge Schubert: aus der Lernzeit des Künstlers* (Vienna, 1940/*R*1977)

F. Walker: 'Schubert's Last Illness', *MMR*, lxxvii (1947), 232

H. Goldschmidt: *Franz Schubert: ein Lebensbild* (Berlin, 1954, 5/1964)

M. J. E. Brown: *Schubert: a Critical Biography* (London, 1958/*R*1977, 2/1961; Ger. trans., 1969)

——: 'Schubert and Salieri', *MMR*, lxxxviii (1958), 211

——: 'Schubert's Early Association with the Kärntnertor-Theater', *MT*, c (1959), 261

——: 'Schubert: Discoveries of the Last Decade', *MQ*, xlvii (1961), 293

F. Hüttenbrenner: 'Anselm Hüttenbrenner und Schuberts H-moll Symphonie', *Zeitschrift des Historischen Vereines für Steiermark*, lii (1961), 12

O. E. Deutsch: 'Der "Mutwille" in Hütteldorf', *ÖMz*, xx (1965), 95

——: 'Ein Scherzgedicht aus der Schubertkreis', *ÖMz*, xxi (1966), 49

P. Ronge: 'Franz Schubert: der Mensch, Geschwister, Vorfahren, Lebenslauf: ein Beitrag zur Genealogie', *Genealogie*, xvi (1967), 721; see also xviii (1969), 534

M.-L. Kupelwieser de Brioni: *Une grande amitié: F. Schubert et L. Kupelwieser* (Paris, 1968)

P. Ronge: 'Katarina Laca a Franz Schubert', *SH*, xii (1968), 261

K. Stekl: 'Schuberts Aufenthalt 1827 in Graz', *Mitteilungen des Steirischen Tonkünstlerbundes*, xli (1969), July–Sept, 3

M. J. E. Brown: 'Schubert: Discoveries of the Last Decade', *MQ*, lvii (1971), 351

O. E. Deutsch: 'Schubert und die Königin Hortense', *ÖMz*, xxvii (1973), 121

H. J. Frölich: *Schubert* (Munich and Vienna, 1978)

H. Osterheld: *Franz Schubert: Schicksal und Persönlichkeit* (Stuttgart, 1978)

E. Sams: 'Schubert's Illness Re-examined', *MT*, cxxi (1980), 15

MUSICAL STYLE

G. Abraham, ed.: *Schubert: a Symposium* (London, 1947/*R*1969)

M. J. E. Brown: *Schubert's Variations* (London, 1954)

H.-W. Berg: *Schuberts Variationswerke* (diss., U. of Freiburg, 1958)

E. G. Porter: 'Schubert's Harmonies', *MR*, xviv (1958), 20

H. Goldschmidt: 'Die Frage der Periodisierung im Schaffen Schuberts', *BMw*, i/2 (1959), p.28

H. Truscott: 'Organic Unity in Schubert's Early Sonata Music', *MMR*. lxxxix (1959), 62

F. Braun: *Studien zur Dynamik in Schuberts Instrumentalmusik* (diss., U. of Tübingen, 1960)

H. Hollander: 'Zur Psychologie des Spätstils in Schuberts Musik', *Musica*, xiv (1960), 565

R. Rhein: *Franz Schuberts Variationswerke* (diss., Saarlandes-U., 1960)

E. Norman-McKay: 'The Interpretation of Schubert's *Decrescendo* and Accent Markings', *MR*, xxii (1961), 108

F. Eibner: 'The Dotted-quaver-and-semiquaver Figure with Triplet Accompaniment in the Works of Schubert', *MR*, xxiii (1962), 281

L. Misch: 'Ein Lieblingsmotiv Schuberts', *Mf*, xv (1962), 146

E. Seidel: *Die Enharmonik in den harmonischen Grossformen Franz Schuberts* (diss., U. of Frankfurt, 1962)

K. P. Bernet Kempers: 'Ganztonreihen bei Schubert', *Organicae voces: Festschrift Joseph Smits van Waesberghe* (Amsterdam, 1963), 7

R. Cox: *Choral Texture in the Music of Franz Schubert* (diss., Northwestern U., 1963)

E. Norman-McKay: 'Rossinis Einfluss auf Schubert', *ÖMz*, xviii (1963), 17

M. Chusid: 'Schubert's Cyclic Compositions of 1824', *AcM*, xxxvi (1964), 37

A. Feil: *Studien zu Schuberts Rhythmik* (Munich, 1966)

W. Riezler: *Schuberts Instrumentalmusik* (Zurich, 1967)

M. Boyd: 'Schubert's Short Cuts', *MR*, xxix (1968), 12

Yu. Khokhlov: *O poslednem periode tvorchestva Shuberta* [The works of Schubert's last period] (Moscow, 1968)

M. K. Whaples: 'On Structural Integration in Schubert's Instrumental Works', *AcM*, xl (1968), 186

R. Bruce: 'The Lyrical Element in Schubert's Instrumental Forms', *MR*, xxx (1969), 131

H. Keller: 'Schuberts Verhältnis zur Sonatenform', *Musa–mens–musici: im Gedenken an Walther Vetter* (Leipzig, 1969), 287

A. Whittall: 'The Sonata Crisis: Schubert in 1828', *MR*, xxx (1969), 124

E. T. Cone: 'Schubert's Beethoven', *MQ*, lvi (1970), 779

D. Schnebel: 'Auf die Suche nach die befreiten Zeit: Versuch über Schubert', *NZM*, cxxxi (1970), 498

M. J. E. Brown: 'Schubert and some Folksongs', *ML*, liii (1972), 173

D. Coren: 'Ambiguity in Schubert's Recapitulations', *MQ*, lx (1974), 568

M. K. Whaples: 'Style in Schubert's Piano Music from 1817 to 1818', *MR*, xxxv (1974), 260

W. S. Newman: 'Freedom of Tempo in Schubert's Instrumental Music',
    MQ, lxi (1975), 528
L. M. Griffel: 'A Reappraisal of Schubert's Methods of Composition',
    MQ, lxiii (1977), 186
W. Gray: 'Schubert the Instrumental Composer', *MQ*, lxiv (1978), 483

ORCHESTRAL WORKS

R. Schumann: 'Die 7. Symphonie von Franz Schubert', *NZM*, xii
    (1840), 81
J. F. Barnett: 'Some Details concerning the Completion and
    Instrumentation of Schubert's Sketch Symphony in E', *PMA*, xvii
    (1890–91), 177
F. Weingartner: *Ratschläge fur Aufführungen klassischer Symphonien*,
    ii (Leipzig, 1919), 1
A. B. Smith: *Schubert*, i: *The Symphonies C major and B minor*
    (London, 1926)
E. Laaff: *Franz Schuberts Sinfonien* (Wiesbaden, 1933)
O. E. Deutsch: 'The Riddle of Schubert's Unfinished Symphony', *MR*,
    i (1940), 36
T. C. L. Pritchard: 'The Unfinished Symphony', *MR*, iii (1942), 10
M. J. E. Brown: 'Schubert's Unfinished Symphony in D', *ML*, xxxi
    (1950), 109 [D615]
O. E. Deutsch: 'The Discovery of Schubert's C major Symphony', *MQ*,
    xxxviii (1952), 528
A. Carse: 'Editing Schubert's Unfinished Symphony', *MT*, xcv (1954),
    143
J. Reed: 'The "Gastein" Symphony Reconsidered', *ML*, xi (1959), 341
E. Laaff: 'Schuberts grosse C-dur-Symphonie: erkennbare Grundlagen
    ihrer Einheitlichkeit', *Festschrift Friedrich Blume* (Kassel, 1963),
    204
M. J. E. Brown: 'Schubert's Italian Overtures', *MR*, xxvi (1965), 303
H. Hollander: 'Die Beethoven-Reflexe in Schuberts grosser C-dur-
    Symphonie', *NZM*, cxxvi (1965), 183
S. Kunze: *Franz Schubert: Sinfonie h-moll: Unvollendete* (Munich,
    1965)
H. Truscott: 'Franz Schubert', *The Symphony*, ed. R. Simpson
    (Harmondsworth, 1966–7, 2/1972), i, 188
P. Hamburger: 'Schuberts "Ufuldente": kendsgeminger og formod-
    ninger' [Schubert's 'Unfinished': facts and assumptions], *Dansk
    musiktidsskrift*, xl (1967), 37
M. J. E. Brown: *Schubert Symphonies* (London, 1970)
G. Abraham: 'Finishing the Unfinished', *MT*, cxii (1971), 547
R. Weber: *Die Sinfonien Franz Schuberts im Versuch einer Struktur-
    wissenschaftlichen Darstellung und Untersuchungen* (diss., U. of
    Münster, 1971)

P. Andraschke: 'Die Retuschen Gustav Mahlers an der 7. Symphonie von Franz Schubert', *AMw*, xxxii (1975), 165

J. Reed: 'How the "Great" C major was written', *ML*, lvi (1975), 18

E. Hilmar: 'Neue Funde, Daten und Dokumente zum symphonischen Werk Franz Schuberts', *ÖMz*, xxxiii (1978), 266

P.-G. Langevin: 'La vraie "Septième" de Schubert et sa résurrection', *SMz*, cxviii (1978), 133, 197

B. Newbould: 'Schubert's Other "Unfinished"', *MT*, cxix (1978), 587

C. Perret-Gentil: 'Le point sur les symphonies inachevées de Schubert et leurs diverses réalisations', *SMz*, cxxi (1981), 76

CHAMBER WORKS

A. B. Smith: *Schubert, ii: Quartet in D minor and Octet* (London, 1927)

O. E. Deutsch: 'The Chronology of Schubert's String Quartets', *ML*, xxiv (1943), 25

H.-M. Sachse: *Franz Schuberts Streichquartette* (Munich, 1958)

H. Truscott: 'Schubert's D minor String Quartet', *MR*, xix (1958), 27

——: 'Schubert's String Quartet in G major', *MR*, xx (1959), 119

M. Chusid: *The Chamber Music of Franz Schubert* (diss., U. of California, Berkeley, 1961)

A. A. Abert: 'Rhythmus und Klang in Schuberts Streichquintett', *Karl Gustav Fellerer zum 60. Geburtstag* (Cologne, 1962), 1

M. Chusid: 'Schubert's Overture for String Quintet and Cherubini's Overture to *Faniska*', *JAMS*, xv (1962), 78

J. A. Westrup: *Schubert Chamber Music* (London, 1969)

M. J. E. Brown: 'Schubert's D minor Quartet: a Footnote', *MT*, cxi (1970), 985

H. Hollander: 'Stil und poetische Idee in Schuberts d-moll-Streichquartett', *NZM*, cxxxi (1970), 239

R. A. Coolidge: 'Form in the String Quartets of Franz Schubert', *MR*, xxxii (1971), 309

K. Marx: 'Einige Anmerkungen zu Schuberts "Forellenquintett" und Oktet', *NZM*, cxxxii (1971), 588

M. Chusid: 'Concerning Orchestral Style in Schubert's Early Chamber Music for Strings', *Zur Aufführungspraxis der Werke Franz Schuberts: Wien 1974*

J. Gillett: 'The Problem of Schubert's G major String Quartet (D.887)', *MR*, xxxv (1974), 281

R. van Hoorickx: 'Schubert's Guitar Quartet', *RBM*, xxxi (1977), 111

M. Willfort: 'Das Urbild des Andante aus Schuberts Klaviertrio Es-dur D.929', *ÖMz*, xxxiii (1978), 277

K. Geiringer: 'Schubert's Arpeggione Sonata and the "Super Arpeggio"', *MQ*, lxv (1979), 513

PIANO WORKS

L. Scheibler: 'Zur Datierung von Schuberts Klaviersonate in A-dur, op.120'; 'Zur Datierung von Schuberts "Letztern Walzer", op.127', *ZIMG*, viii (1906–7), 485; 487

H. Wetzel: 'Schuberts Werke für Klavier zu vier Hände', *Die Musik*, vi (1906–7), 36

W. Kahl: 'Das lyrische Klavierstück Schuberts und seine Vorgänger seit 1810', *AMw*, iii (1921), 54, 99

H. Költzsch: *Franz Schubert in seinen Klaviersonaten* (Leipzig, 1927/*R*1976)

M. J. E. Brown: 'An Introduction to Schubert's Sonatas of 1817', *MR*, xii (1951), 35

W. G. Hill: 'The Genesis of Schubert's Posthumous Sonata in B flat major', *MR*, xii (1951), 269

L. Nowak: 'Das Autograph von Schuberts Rondo in D-dur, op.138', *ÖMz*, viii (1953), 325

H. Truscott: 'The Two Versions of Schubert's op.122', *MR*, xiv (1953), 89

P. Mies: 'Der zyklische Charakter der Klaviertänze bei Franz Schubert', *Kongressbericht: Wien Mozartjahr 1956*, 408

H. Truscott: 'Schubert's Unfinished Sonata in C major', *MR*, xviii (1957), 114

A. Weinmann: 'Eine Plagiatsbeschildigung gegen Schubert', *ÖMz*, xii (1957), 19 [Trauerwalzer]

M. J. E. Brown: 'Schubert's "Trauer-Walzer"', *MMR*, xc (1960), 124

P. Mies: 'Die Entwürfe Franz Schuberts zu den letzten drei Klaviersonaten von 1828', *BMw*, ii/3 (1960), 52

P. Badura-Skoda: 'Unbekannter Eigenschriften bekannter Schubert-Werke', *NZM*, cxxii (1961), 502 [4 Impromptus D935]

A. Brendel: 'Die beiden Versionen von Schuberts "Wanderer-Fantasie"', *ÖMz*, xvii (1962), 56

M. J. E. Brown: 'Eine unbekannte Schubert-Handschrift', *NZM*, cxiv (1963), 92

——: 'Schubert: Three Dance-music Manuscripts', *Festschrift Otto Erich Deutsch* (Kassel, 1963), 226

A. L. Hanna: *A Statistical Analysis of some Style Elements in the Solo Piano Sonatas of Franz Schubert* (diss., Indiana U., 1965)

P. Radcliffe: *Schubert Piano Sonatas* (London, 1967)

F. Bisogni: 'Rilievi filologici sulle sonate giovanili di Franz Schubert (1815–17)', *RIM*, ii (1968), 453

M. J. E. Brown: 'Schuberts Fuge in E-moll', *ÖMz*, xxiii (1968), 65

R. van Hoorickx: 'A Schubert Autograph at the Brussels Conservatoire', *RBM*, xxii (1968), 109 [6 Polonaises op.61, D824]

——: 'Two Schubert Dances', *MT*, cix (1968), 532

M. Hughes, L. Moss and C. Schachter: 'Analysis Symposium', *JMT*, xii (1968), 184–239; see also *JMT*, xiii, (1969), 128, 218 [Moment musical op.94 no.1 D780]

R. Klein: 'Schuberts "Kupelwieser-Walzer": Information zu seiner Überlieferung', *ÖMz*, xxiii (1968), 79

A. Tyson: 'Schubert and *Terpsichore*', *MT*, cix (1968), 812

D. A. Weekley: *The One-piano, Four-hand Compositions of Franz Schubert: Historical and Interpretative Analysis* (diss., Indiana U., 1968)

K. Stekl: 'Zur Auffindung eines unbekannten Klavierwerkes von Franz Schubert', *Mitteilungen des Steirischen Tonkünstlerbundes*, xxxix (1969), Jan–March, 1 ['Grazer Fantasie' D605*a*]

W. Dürr: 'Eine unbekannte Fantasia von Schubert', *ÖMz*, xxiv (1969), 569

R. van Hoorickx: 'Franz Schubert (1797–1828): List of the Dances in Chronological order', *RBM*, xxv (1971), 68

K. Stekl: 'Zwei wiederaufgefundene Schubert-Ländler', *Steirische Sängerzeitung*, xli (1971), 1 [D679]

J. P. Vogel: 'Die "Grazer Fantasie" von Franz Schubert', *Mf*, xxiv (1971), 168

K. M. Komma: 'Franz Schuberts Klaviersonate a-moll op.posth. 164 (D537)', *Zeitschrift für Musiktheorie*, iv/2 (1972), 2

K. Musiol: '"Sieben leichte Variationen in G-Dur", ein verschollenes Jugendwerk von Franz Schubert', *Mf*, xxviii (1975), 202

F. Bisogni: 'Rilievi filologici sulle sonate della maturità di Franz Schubert (1817–1828)', *RIM*, xi (1976), 71

W. Dürr: '"Sieben leichte Variationen in G" – von Schubert?' *Mf*, xxix (1976), 175

E. Sams: 'Schubert's Piano Duets', *MT*, cxvii (1976), 120

SACRED WORKS

E. Prout: 'Franz Schubert's Masses', *MMR*, i (1871), 2, 13, 26, 39, 53, 69, 84

O. Wissig: *Franz Schuberts Messen* (Leipzig, 1909)

M. J. E. Brown: 'Schubert's Settings of the "Salve regina" ', *ML*, xxxvii (1956), 234

K. Pfannhauser: 'Zur Es-Dur-Messe von Franz Schubert', *NZM*, cxix (1958), 435

A. Bamer: 'Franz Schuberts Messen', *Singende Kirche*, viii (1960), 172; also in *Musica sacra*, lxxx (1960), 41

R. van Hoorickx: 'Schubert's "Pastoral" Mass', *ML*, xlii (1961), 53

R. S. Stringham: *The Masses of Franz Schubert* (diss., Cornell U., 1964)

K. J. Nafziger: *The Masses of Haydn and Schubert: a Study in the Rise of Romanticism* (diss., U. of Oregon, 1970)

F. Burkhart: 'Franz Schuberts "Deutsche Messe"', *ÖMz*, xxxi (1976), 565

D. Finke-Hecklinger: 'Franz Schuberts Messe in As', *ÖMz*, xxxiii (1978), 185

R. van Hoorickx: 'Schubert and the Bible', *MT*, cxix (1978), 953

STAGE WORKS

F. Liszt: 'Alfonso und Estrella', *Gesammelte Schriften*, iii/1, trans. L. Ramann (Leipzig, 1881), 68

R. Krott: *Die Singspiele Schuberts* (diss., U. of Vienna, 1921)

M. J. E. Brown: 'Schubert's Two Major Operas', *MR*, xx (1959), 104

E. Norman-McKay: 'Schubert's Incidental Music to "Rosamunde"', *MR*, xxi (1960), 8

——: 'Publisher's Errors in Schubert's Overture to "Die Zauberharfe"', *MR*, xxiii (1962), 128

——: *The Stage-works of Schubert, considered in the Framework of Austrian Biedermeier Society* (diss., U. of Oxford, 1962–3)

F. Racek: 'Franz Schuberts Singspiel "Der häusliche Krieg" und seine jetzt aufgefundene Ouvertüre', *Biblos*, xii (1963), 136

E. Norman-McKay: 'Schubert's Music for the Theatre', *PRMA*, xciii (1966–7), 51

M. J. E. Brown: 'Schubert's *Fierrabras*', *MT*, cxii (1971), 338

M. J. Citron: *Schubert's Seven Complete Operas: a Musico-dramatic Study* (diss., U. of North Carolina, 1971)

W. Szmolyan: 'Schubert als Opernkomponist', *ÖMz*, xxvi (1971), 282

G. R. Cunningham: *Franz Schubert als Theaterkomponist* (diss., U. of Freiburg, 1974)

R. van Hoorickx: 'Les opéras de Schubert', *RBM*, xxviii–xxx (1974–6), 238

P. Branscombe: 'Schubert and his Librettists – 1', *MT*, cxix (1978), 943

O. E. Deutsch: 'Schuberts "Rosamunde" im Theater an der Wien', *ÖMz*, xxxiii (1978), 179

E. Forbes: 'Schubert's "Claudine"', *Opera*, xxix (1978), 1168

CHORAL WORKS

V. Keldorfer: 'Schuberts Chorschaffen', *ÖMz*, xiii (1958), 257

P. Mies: 'Interessantes Schubertfragment aufgefunden: "Die Allmacht" für gemischten Chor', *Lied und Chor*, li (1959), 139

A. Niemeyer: 'Franz Schuberts "Lazarus"-Fragment und seine Beziehung zur Textdichtung', *GfMKB, Leipzig 1966*, 300

R. van Hoorickx: 'Schuberts Trio "Die Advokaten"', *RBM*, xxv (1971), 46

A. Weinmann: 'Eine österreichische Volkshymne von Franz Schubert', *ÖMz*, xxvii (1972), 430

SONGS

H. de Curzon: *Les Lieder de Franz Schubert* (Paris, 1899)

L. Scheibler: 'Franz Schuberts einstimmige Lieder nach österreichischen Dichtern', *Musikbuch für Österreich*, v (1908), 3–35

M. Bauer: *Die Lieder Franz Schuberts*, i (Leipzig, 1915) [only 1 vol. pubd]

H. G. Fiedler: 'Schubert's Poets', *ML*, vi (1925), 68

O. E. Deutsch: *Die Originalausgaben von Schuberts Goethe-Lieder* (Vienna, 1926)

R. Capell: *Schubert's Songs* (London, 1928/*R*1977, rev. 3/1973 by M. Cooper)

P. Mies: *Schubert der Meister des Liedes* (Berlin, 1928)

E. G. Porter: *The Songs of Schubert* (London, 1937)

F. Schnapper: *Die Gesänge des jungen Schubert vor dem Durchbruch des romantischen Liedprinzipes* (Berne and Leipzig, 1937)

E. Schaeffer: 'Schubert's "Winterreise"', *MQ*, xxiv (1938), 39

G. Mackworth-Young: 'Goethe's "Prometheus" and its Settings by Schubert and Wolf', *PRMA*, lxxix (1952–3), 53

M. J. E. Brown: 'Some Unpublished Schubert Songs and Song Fragments', *MR*, xv (1954), 93

T. G. Georgiades: '*Das Wirtshaus* von Schubert und das Kyrie aus dem gregorianschen Requiem', *Gegenwart im Geiste: Festschrift für Richard Benz* (Hamburg, 1954), 126

H. Haas: *Über die Bedeutung der Harmonik in den Liedern Franz Schuberts* (Bonn, 1957)

H. Brandenburg: 'Die "Winterreise" als Dichtung: eine Ehrenrettung für Wilhelm Müller', *Aurora*, xviii (1958), 57

M. J. E. Brown: 'Schubert's "Wilhelm Meister"', *MMR*, lxxxviii (1958), 4

A. E. F. Dickinson: 'Fine Points in "The Erl King"', *MMR*, lxxxviii (1958), 141

J. Mainka: *Das Liedschaffen Franz Schuberts in den Jahren 1815 und 1816: Schuberts Auseinandersetzung mit der Liedtradition des 18. Jahrhunderts* (diss., Humboldt U., Berlin, 1958)

J. L. Broeckx: 'Het vraagstuk van de tekstbehandeling in Schuberts Winterreise', *Antwerpen jb 1959*, 51–81

J. Kramarz: *Das Rezitativ im Liedschaffen Franz Schuberts* (diss., Free U. of Berlin, 1959)

E. G. Porter: *Schubert's Song-technique* (London, 1961)

J. Kerman: 'A Romantic Detail in Schubert's *Schwanengesang*', *MQ*, xlviii (1962), 36

V. Levi: 'Le arie e ariette di Schubert su testo italiano', *SMw*, xxv (1962), 307

G. Spies: *Studien zum Liede Franz Schuberts: Vorgeschichte, Eigenart und Bedeutung der Strophenvarierung* (diss., U. of Tübingen, 1962)

W. Gerstenberg: 'Schubertiade: Anmerkungen zu einigen Liedern', *Festschrift Otto Erich Deutsch* (Kassel, 1963), 232

P. Hauschild: *Studien zur Liedmelodie Franz Schuberts* (diss., U. of Leipzig, 1963)

A. Holschneider: 'Zu Schuberts "Frühlingsglaube"', *Festschrift Otto Erich Deutsch* (Kassel, 1963), 240

A. C. Bell: *The Songs of Schubert* (Lowestoft, 1964)

M. E. Grebe: 'Estudio analítico de "Der stürmische Morgen"': un enfoque metodológico', *Revista musical chilena* (1964), no.18, p.87

M. J. E. Brown: 'Die Handschriften und Frühausgaben von Schuberts "Die Forelle"', *ÖMz*, xx (1965), 578

E. Seidel: 'Ein chromatisches Harmonisierungsmodell in Schuberts "Winterreise"', *GfMKB, Leipzig 1966*, 437; see also *AMw*, xxvi (1965), 285

J. M. Stein: 'Schubert's Heine Songs', *Journal of Aesthetics and Art Criticism*, xxiv (1966), 559

G. Baum: 'Schubert–Müllers *Winterreise* – neu gesehen', *NZM*, cxxviii (1967), 78

M. J. E. Brown: *Schubert Songs* (London, 1967)

T. G. Georgiades: *Schubert: Musik und Lyrik* (Göttingen, 1967)

P. Hamburger: 'Reprisebehandlingen i den Schubert'ske lied', *Dansk musiktidsskrift*, xliii (1967), 163, 196

F. D. Stovall: *Schubert's Heine Songs: a Critical and Analytical Study* (diss., U. of Texas, 1967)

M. J. E. Brown: 'The Therese Grob Collection of Songs by Schubert', *ML*, xlix (1968), 122

R. van Hoorickx: 'Notes on a Collection of Schubert Songs copied from Early Manuscripts around 1821–5', *RBM*, xxii (1968), 86

I. Kecskeméti: 'Eine wieder aufgetauchte Eigenschrift Schuberts', *ÖMz*, xxiii (1968), 70 [*Die Nacht* D534]

D. C. Ossenkop: *The Earliest Setting of German Ballads for Voice and Clavier* (diss., Columbia U., 1968)

L. E. Peake: *The Song Cycle: a Preliminary Inquiry into the Beginnings of the Romantic Song Cycle and the Nature of an Art Form* (diss., Columbia U., 1968)

E. T. Simpson: *A Study, Analysis and Performance of the Schwanengesang of Franz Schubert D.957* (diss., Columbia U., 1968)

D. Berke: 'Zu einigen anonymen Texten Schubertscher Lieder', *Mf*, xxii (1969), 485

J. Chailley: 'Le "Winterreise" et l'énigme de Schubert', *SM*, xi (1969), 107

J. P. Larsen: 'Zu Schuberts Vertonung des Liedes *Nur wer die Sehnsucht kennt*', *Musa–mens–musici: im Gedenken an Walther Vetter* (Leipzig, 1969), 277

E. Schwarmath-Tarján: *Musikalischer Bau und Sprachvertonung in Schuberts Liedern* (Tutzing, 1969)

H. H. Eggebrecht: 'Prinzipien des Schubert-Liedes', *AMw*, xxvii (1970), 89

D. B. Greene: 'Schubert's *Winterreise*: a Study in the Aesthetics of Mixed Media', *Journal of Aesthetics and Art Criticism*, xxix (1970), 181

G. Maier: *Die Lieder Johann Rudolf Zumsteegs und ihr Verhältnis zu Schubert* (diss., U. of Tübingen, 1970)

E. Brody and R. A. Fowkes: *The German Lied and its Poetry* (New York, 1971)

G. Estermann: *Die Klavierbegleitung im Sololied bei Schubert und Schumann* (diss., U. of Innsbruck, 1971)

D. Fischer-Dieskau: *Auf den Spuren der Schubert-Lieder: Werden, Wesen, Wirkung* (Wiesbaden, 1971; Eng trans., 1976)

W. Gray: 'The Classical Nature of Schubert's Lieder', *MQ*, lvii (1971), 62

W. Wiora: *Das Deutsche Lied* (Wolfenbüttel and Zurich, 1971)

W. Gerstenberg: 'Der Rahmen der Tonalität im Liede Schuberts', *Musicae scientiae collectanea: Festschrift Karl Gustav Fellerer* (Cologne, 1973), 147

B. Kinsey: 'Schubert and the Poems of Ossian', *MR*, xxiv (1973), 22

H. Lowen Marshall: 'Symbolism in Schubert's *Winterreise*', *Studies in Romanticism*, xii (1973), 607

S. Sorensen: 'Baek-motiver i Schuberts sange', *Festschrift Gunnar Heerup* (Egtved, 1973), 217

J. H. Thomas: 'Schubert's Modified Strophic Songs with Particular Reference to *Schwanengesang*', *MR*, xxiv (1973), 83

J. Armitage-Smith: 'Schubert's *Winterreise*, Part I: the Sources of the Musical Text', *MQ*, lx (1974), 20

M. Flothuis: 'Franz Schubert's Compositions to Poems from Goethe's *Wilhelm Meisters Lehrjahre*', *Notes on Notes: Selected Essays* (Buren, 1974), 87–138

M. and L. Schochow, eds.: *Franz Schubert: die Texte seiner einstimmig komponierten Lieder und ihre Dichter* (Hildesheim and New York, 1974)

J. Chailley: *Le voyage d'hiver de Schubert* (Paris, 1975)

A. Feil: *Franz Schubert: Die schöne Müllerin, Winterreise* (Stuttgart, 1975)

G. Moore: *The Schubert Song Cycles* (London, 1975; Ger. trans., 1975)

A. Spirk: 'Theorie, Beschreibung und Interpretation in der Lied-Analyse', *AMw*, xxxiv (1977), 225

J. Reed: '*Die schöne Müllerin* reconsidered', *ML*, lix (1978), 411

E. Sams: 'Notes on a Magic Flute: the Origins of the Schubertian Lied', *MT*, cxix (1978), 947

W. Szmolyan: 'Schubert als Singspiel-Komponist', *ÖMz*, xxxiii (1978), 215

R. van Hoorickx: 'A Schubert Song Rediscovered', *MT*, cxxi (1980), 97

C. S. Brauner: 'Irony in the Heine Lieder of Schubert and Schumann', *MQ*, lxvii (1981), 261

A. Walker: 'Liszt and the Schubert Song Transcriptions', *MQ*, lxvii (1981), 50

GENERAL STUDIES

R. Schumann: *Gesammelte Schriften über Musik und Musiker* (Leipzig, 1854, 5/1914/R1969)

H. Kreissle von Hellborn: *Franz Schubert* (Vienna, 1865; Eng. trans., 1869)

A. Reissmann: *Franz Schubert: sein Leben und seine Werke* (Berlin, 1873)

H. F. Frost: *Franz Schubert* (London, 1881, 2/1923)

A. Dvořák: 'Franz Schubert', *Century Magazine*, lxviii (1894), 341

R. Heuberger: *Franz Schubert* (Berlin, 1902, rev. 3/1920 by H. von der Pforten)

W. Klatte: *Franz Schubert* (Berlin, 1907)

W. Dahms: *Schubert* (Berlin, 1912)

O. Bie: *Franz Schubert: sein Leben und sein Werk* (Berlin, 1925; Eng. trans., 1928)

D. F. Tovey: 'Franz Schubert', *The Heritage of Music*, ed. H. J. Foss, i (Oxford, 1927), 82–122

P. Stefan: *Franz Schubert* (Berlin, 1928)

R. Bates: *Schubert* (London, 1934)

W. Vetter: *Franz Schubert* (Potsdam, 1934)

B. Paumgartner: *Franz Schubert* (Zurich, 1943, 2/1947)

A. Hutchings: *Schubert* (London, 1945, rev. 4/1973)

A. Einstein: *Schubert* (London, 1951/R1971; Ger. orig., 1952)

W. Vetter: *Der Klassiker Schubert* (Leipzig, 1953)

P. Mies: *Franz Schubert* (Leipzig, 1954)

T. Marek: *Schubert* (Kraków, 1955)

F. Hug: *Franz Schubert: Leben und Werk eines Frühvollendeten* (Frankfurt am Main, 1958)

H. Wagemans: *Schubert* (Haarlem, 1958)

M. Erdelyi: *Franz Schubert* (Budapest, 1962)

L. Kusche: *Franz Schubert: Dichtung und Wahrheit* (Munich, 1962)

J. E. van Ackere: *Schubert en de romantiek* (Antwerp, 1963)

K. Kobald: *Franz Schubert* (Vienna, Munich and Zurich, 1963)

A. Kolb: *Schubert* (Gütersloh, 1964)

J. Bruyr: *Franz Schubert: l'homme et son oeuvre* (Paris, 1965)

F. de Eaubonne and M.-R. Hofmann: *La vie de Schubert* (Paris, 1965)

M. J. E. Brown: *Essays on Schubert* (London, 1966/R1977)

W. Marggraf: *Franz Schubert* (Leipzig, 1967)

J. Reed: *Schubert: the Final Years* (London, 1972)

R. van Hoorickx: 'Old and New Schubert Problems', *MR*, xxxv (1974), 76

——: 'Schubert's Reminiscences of his Own Works', *MQ*, lx (1974), 373

O. E. Deutsch: 'Schubert und Grillparzer', *ÖMz*, xxxii (1977), 497

P. Badura-Skoda: 'Fehlende und überzählige Takte bei Schubert und Beethoven', *ÖMz*, xxxiii (1978), 284

O. Biba: 'Franz Schubert in Niederösterreich', *ÖMz*, xxxiii (1978), 359

O. Brusatti: 'Desiderata der Schubert-Forschung', *ÖMz*, xxxiii (1978), 295

R. Klein: 'Begriff und Geschichte der Schubertiaden', *ÖMz*, xxxiii (1978), 209
E. Badura-Skoda and P. Branscombe, eds.: *Schubert Studies: Problems of Style and Chronology* (Cambridge, 1982)

COMMEMORATIVE

Die Musik, vi/7–8 (1906–7)
'Die intime Schubert', *Die moderne Welt* (Vienna, 1 Dec 1925) [Schubert suppl.]
Internationaler Kongress für Schubertforschung: Wien 1928
A. Weiss: *Franz Schubert: eine Festgabe* (Vienna, 1928)
MQ, xiv/4 (1928)
ML, ix/4 (1928)
ReM, x/1–3 (1928–9)
Ars (Buenos Aires, 1961), no.92
ÖMz, xxvii/4 (1972) [on Schubert interpretation]
ÖMz, xxxiii/6 (1978)
ÖMz, xxxiii/11 (1978)
MT, cxix/11 (1978)
19th Century Music, iii/2 (1979)

Index